DATE DUE

Techniques of Physics

Editor

N.H. MARCH

Department of Theoretical Chemistry; University of Oxford, Oxford, England

Techniques of physics find wide application in biology, medicine, engineering and technology generally. This series is devoted to techniques which have found and are finding application. The aim is to clarify the principles of each technique, to emphasize and illustrate the applications, and to draw attention to new fields of possible employment.

Quantitative Coherent Imaging

Theory, methods and some applications

J. M. BLACKLEDGE

*Department of Applied Computing and Mathematics,
Cranfield Institute of Technology,
Bedford UK*

ACADEMIC PRESS

Harcourt Brace Jovanovich, Publishers

*London   San Diego   New York
Berkeley   Boston   Sydney   Tokyo   Toronto*

Academic Press Limited
24–28 Oval Road
London NW1

US edition published by
Academic Press Inc.
San Diego, CA 92101

British Library Cataloguing in Publication Data

Blackledge, Jonathan M.
Quantitative coherent imaging
1. Imaging
I. Title
535'.32

ISBN 0-12-103300-7

Typeset by the author using T$_E$X
Printed in Great Britain by the University Press, Cambridge

Preface

Quantitative coherent imaging is concerned with the principles of interpreting the structure and material properties of objects by the way in which they scatter electromagnetic and acoustic radiation. The main theme of the work is the theory, methods and some of the applications of coherent imaging. This has been the focus of some of the author's research at King's College, London and Cranfield Institute of Technology, Bedford.

The book is divided into three parts. Part One is concerned with the mathematical and computational background to the subject. After presenting some of the general concepts and basic methods in Chapter 1, a detailed discussion of the Fourier transform is provided in Chapter 2. This transform is one of the most important results in imaging science and it is therefore an essential chapter for newcomers to the subject. Chapter 3 formulates some of the analytical methods and results that are required to compute a scattered field. Mathematical details on some of the equations that are used in later chapters are also presented in this chapter.

Part Two is concerned with the theory of quantitative coherent imaging. Here, the theoretical foundations used in a variety of applications are presented. Both acoustic and electromagnetic imaging systems are discussed. Chapter 4 considers techniques for imaging layered materials and the theory of scattering in one dimension which is used to study imagery of this type. Chapter 5 discusses projection tomography. Here, it is assumed that the probe (i.e. the radiation field) used to interrogate an object can be described in terms of a sequence of rays which may be traced through the object. Chapter 6 deals with a relatively new development which is known as diffraction tomography. The aim of this method of imaging is to interpret the internal structure and composition of an object by the way in which it diffracts radiation. Two types of diffraction tomography are discussed where the object is interrogated with a wave oscillating at a fixed frequency and a short pulse of radiation. Chapter 7 discusses synthetic aperture imaging. Attention is focused on the use of radar for imaging the surface of the earth. A mathematical model is presented to describe the scattering of a pulse of microwave radiation by the ground surface.

Part Three discusses some of the data-processing techniques which are common to most types of imagery. Details are presented on methods of deconvolution (Chapters 8, 9 and 10), image enhancement and noise reduction (Chapters 11 and 12 respectively).

The emphasis throughout is on the mathematical foundations of the subject which are common to a variety of disciplines. In some cases, examples have been provided to illustrate the conversion of a theoretical processing scheme into a digital computer program. FORTRAN 77 is used throughout for this purpose. Subroutines are presented which have been written and compiled on a Digital Electronics Corporation VAX/VMS 11/780 computer.

This book is designed to serve the reader with enough formal detail for him to acquire a firm foundation on which to build further. References to other useful texts and key scientific papers are included at the end of each chapter for this purpose.

An attempt has been made to cut through the jargon that characterizes different fields of research in imaging science and present an account of the fundamental physical principles which are common to nearly all imaging systems. This is done by illustrating the similarity of the underlying mathematical models that are used in practice to process data on the scattered field in a variety of applications. In this sense, the approach has been to unify the principles of coherent imaging and provide a text that covers the theoretical foundations of imaging science in an integrated and complete form.

J. M. Blackledge

Acknowledgements

Some of the work discussed in this book is the result of research which has been supported by the UK Science and Engineering Research Council (Grant Reference Number: B/80303414), British Coal (Research Contract Reference Number: PLG2743), British Petroleum (Consultancy) and the UK Ministry of Defence, Royal Signals and Radar Establishment (Research Contract Reference Number: MOD 2166/019 'RSRE'). The author is grateful to the organizations named above for their financial support and to Professor R.E. Burge (King's College) for his help and advice.

The seismic data used in chapters 4 and 11 is presented with the permission of British Coal (Geophysics Unit). The radar data used in Chapter 7 is presented with the permission of the UK Ministry of Defence. The ultrasonic images discussed in Chapter 4 and the X-ray computer tomogram presented in Chapter 5 are reproduced with the permission of the Editor's of the Lancet and Harvard University Press respectively.

Contents

You British asses, who expect to hear ever some new thing. I've nothing to tell, but what I fear may be a true thing. For Tait comes with his plummet and his line, quick to detect your old stuff, now dressed in what you call a fine popular lecture.

James Clerk Maxwell,

PART ONE

Mathematical and Computational Background

1 Introduction

In recent years there has been a rapid advance in the science and technology of information processing and analysis. Previously, the large majority of research and development in this subject was almost exclusively stimulated by the need for military intelligence. Now it is important in all physical and biological sciences.

Over the past twenty years in particular, many important developments have occurred in information science. This has been due to a massive increase in the speed, power and availability of digital computers. One area of information technology which has grown rapidly as a result of this has been imaging science. This subject has become increasingly important because of the growing demand to obtain information about the structure, composition a behaviour of objects without having to inspect them visually. Many techniques have been developed for this purpose using different types of radiation over a wide band of frequencies. However, in each case, the underlying principle that is used to obtain an image is the same and is known generally as the reconstruction or inverse problem.

In simple terms, and in the context of imaging science, the reconstruction problem is concerned with evaluating the structure of an object from observations on how it modifies certain properties of a probe - the field of radiation that is used to interrogate an object. In practice, this usually involves finding a method of inverting certain classes of integral equations. The exact form of integral equation depends upon the details of the model that is used to describe the interaction between the probe and the object. This book is concerned with the variety of mathematical models and reconstruction methods which are used to provide detailed quantitative information about the structure and material properties of an object by the way in which it scatters radiation.

1.1 SIGNALS AND IMAGES

A large proportion of information comes in the form of electrical wave-forms called signals. Information can also be encoded in two- dimensional signals. These are called images. In both cases, certain processes are usually required to extract useful information. The subject which is concerned with the theory and applications of these processes for the analysis and interpretation of signals and images is called signal or image processing. The only basic difference between signal processing and image processing is the dimension. However, in practice there are other more subtle differences which stem from the precise nature of the mathematical techniques which are used in each case.

Electrical waveforms are known generally as analogue signals and methods of processing them can be performed using an analogue computer. Another way of processing and analysing signals can be obtained by converting them into a set of numbers or digits. This is known as digital conversion and signals of this type are called digital signals. Each number of a digital signal is a sample of the original analogue signal. Digital conversion can also be carried out on images. This provides a two-dimensional array of numbers - a digital image. In this case, the individual samples or picture elements are referred to as pixels. The advantage of working with digital signals is that they can be stored easily (on magnetic tape for example) and can then be processed numerically using a digital computer.

1.2 QUANTITATIVE COHERENT IMAGING

Most imaging systems can be divided into two distinct classes: coherent imaging and incoherent imaging. The basic difference between these two types of imaging is determined by a single parameter called the phase. Coherent imaging is based on recording spatial and/or temporal variations in both the intensity of the scattered field and its phase. Incoherent imaging is based on recording fluctuations in just the intensity of the scattered field. Coherent imaging systems utilize relatively low frequency radiation (i.e. frequencies in the range of $10\text{-}10^{10}$ Hz). At these frequencies it is technically possible to record the time history of the scattered field. Incoherent images are time averaged intensity distributions of very high frequency wavefields such as light (frequency $\sim 10^{14}$ Hz), X-rays (frequency $\sim 10^{18}$ Hz) and γ-rays (frequency $\sim 10^{20}$ Hz). In this case, the frequency of the radiation is to high for the variations in time of the wavefield to be measured. A well known example of an incoherent image is the photograph.

Both coherent and incoherent imaging systems record and process information which is related to the spectral characteristics of an object. However, it is important to realize that the characteristic spectrum of an imaged object is not necessarily that of the object itself but rather the result of a physical interaction between the probe and the object. Most images only provide information on the structure of an object according to the way in which it scatters radiation. They do not necessarily provide information about the properties of the material from which the object is composed. Different properties of a material can scatter certain types of radiation in a variety of ways. By using this effect to provide information on the material properties as well as the structure of an object, a quantitative interpretation of the object is obtained. This is known as quantitative imaging. Although some methods of incoherent imaging are discussed in this book, it is primarily concerned with coherent imaging methods which allow a quantitative interpretation of the imaged object to be obtain - hence the title, *Quantitative Coherent Imaging*.

1.3 BASIC EQUATIONS AND PROBLEMS

To extract useful information from a signal or image, a mathematical model for the data must be established. There is one particular equation that is used extensively for this purpose. This equation is given by:

$$\text{Data} = (\text{Instrument function}) \text{ Convolved } (\text{Information})$$

$$+ \text{ Noise}$$

The instrument function describes the way in which an instrument responds to a given train of information. It has a variety of names which depend on the context in which the above equation is used. In signal analysis the instrument function describes the way in which the information is spread about a single spike. Hence, in this case, the instrument function is referred to as the spike spread function. In image analysis, it describes how information is spread about a point and is therefore known as the point spread function. Convolution is a mathematical operation which can be thought of as smoothing or blurring the information in a way that is determined by the characteristics of the instrument function. The instrument function is therefore sometimes referred to as the smoothing or blurring function. In addition to this effect, data can be perturbed by a whole range of external, unwanted disturbances which gives rise to the noise term.

There are two basic problems which are fundamental to imaging science in general. In the light of the equation above, these problems can be summarized as follows:

1. Given the data together with an estimate of the instrument function and a valid statistical model for the noise, recover the information.

2. By employing suitable physical models, interpret the information that is present in the data.

Problems 1 and 2 above are the basis for a variety of applications. Examples include the analysis and interpretation of speech signals, imaging the surface of the earth with radar, active and passive sonar, investigating the internal structure and composition of the earth using seismic waves and using ultrasound to determine the pathological state of human tissues. In each case, the act of recording the relevant data involves setting up an experiment with a given instrument function and certain noise statistics. In each case, the problem is to recover and interpret the information that is present in the data.

The information that is present in the data generated by a coherent imaging system is related to the way in which the radiation is scattered by the imaged object. To interpret this information, we must therefore establish a mathematical model for the scattering mechanism that takes place. The behaviour of the scattered field is compounded in a characteristic function which depends on the type and material properties of the scattering object. This function is known generally as the object function. Our basic coherent imaging equation can therefore be written in the form

Data = (Point Spread Function) Convolved (Object Function)

+ Noise

This equation is known as the imaging equation. It is based on a mathematical description for scattering that is linear. This is the same as assuming that the scattered field is generated by single scattering alone and that multiple scattering is negligible. The exact form of the point spread function depends upon the type and properties of the imaging system whereas the form of the object function depends upon the type of physical interaction that takes place. In this book (part 2 in particular), emphasis is placed on literally finding a mathematical expression for the object function in terms of a more fundamental set of material parameters. Two cases are considered:

1. **Electromagnetic imaging,** where the probe is an electromagnetic wave and the material parameters are the permittivity, permeability and conductivity.

2. **Acoustic imaging,** where the probe is an acoustic wave and the material parameters are the density, compressibility and the viscosity.

In both cases, the basic problem is the same and primarily involves:

(i) Designing an algorithm to compute the object function given certain data on the scattered field and estimates of the point spread function in the presence of experimental noise.

(ii) Finding a way to recover the appropriate set of material parameters from the object function.

Both (i) and (ii) above are inverse problems. The recovery of the object function from the data is an inverse problem which is known generally as deconvolution. In one way or another, deconvolution is common to all imaging systems. It is the basis for the large majority of the reconstruction methods that are presented in this book and is discussed at length in part 3.

1.4 RESOLUTION, DISTORTION, FUZZINESS AND NOISE

The 'quality' of a coherent image is described by four distinct features:

1. **Resolution**

2. **Distortion**

3. **Fuzziness**

4. **Noise**

Resolution is determined primarily by experimental parameters such as the wavelength of the radiation that is used to probe an object and scattered by it. Two other important parameters that effect the resolution are the size of the aperture used to observe the scattered field and the beamwidth of the probe used to illuminate the object. In terms of the imaging equation, the resolution of an image is determined by the spread (the local spatial extent) of the point spread function.

In contrast to resolution, distortion and fuzziness are determined by the type of physical model used to design the data processing algorithm. These effects are associated with two distinct physical aspects of the imaging system. Distortion is related to the geometry of the system and, in particular, the type of model that is used to describe the propagation of the probe from the source to scatterer and from the scatterer to detector. If an inversion algorithm is used to invert data which is based on a model for the probe that is inaccurate, then distortion will occur. The amount of distortion depends on how well the theoretical model describes the behaviour of the probe. In turn, this is determined by the accuracy of the point spread function.

Image fuzziness is related to the physical model used to describe the type and material properties of a scatterer. Fuzziness occurs when the physical model used to design an inversion algorithm fails to describe all the properties of the material and hence, the variety of scattering that can occur. The degree of image fuzziness is determined by the accuracy of the mathematical model adopted for the object function and can lead to errors in the way an image is interpreted.

The noise in an image is a combination of effects due to a whole range of unwanted disturbances and interference. In practice, because the noise is multifaceted, it is not possible to define it uniquely. For this reason, models are used to construct a suitable probability distribution function for the noise which is statistically compatible with the experiment. In general, noise accounts for all the non-ideal effects that may occur in a coherent imaging system.

In terms of the coherent imaging equation, i.e.

Coherent Image = | (Point Spread Function) Convolved

(Object Function) + Noise|

we can summarize resolution, distortion, image fuzziness and noise in the following way:

Resolution is determined by the spread of the point spread function.

Distortion is determined by the accuracy of the mathematical model for the point spread function.

Fuzziness is determined by the accuracy of the mathematical model for the object function.

Noise is determined by the accuracy of the convolution model for the data.

The aim of a coherent imaging system is to obtain data on the scattered field which provides a coherent image with minimal noise, fuzziness and distortion and maximum resolution.

1.5 ABOUT THIS BOOK

In this book, an attempt has been made to establish the underlying physical principles which link a variety of different imaging methods and systems. In each case, it is shown how, starting with an appropriate physical model, a solution for the scattered field can be obtained which provides mathematical expressions for the point spread function and the object function.

Part 1 is devoted to the essential mathematical and computational background to the subject which the reader should be acquainted with in order to comprehend the rest of the work. The second part discusses the application of the scattering theory presented in Chapter 3 to coherent imaging. In part 3, some methods of digital data processing are covered which are primarily concerned with the problem of deconvolving the data to recover the object function. Methods of image enhancement and noise reduction are also presented in part 3.

To illustrate the principal results, a number of different imaging methods have been introduced. These include, seismic imaging and medical imaging with ultrasound, two related imaging methods known as projection tomography and diffraction tomography and a method of imaging the surface of the earth using microwaves called synthetic aperture radar or SAR. In each case, the physical principles that are involved are discussed and examples are provided to illustrate the variety of phenomena that can occur and be used for the purposes of interpreting the structure of an object and its physical state.

2 Fourier transforms

The Fourier transform is used extensively in many branches of science and engineering. It is particularly important in signal processing.

In this chapter, the Fourier transform is discussed at length and important theorems, properties and results are derived. Digital methods for computing the discrete Fourier transform and some of its applications are presented at the end of this chapter.

2.1 THE DIRAC DELTA FUNCTION

The Dirac delta function (herein referred to as the delta function) occurs in many different fields of mathematics and mathematical physics. It is particularly important in the theory of data processing and is required to formulate many useful results. We shall therefore start by defining a delta function and study some of its properties.

One dimension

In one dimension, the delta function may be written symbolically as

$$\delta(x) = \begin{cases} 0, & x \neq 0 \\ \infty, & x = 0 \end{cases}$$

This definition, shows that the delta function can be thought of in terms of an infinitely high, infinitely thin spike. Physically, such a function is meaningless. In other words, a delta function cannot really exist. It should therefore be thought of more as a symbol through which we may define certain useful properties. These properties will be discussed shortly.

In the symbolic definition given above, the delta function is singular at $x = 0$. The position of the singularity can be changed by writing the delta function as $\delta(x - x_0)$. The singularity is then taken to occur at $x = x_0$ and we obtain a more general (symbolic) definition for the delta function of the form

$$\delta(x - x_0) = \begin{cases} 0, & x \neq x_0 \\ \infty, & x = x_0 \end{cases}$$

The shifting property and other related properties

One of the most important properties of the delta function and the one that makes it particularly useful is expressed by the following equation

1. $\int\limits_{-\infty}^{\infty} f(x)\delta(x - x_0)dx = f(x_0)$

where f is a continuous function in the locality of x_0.

This property is known as the shifting or sampling property of the delta function. From this result, we note that if $x_0 = 0$, then

2. $\int\limits_{-\infty}^{\infty} f(x)\delta(x)dx = f(0)$

and if $f(x) = 1$, then

3. $\int\limits_{-\infty}^{\infty} \delta(x)dx = 1$

The shifting property of the the delta function also applies to definite integrals. In this case, because $\delta(x - x_0)$ vanishes when $x \neq x_0$, we have

4. $\int\limits_{a}^{b} f(x)\delta(x - x_0)dx = f(x_0), \quad a \leq x_0 \leq b$

If x_0 lies outside the range of values between a and b, then this integral is zero.

Two dimensions

In two dimensions, the delta function may be defined in the same way. In order to distinguish between different dimensions, it is common to label the two-dimensional delta function with the superscript 2. Similarly, the superscript 3 is used to denote a three-dimensional delta function. The dimension of any position vector associated with the delta function is then inferred from the value of this superscript. Thus, in two dimensions, the delta function can be written in the form

$$\delta^2(\mathbf{r} - \mathbf{r}_0) = \begin{cases} 0, & \mathbf{r} \neq \mathbf{r}_0 \\ \infty, & \mathbf{r} = \mathbf{r}_0 \end{cases}$$

where

$$\mathbf{r} = \hat{\mathbf{x}}x + \hat{\mathbf{y}}y$$

and

$$\mathbf{r}_0 = \hat{\mathbf{x}}x_0 + \hat{\mathbf{y}}y_0$$

Here, $\hat{\mathbf{x}}$ and $\hat{\mathbf{y}}$ are unit vectors pointing in the x and y directions respectively. In Cartesian coordinates, this function is separable and can be written in the form

$$\delta^2(\mathbf{r} - \mathbf{r}_0) = \delta(x - x_0)\delta(y - y_0)$$

The shifting property of this function is expressed by the equation

$$\int\limits_{-\infty}^{\infty} f(\mathbf{r})\delta^2(\mathbf{r} - \mathbf{r}_0)d^2\mathbf{r} = f(\mathbf{r}_0)$$

If A defines a 2D finite region of space, then we have

$$\int\limits_{A} f(\mathbf{r})\delta^2(\mathbf{r} - \mathbf{r}_0)d^2\mathbf{r} = f(\mathbf{r}_0), \quad \mathbf{r}_0 \in A$$

The sign $\in$ signifies that the position vector $\mathbf{r}_0$ is 'in' the region of space denoted by A. If $\mathbf{r}_0$ is 'not in' A (the notation for this statement being $\mathbf{r}_0 \notin A$), then the above integral in zero, i.e.

$$\int\limits_{A} f(\mathbf{r})\delta^2(\mathbf{r} - \mathbf{r}_0)d^2\mathbf{r} = 0, \quad \mathbf{r}_0 \notin A$$

Alternative representations

Because the delta function is so highly discontinuous, it is often useful to define it in terms of the limit of a continuous function. A number of functions can be used for this purpose which are known as auxiliary functions. A function which is particularly important in the theory of signal processing is the sinc function defined by

$$\text{sinc}(x) = \frac{\sin(x)}{x}$$

Using this result, we can construct the following auxiliary function:

$$\delta(\alpha, x) = \frac{\alpha}{\pi} \text{sinc}(\alpha x)$$

This function has its maximum value at $x = 0$ where $\text{sinc}(0) = 1$ and $\delta(x, \alpha) = \alpha/\pi$. As the value of α increases, the sinc function contracts and the value of $\delta(\alpha, x)$ increases (see figure 2.1). Eventually, as α approaches infinity, the sinc function contracts to a single spike at $x = 0$ and $\delta(\alpha, x)$ becomes infinitely large. Hence, we can write

$$\delta(x) = \lim_{\alpha \to \infty} \delta(\alpha, x)$$

This particular auxiliary function provides another important representation for the delta function. This representation shall be used many times throughout this book and is obtained by noting that

$$\delta(\alpha, x) = \frac{1}{2\pi} \int_{-\alpha}^{\alpha} \exp(ikx)dk$$

From this result, we get

$$\delta(x) = \frac{1}{2\pi} \int_{-\infty}^{\infty} \exp(ikx)dk \tag{2.1.1}$$

Similarly, in two dimensions, we have

$$\delta(x)\delta(y) = \frac{1}{(2\pi)^2} \int_{-\infty}^{\infty} \exp(ik_x x)dk_x \int_{-\infty}^{\infty} \exp(ik_y y)dk_y$$

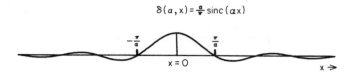

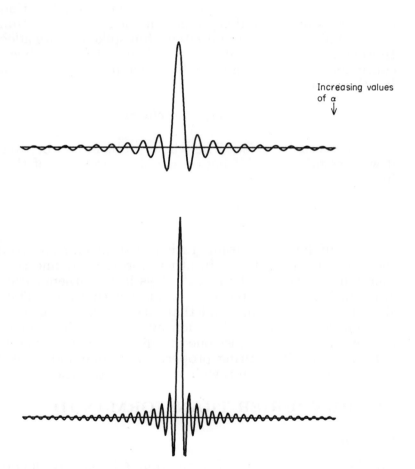

Figure 2.1 Behaviour of the auxiliary function $\delta(\alpha, x) = (\alpha/\pi)\sinc(\alpha x)$ for increasing values of α

or alternatively, using vector notation

$$\delta^2(\mathbf{r}) = \frac{1}{(2\pi)^2} \int\limits_{-\infty}^{\infty} \exp(i\mathbf{k} \cdot \mathbf{r}) d^2\mathbf{r}$$

where

$$\mathbf{k} = \hat{\mathbf{x}}k_x + \hat{\mathbf{y}}k_y$$

In terms of a physical picture for the delta function, the contraction of an auxiliary function such as the sinc function to an infinitely high and infinitely thin spike is quite adequate. However, mathematically it is still unsatisfactory because a continuous function cannot reduce to a discontinuous function. In other words, the limit

$$\delta(x) = \lim_{\alpha \to \infty} \delta(\alpha, x)$$

does not actually exist. The whole problem can be overcome if we recognize the shifting or sampling property of the delta function,

$$\int\limits_{-\infty}^{\infty} f(x)\delta(x - x_0)dx = f(x_0)$$

to be a fundamental result, rather than attempting to define the delta function itself. In other words, we define the delta function in terms of the role it plays in a mathematical operation rather than in terms of what it actually is. Thus, one should always bear in mind that, strictly speaking, the delta function is not really a function even though it is referred to as one. It is actually just one of infinitely many different distributions but its shifting property is unique and is the main reason why it has such a wide range of applications.

2.2 THE FOURIER TRANSFORM IN 1D

Notation

The Fourier transform of a function f is usually denoted by the upper case F. If the function in question is already upper case F, then the Fourier transform is denoted by writing a tilde above this function. The Fourier transform is then given by $\widetilde{F}$.

The basic transform

Using the notation above, the Fourier transform of f can be written in the form

$$F(k) = \hat{F}_1 f(x) = \int_{-\infty}^{\infty} f(x) \exp(-ikx) dx \qquad (2.2.1)$$

The operator $\hat{F}_1$ is known as the Fourier operator. The hat denotes that $\hat{F}_1$ is a mathematical operator and the subscript 1 denotes the dimension of the operator.

Physical interpretation

Physically, the Fourier transform of a function provides a quantitative picture of the frequency content of the function. This is important in a wide range of physical problems and is fundamental to the processing and analysis of signals and images. The variable k has dimensions that are reciprocal to those of the variable x. There are two important cases which arize in imaging science:

1. x - time in seconds; k - temporal frequency in cycles per second (Hertz).

In this case, k is referred to as the angular frequency which is given by $2\pi \times$ frequency.

2. x - distance in metres; k - spatial frequency in cycles per metre.

Here, k is known as the wavenumber and is given by

$$k = \frac{2\pi}{\lambda}$$

where λ is the wavelength. The Fourier transform is just one of a variety of integral transforms but it has certain properties which make it particularly versatile and easy to work with. This was expressed eloquently by Lord Kelvin, who stated that: 'Fourier's theorem is not only one of the most beautiful results of modern analysis, but it may be said to furnish an indispensable instrument in the treatment of nearly every recondite question in modern physics.'

17

Sufficient condition

The sufficient condition for the existence of the Fourier transform is that f is square integrable, i.e.,

$$\int_{-\infty}^{\infty} \mid f(x) \mid^2 \, dx < \infty$$

The spectrum

The Fourier transform of a function is called the spectrum. It is a complex function which can be written in the form

$$F(k) = F_r(k) + iF_i(k)$$

or alternatively as

$$F(k) = A(k) \exp[i\theta(k)]$$

where

$$A = \mid F \mid = \sqrt{F_r^2 + F_i^2}$$

and

$$\theta = \tan^{-1} \left(\frac{F_i}{F_r} \right)$$

The functions F_r and F_i are the real and imaginary parts of the Fourier transform respectively. If $f(x)$ is a real valued function, then the real and imaginary parts of its Fourier transform are given by

$$F_r(k) = \int_{-\infty}^{\infty} f(x) \cos(kx) dx$$

and

$$F_i(k) = \int_{-\infty}^{\infty} f(x) \sin(kx) dx$$

The functions F, A and θ are defined as follows:

F - complex spectrum

A - amplitude spectrum

θ - phase spectrum

In addition to these functions, the function

$$A^2 = \mid F \mid^2$$

is also important in Fourier analysis. This function is known as the power spectrum.

The DC level

The value of the spectrum at $k = 0$ is called the DC (after Direct Current) level and is given by the integral of f, i.e.

$$\text{DC level} = F(0) = \int\limits_{-\infty}^{\infty} f(x)dx$$

The inverse Fourier transform

The function $f(x)$ can be recovered from $F(k)$ by employing the inverse Fourier transform which is given by

$$f(x) = \hat{F}_1^{-1} F(k) = \frac{1}{2\pi} \int\limits_{-\infty}^{\infty} F(k)\exp(ikx)dk$$

The operator $\hat{F}_1^{-1}$ is the inverse Fourier operator. The superscript -1 is used to denote that this operator is an inverse operator (NB it does not mean $1/\hat{F}_1$). The proof for this inversion is based on the properties of the delta function discussed in section 2.1. Multiplying both side of equation (2.2.1) by $\exp(ikx')$ and integrating over k from $-\infty$ to ∞ we can write

$$\int\limits_{-\infty}^{\infty} F(k)\exp(ikx')dk = \int\limits_{-\infty}^{\infty} dx f(x) \int\limits_{-\infty}^{\infty} \exp[ik(x'-x)]dk$$

From equation (2.1.1), we have

$$\int\limits_{-\infty}^{\infty} \exp[ik(x'-x)]dk = 2\pi\delta(x'-x)$$

19

By substituting this result into the previous equation and using the shifting property of the delta function, we get

$$\int_{-\infty}^{\infty} F(k)\exp(ikx')dk = \int_{-\infty}^{\infty} dx f(x)2\pi\delta(x'-x) = 2\pi f(x')$$

or

$$f(x) = \frac{1}{2\pi}\int_{-\infty}^{\infty} F(k)\exp(ikx)dk$$

Alternative definitions and representations

Some authors prefer to define the forward and inverse Fourier transforms as

$$F(k) = \frac{1}{2\pi}\int_{-\infty}^{\infty} f(x)\exp(-ikx)dx$$

$$f(x) = \int_{-\infty}^{\infty} F(k)\exp(ikx)dk$$

or

$$F(k) = \frac{1}{\sqrt{2\pi}}\int_{-\infty}^{\infty} f(x)\exp(-ikx)dx$$

$$f(x) = \frac{1}{\sqrt{2\pi}}\int_{-\infty}^{\infty} F(k)\exp(ikx)dk$$

Also it is a matter of convention that F is called the Fourier transform of f when $-i$ occurs in the exponential and that f is the inverse Fourier transform of F when i appears in the exponential. The exact form of the forward and inverse Fourier transforms that are used does not really matter and the user may choose the definition which he or she likes the best. What does matter is that consistency with a given definition is maintained throughout a calculation. In this book the definitions

$$F(k) = \int_{-\infty}^{\infty} f(x)\exp(-ikx)dx$$

and

$$f(x) = \frac{1}{2\pi} \int_{-\infty}^{\infty} F(k)\exp(ikx)dk$$

are used throughout. Collectively, these integral transforms are known as Fourier transform pairs.

To avoid constantly having to write integral signs and specify the forward or inverse Fourier transform in full, we can make use of the symbolic form

$$f(x) \Longleftrightarrow F(k)$$

which means that F is the Fourier transform of f and f is the inverse Fourier transform of F. This notation is useful when we want to indicate the relationship between a mathematical operation on f and its effect on F. Mathematical operations on f are referred to a operations in real, x-space or image space. Similarly, operations on F are referred to as operations in Fourier space or k-space.

Bandlimited functions

If a complex spectrum $F(k)$ is such that

$$F(k) = 0, \quad |\,k\,| > K$$

then the inverse Fourier transform is given by

$$f(x) = \frac{1}{2\pi} \int_{-K}^{K} F(k)\exp(ikx)dk$$

In this case, f is known as a bandlimited function. A bandlimited function is therefore a function that is composed of frequencies which are limited to a particular finite band. If $f(x)$ is such that

$$f(x) = 0, \quad |\,x\,| > X$$

then its complex spectrum is given by

$$F(k) = \int_{-X}^{X} f(x)\exp(-ikx)dx$$

In this case, f is referred to as a space (x - distance in metres) or time (x - time in seconds) limited signal. In practice, all signals are of a finite duration and are therefore space/time limited. They are also usually bandlimited for a variety of different physical reasons.

Differentiation

Using the notation

$$f(x) \Longleftrightarrow F(k)$$

we have

$$\frac{d}{dx} f(x) \Longleftrightarrow ik F(k)$$

since

$$\frac{d}{dx} f(x) = \frac{1}{2\pi} \frac{d}{dx} \int\limits_{-\infty}^{\infty} F(k) \exp(ikx) dk$$

$$= \frac{1}{2\pi} \int\limits_{-\infty}^{\infty} ik F(k) \exp(ikx) dk$$

Differentiating n times,

$$\frac{d^n}{dx^n} f(x) \Longleftrightarrow (ik)^n F(k)$$

Important results

There are numerous texts which provide lists of Fourier transforms of functions $f(x)$ in those cases where the Fourier integral can be computed analytically. Some of these texts are referenced at the end of this chapter (e.g. Bates H, *Tables of Integral Transforms*, McGraw-Hill, 1954). Here, we present some results which are particularly important in signal analysis and are used in both this and later chapters.

1. Fourier transform of the tophat function The Top Hat function (so called because of its shape) is given by

$$H(x) = \begin{cases} 1, & |x| \le X \\ 0, & |x| > 0 \end{cases}$$

The Fourier transform of this function is

$$\int_{-\infty}^{\infty} H(x) \exp(-ikx)dx = \int_{-X}^{X} \exp(-ikx)dx$$

$$= \frac{1}{ik}[\exp(ikX) - \exp(-ikX)] = 2\frac{\sin(kX)}{k} = 2X \operatorname{sinc}(kX)$$

2. Fourier transform of the cosine function Consider the cosine function $\cos(k_0 x)$, where k_0 is a constant which determines the rate at which this function fluctuates about zero. To compute the Fourier transform of this function we first write it in terms of complex exponentials, i.e.

$$\cos(k_0 x) = \frac{\exp(ik_0 x) + \exp(-ik_0 x)}{2}$$

The Fourier transform of this function can then be written as (using equation (2.1.1))

$$\int_{-\infty}^{\infty} \cos(k_0 x) \exp(-ikx)dx = \frac{1}{2} \int_{-\infty}^{\infty} \exp[-i(k - k_0)x]dx$$

$$+ \frac{1}{2} \int_{-\infty}^{\infty} \exp[-i(k + k_0)x]dx = \pi[\delta(k - k_0) + \delta(k + k_0)]$$

3. Fourier transform of the sine function By defining $\sin(k_0 x)$ in terms of complex exponentials, i.e.

$$\sin(k_0 x) = \frac{\exp(ik_0 x) - \exp(-ik_0 x)}{2i}$$

we get

$$\int_{-\infty}^{\infty} \sin(k_0 x) \exp(-ikx)dx = \frac{1}{2i} \int_{-\infty}^{\infty} \exp[-i(k - k_0)x]dx$$

$$- \frac{1}{2i} \int_{-\infty}^{\infty} \exp[-i(k + k_0)]dx = i\pi[\delta(k + k_0) - \delta(k - k_0)]$$

4. Fourier transform of the sign function

The sign function $\text{sgn}(x)$ is defined by

$$\text{sgn}(x) = \begin{cases} 1, & x > 0 \\ -1, & x < 0 \end{cases}$$

The Fourier transform of this function can be obtained by computing the Fourier transform of $\exp(-\epsilon \mid x \mid) \text{sgn}(x)$ over the interval $[-a, a]$ and then letting $a \to \infty$ and $\epsilon \to 0$. Thus,

$$\int_{-\infty}^{\infty} \text{sgn}(x) \exp(-ikx) dx = \lim_{\epsilon \to 0} \lim_{a \to \infty} \left(\int_{0}^{a} \exp(-\epsilon \mid x \mid) \exp(-ikx) dx \right.$$

$$\left. - \int_{-a}^{0} \exp(-\epsilon \mid x \mid) \exp(-ikx) dx \right)$$

$$= \lim_{\epsilon \to 0} \lim_{a \to \infty} \left(\int_{0}^{a} \exp(-\epsilon x) \exp(-ikx) dx - \int_{0}^{a} \exp(-\epsilon x) \exp(ikx) dx \right)$$

$$= \lim_{\epsilon \to 0} \lim_{a \to \infty} \left(\frac{\exp[-a(\epsilon - ik)]}{\epsilon - ik} - \frac{\exp[-a(\epsilon + ik)]}{\epsilon + ik} + \frac{1}{\epsilon + ik} - \frac{1}{\epsilon - ik} \right)$$

$$= \lim_{\epsilon \to 0} \left(\frac{-2ik}{(\epsilon + ik)(\epsilon - ik)} \right) = \frac{2}{ik}$$

Hence,

$$\text{sgn}(x) \iff \frac{2}{ik}$$

5. Fourier transform of the Heaviside step function

The Heaviside step function is defined by

$$S(x) = \begin{cases} 1, & x > 0 \\ 0, & x < 0 \end{cases}$$

To obtain the Fourier transform of this function, we write it in terms of the sign function, i.e.

$$S(x) = \frac{1}{2}[1 + \text{sgn}(x)]$$

We then get,

$$\int_{-\infty}^{\infty} S(x)\exp(-ikx)dx = \frac{1}{2}\int_{-\infty}^{\infty} \text{sgn}(x)\exp(-ikx)dx + \frac{1}{2}\int_{-\infty}^{\infty} \exp(-ikx)dx$$

$$= \pi\left(\delta(x) - \frac{i}{\pi k}\right)$$

6. Fourier transform of 1/x

Using the result $\text{sgn}(x) \Longleftrightarrow 2/ik$, we have

$$\frac{1}{2\pi}\int_{-\infty}^{\infty} \frac{2}{ik}\exp(ikx)dk = \text{sgn}(x)$$

Interchanging x and k and changing the sign of i, this equation becomes

$$\int_{-\infty}^{\infty} \frac{1}{x}\exp(-ikx)dx = -i\pi\,\text{sgn}(k)$$

Hence, we can write

$$\frac{1}{x} \Longleftrightarrow -i\pi\,\text{sgn}(k)$$

Note, by taking the inverse Fourier transform of $-i\pi\,\text{sgn}(k)$, we get

$$\frac{i}{\pi x} = \frac{1}{2\pi}\int_{-\infty}^{\infty} \text{sgn}(k)\exp(ikx)dk$$

This result shall be used in later work on the Hilbert transform.

Important theorems

1. Addition theorem The Fourier transform of the sum of two functions f and g is equal to the sum of their Fourier transforms F and G respectively.

Proof:

$$\int_{-\infty}^{\infty} [f(x) + g(x)]\exp(-ikx)dx$$

$$= \int_{-\infty}^{\infty} f(x)\exp(-ikx)dx + \int_{-\infty}^{\infty} g(x)\exp(-ikx)dx = F(k) + G(k)$$

2. Similarity theorem The Fourier transform of $f(ax)$ is $(1/a)F(k/a)$.

Proof:

$$\int_{-\infty}^{\infty} f(ax)\exp(-ikx)dx = \frac{1}{a}\int_{-\infty}^{\infty} f(ax)\exp\left(i\frac{k}{a}ax\right)d(ax)$$

$$= \frac{1}{a}F\left(\frac{k}{a}\right)$$

3. Shift theorem The Fourier transform of $f(x-a)$ is given by $\exp(-ika)F(k)$.

Proof:

$$\int_{-\infty}^{\infty} f(x-a)\exp(-ikx)dx = \int_{-\infty}^{\infty} f(x-a)\exp[-ik(x-a)]\exp(-ika)d(x-a)$$

$$= \exp(-ika)F(k)$$

4. Parseval's theorem If f and g have Fourier transforms F and G respectively, then

$$\int_{-\infty}^{\infty} f(x)g^*(x)dx = \frac{1}{2\pi}\int_{-\infty}^{\infty} F(k)G^*(k)dk$$

where g^* is the complex conjugate of g and G^* is the complex conjugate of G.

Proof:

$$\int_{-\infty}^{\infty} f(x)g^*(x)dx = \int_{-\infty}^{\infty} g^*(x)\left(\frac{1}{2\pi}\int_{-\infty}^{\infty} F(k)\exp(ikx)dk\right)dx$$

$$= \frac{1}{2\pi}\int_{-\infty}^{\infty} F(k)\left(\int_{-\infty}^{\infty} g^*(x)\exp(ikx)dx\right)dk$$

$$= \frac{1}{2\pi} \int\limits_{-\infty}^{\infty} F(k) \left(\int\limits_{-\infty}^{\infty} g(x) \exp(-ikx)dx \right)^{*} dk$$

$$= \frac{1}{2\pi} \int\limits_{-\infty}^{\infty} F(k)G^{*}(k)dk$$

5. Rayleigh's theorem (also known as the energy theorem) If f has Fourier transform F, then,

$$\int\limits_{-\infty}^{\infty} \mid f(x) \mid^2 dx = \frac{1}{2\pi} \int\limits_{-\infty}^{\infty} \mid F(k) \mid^2 dk$$

Proof: The proof follows from setting $g = f$ in Parseval's theorem.

2.3 CONVOLUTION AND CORRELATION

Notation

In this section and throughout the rest of this book, convolution shall be denoted by the symbol $\otimes$ and correlation by the symbol $\odot$. Other symbols that are sometimes used (by other authors) are the six sided star $*$ to denote convolution and the five sided star $\star$ to denote correlation.

Convolution

The convolution of two functions f and g in one dimension is defined by the operation

$$f \otimes g = \int\limits_{-\infty}^{\infty} f(x)g(x' - x)dx$$

This is a convolution over the interval $[-\infty, \infty]$. If f and g are of finite extent $\mid x \mid \leq X$, then the convolution is finite and given by

$$f \otimes g = \int\limits_{-X}^{X} f(x)g(x' - x)dx$$

Using this notation, the shifting property of the delta function discussed in section 2.1 can be written as

$$f(x) \otimes \delta(x) = f(x)$$

Hence, the convolution of a function with the delta function replicates the function.

Correlation

The correlation (also known as cross-correlation) of two functions f and g in one dimension is defined by the operation

$$f \odot g = \int\limits_{-\infty}^{\infty} f(x)g(x - x')dx$$

This is very similar to convolution except that the function g is not reversed (i.e. g is a function of $x - x'$ not $x' - x$) - a seemingly small but very important difference. When the functions are complex, we define the complex correlation

$$f^* \odot g = \int\limits_{-\infty}^{\infty} f^*(x)g(x - x')dx$$

Apart from the complex conjugate, the important difference between correlation and convolution is that in correlation the function g is not flipped about the origin as in convolution. In fact, for real functions,

$$f(x) \otimes g(x) = f(x) \odot g(-x)$$

Hence, correlation is really just a special form of convolution.

Physical interpretation

Physically, convolution can be thought of as a 'blurring' or 'smearing' of one function by another. Convolution integrals occur in a wide variety of physical problems. They are particularly important in signal and image analysis where convolution equations are used to describe signals and images of many different types. A large proportion of signal and image processing is in one way or another concerned with an inverse process known as deconvolution. This important operation is discussed in detail in part 3.

Autoconvolution and autocorrelation

Two other definitions which are important in the context of convolution and correlation are:

Autoconvolution

$$f \otimes f = \int\limits_{-\infty}^{\infty} f(x)f(x' - x)dx$$

Autocorrelation

$$f \odot f = \int\limits_{-\infty}^{\infty} f(x)f(x - x')dx$$

The convolution theorem

The convolution theorem is one of the most important results of Fourier theory. It is related to nearly every aspect of signal and image processing and is used repeatedly throughout this book. The theory is as follows and should be committed to memory: The convolution of two functions in real space is the same as the product of their Fourier transforms in Fourier space.

Proof: Writing

$$f(x) = \frac{1}{2\pi} \int\limits_{-\infty}^{\infty} F(k) \exp(ikx)dk$$

$$g(x) = \frac{1}{2\pi} \int\limits_{-\infty}^{\infty} G(k) \exp(ikx)dk$$

and using equation (2.2.1), we have,

$$f \otimes g = \frac{1}{(2\pi)^2} \int\limits_{-\infty}^{\infty} dx \int\limits_{-\infty}^{\infty} F(k) \exp(ikx)dk \int\limits_{-\infty}^{\infty} G(k') \exp[ik'(x' - x)]dk'$$

29

$$= \frac{1}{2\pi} \int\limits_{-\infty}^{\infty} dk F(k) \int\limits_{-\infty}^{\infty} dk' G(k') \exp(ik'x') \frac{1}{2\pi} \int\limits_{-\infty}^{\infty} \exp[ix(k - k')] dx$$

$$= \frac{1}{2\pi} \int\limits_{-\infty}^{\infty} dk F(k) \int\limits_{-\infty}^{\infty} dk' G(k') \exp(ik'x') \delta(k - k')$$

$$= \frac{1}{2\pi} \int\limits_{-\infty}^{\infty} F(k) G(k) \exp(ikx') dk$$

Hence,

$$f(x) \otimes g(x) \Longleftrightarrow F(k)G(k)$$

This theorem is sometimes referred to as the Fultung theorem from the German word 'Fultung' meaning 'folding'. The convolution theorem also holds in Fourier space. That is, the convolution of two complex spectra is equal to the Fourier transform of the product of these functions in real space, or

$$f(x)g(x) \Longleftrightarrow \frac{1}{2\pi} F(k) \otimes G(k)$$

This result is sometimes referred to as the product theorem.

The correlation theorem

The correlation theorem follows from the convolution theorem and can be written in the form

$$f(x) \odot g(x) \Longleftrightarrow F(-k)G(k)$$

f and g real,

$$f^*(x) \odot g(x) \Longleftrightarrow F^*(k)G(k)$$

f and g complex. If f is a real function, then the real part of its Fourier transform $F(k)$ is symmetric and the imaginary part of $F(k)$ is asymmetric, i.e.

$$F_r(-k) = F_r(k)$$

and

$$F_i(-k) = -F_i(k)$$

In this case

$$F(-k) = F_r(-k) + iF_i(-k)$$

30

$$= F_r(k) - iF_i(k) = F^*(k)$$

and thus, for real functions f and g, we can write

$$f(x) \odot g(x) \Longleftrightarrow F^*(k)G(k)$$

The autoconvolution theorem

From the convolution theorem we have

$$f(x) \otimes f(x) \Longleftrightarrow [F(k)]^2$$

The autocorrelation theorem

From the correlation theorem, we get

$$f(x) \odot f(x) \Longleftrightarrow F(-k)F(k)$$

f real,

$$f^*(x) \odot f(x) \Longleftrightarrow |F(k)|^2$$

f complex.

   This theorem has a unique feature which is that information about the phase of F is entirely missing from $|F|^2$ in contrast to the autoconvolution theorem where information about the phase of the spectrum is retained. Hence, the autocorrelation function $f^* \odot f$ contains no information about the phase of the Fourier components of f and is consequently unchanged if the phase changes.

Important properties

1. Convolution is commutative

$$f \otimes g = g \otimes f$$

2. Convolution is associative

$$f \otimes (g \otimes h) = (f \otimes g) \otimes h$$

Multiple convolutions can therefore be carried out in any order.

3. Convolution is distributive

$$f \otimes (g + h) = f \otimes g + f \otimes h$$

4. Derivative of a convolution

$$\frac{d}{dx}[f(x) \otimes g(x)] = f(x) \otimes \frac{d}{dx}g(x) = g(x) \otimes \frac{d}{dx}f(x)$$

5. Correlation does not commute

$$f \odot g \neq g \odot f$$

The proof of these results is left as an exercise for the reader.

2.4 MODULATION AND DEMODULATION

If $f(x)$ is a bandlimited function with spectrum $F(k), \mid k \mid \leq K$, then multiplying this function by $\cos(k_0 x)$ shifts or modulates the location of the centre of $F(k)$ from $k = 0$ to $k = \pm k_0$. This process is known as modulation and is described mathematically by the following:

$$f(x)\cos(k_0 x) \Longleftrightarrow F(k) \otimes \pi[\delta(k - k_0) + \delta(k + k_0)]$$

$$\|$$

$$\pi[F(k - k_0) + F(k + k_0)]$$

A modulated spectrum of this kind is known as a sideband spectrum. If the original spectrum has its centre at $k = 0$, then it is known as a baseband spectrum. Shifting a sideband spectrum back to baseband is called demodulation. This is done by multiplying again by a cosine function oscillating at the same frequency k_0 - a process that is described mathematically by

$$f(x)\cos(k_0)\cos(k_0 x) \Longleftrightarrow \pi[F(k - k_0) + F(k + k_0)] \otimes \pi[\delta(k - k_0) + \delta(k + k_0)]$$

$$\|$$

$$\pi^2[2F(k) + F(k - 2k_0) + F(k + 2k_0)]$$

By neglecting the part of the spectrum which is modulated to $\pm 2k_0$ by this process, the baseband spectrum $F(k)$ can be extracted. In practice, this is achieved by applying a suitable lowpass filter (see section 2.7).

2.5 THE HILBERT TRANSFORM AND QUADRA-TURE DETECTION

The Hilbert transform $q(x)$ of a real function $f(x)$ is defined by

$$q(x) = \hat{H}f(x) = \frac{1}{\pi} \int\limits_{-\infty}^{\infty} \frac{f(x')}{x - x'} dx'$$

The operator $\hat{H}$ is used to denote the Hilbert transform. Notice, that this operator is a just a convolution - a convolution of $f(x)$ with $1/\pi x$. Hence, we may write the Hilbert transform in the following way

$$q(x) = \frac{1}{\pi x} \otimes f(x)$$

Using the convolution theorem and noting that

$$\hat{F}_1\left(\frac{1}{\pi x}\right) = -i \operatorname{sgn}(k)$$

the Fourier transform of q can be written as

$$Q(k) = -i \operatorname{sgn}(k) F(k)$$

Hence,

$$q(x) = \hat{F}_1^{-1}[-i \operatorname{sgn}(k) F(k)]$$

This result provides a method of computing the Hilbert transform, thus:

1. Take the Fourier transform of the function.

2. Multiply the result by $-i \operatorname{sgn}(k)$.

3. Compute the inverse Fourier transform.

Quadrature detection

The Hilbert transform of a signal is often referred to as the quadrature signal which is why it is usually denoted by the letter q. Electronic or digital systems which perform Hilbert transforms are also known as quadrature filters. Electronic quadrature filters are usually employed in systems where the signal is a continuous wave or a narrowband signal (i.e. a signal whose bandwidth is a small percentage of the dominant carrier frequency). These filters operate on the basis that if $y(x)$ is a real valued, bandlimited signal with a spectrum $Y(k), |k| \leq K$ and

$$f(x) = y(x) \cos(k_0 x)$$

where $k_0 > K$, then the quadrature signal can be obtained by simply multiplying $y(x)$ by $\sin(k_0 x)$, i.e.

$$q(x) = y(x) \sin(k_0 x)$$

Proof: The above result can be proved by analysing the Fourier transform of $f(x)$ which is given by (using the convolution theorem)

$$F(k) = Y(k) \otimes \pi[\delta(k - k_0) + \delta(k + k_0)]$$

$$= \pi[Y(k - k_0) + Y(k + k_0)]$$

Now, the spectrum of the Hilbert transform of F is obtained by multiplying F by $-i\,\text{sgn}(k)$. Hence, provided $k_0 > K$,

$$Q(k) = -i\pi\,\text{sgn}(k)[Y(k - k_0) + Y(k + k_0)]$$

$$= i\pi[Y(k + k_0) - Y(k - k_0)]$$

$$= Y(k) \otimes i\pi[\delta(k + k_0) - \delta(k - k_0)]$$

In real space, the last equation is

$$q(x) = y(x) \sin(k_0 x)$$

which completes the proof.

The quadrature filter is mostly used in systems where frequency demodulation is required to extract a baseband signal from a narrowband signal. It is used in coherent electromagnetic imaging systems where the frequency of the radiation is relatively high - ranging from about 10 MHz (short radio waves) to 10 GHz (microwaves). The real signal f is demodulated by multiplying it by the appropriate cosine wave and the quadrature signal is obtained by multiplying the signal by the appropriate sine wave. In systems where baseband signals are recorded, the quadrature signal is usually obtained by computing the Hilbert transform digitally. Baseband signals are produced in acoustic imaging systems where the frequency of the radiation is relatively low - ranging from 100 Hz (seismic waves) to 10 MHz (ultrasound).

2.6 THE ANALYTIC SIGNAL

In signal analysis (where the independent variable is usually time), a real valued signal can be represented in terms of the so called analytic signal. The analytic signal is important because it is from this signal that the amplitude, phase and frequency modulations of the original real valued signal can be determined.

If $f(x)$ is a real valued signal with spectrum $F(k)$, then $f(x)$ can be computed from $F(k)$ via the inverse Fourier transform

$$f(x) = \frac{1}{2\pi} \int\limits_{-\infty}^{\infty} F(k) \exp(ikx) dk$$

This involves integrating over k from $-\infty$ to ∞. The analytic signal is obtained by integrating only over the positive half of the spectrum which contains the physically significant frequencies (i.e. integrating over k from 0 to ∞). Hence, if s is used to denote the analytic signal of f, then we have by definition

$$s(x) = \frac{1}{\pi} \int\limits_{0}^{\infty} F(k) \exp(ikx) dk$$

From this result it is possible to obtain an expression for s in terms of f. This is done by transforming s into Fourier space and analysing the spectral properties of the analytic signal. In Fourier space, the analytic signal can be written (from the last equation) as

$$S(k) = 2U(k)F(k)$$

where S and F are the Fourier transforms of s and f respectively and $U(k)$ is the unit step function given by

$$U(k) = \begin{cases} 1, & k > 0 \\ 0, & k < 0 \end{cases}$$

We now employ a simple but useful analytical trick by writing the step function in the form

$$U(k) = \frac{1}{2} + \frac{1}{2} \operatorname{sgn}(k)$$

where

$$\text{sgn}(k) = \begin{cases} 1, & k > 0 \\ -1, & k < 0 \end{cases}$$

The inverse Fourier transform of this function can then be written as

$$u(x) = \frac{1}{2\pi} \int\limits_{-\infty}^{\infty} \frac{1}{2} \exp(ikx)dk + \frac{1}{2\pi} \int\limits_{-\infty}^{\infty} \frac{1}{2} \text{sgn}(k) \exp(ikx)dk$$

$$= \frac{1}{2}\delta(x) + \frac{i}{2\pi x}$$

where we have used the results

$$\delta(x) = \frac{1}{2\pi} \int\limits_{-\infty}^{\infty} \exp(ikx)dk$$

and

$$\frac{1}{2\pi} \int\limits_{-\infty}^{\infty} \text{sgn}(k) \exp(ikx)dk = \frac{i}{\pi x}$$

Now, since

$$2U(k)F(k) \Longleftrightarrow 2u(x) \otimes f(x)$$

we have

$$s(x) = 2u(x) \otimes f(x)$$

$$= f(x) \otimes \left(\delta(x) + \frac{i}{\pi x}\right)$$

$$= f(x) + \frac{i}{\pi x} \otimes f(x)$$

or

$$s(x) = f(x) + iq(x)$$

where q is the Hilbert transform of f, i.e.

$$q(x) = \frac{1}{\pi x} \otimes f(x)$$

From this result it is clear that the analytic signal associated with a real valued function f can be obtained by computing its Hilbert transform to provide the quadrature component.

This process is called quadrature detection. Note that the analytic signal is a complex function and therefore contains both amplitude and phase information. The important feature about the analytic signal is that its spectrum (by definition) is zero for all values of k less than zero. This type of spectrum is known as a single sideband spectrum because the negative half of the spectrum is zero. An analytic signal is therefore a single sideband signal.

Attributes of the analytic signal

As with any other complex function, the behaviour of the analytic signal can be analysed using an argand diagram and may be written in the form

$$s(x) = A(x)\exp[i\theta(x)]$$

where

$$A = \sqrt{f^2 + q^2}$$

and

$$\theta = \tan^{-1}\left(\frac{q}{f}\right)$$

Physically, the parameter A describes the average dynamical behaviour of the amplitude modulations of f. For this reason, it is sometimes referred to as the amplitude envelope. The parameter θ measures the phase of the signal at an instant in time and is therefore known as the instantaneous phase. Because the arctangent function is periodic, this parameter is multivalued. Hence, strictly speaking, the analytic function should be written as

$$s = A\exp[i(\theta + 2\pi n)]; \quad n = 0, \pm 1, \pm 2, ...$$

If we confine the value of the phase to a fixed period (i.e. we compute the phase using only one particular value of n), then it is referred to as the wrapped phase. In this case, there is only one unique value of the phase within a fixed period. However, any other interval of length 2π can be chosen. Any particular choice, decided upon in advance, is called the principal range. The value of the phase within this range, is called the principal value.

An alternative way of defining the phase can be obtained by taking the natural logarithm of the analytic signal. This yields the equation

$$\ln s = \ln A + i(\theta + 2\pi n)$$

from which it follows that

$$\theta + 2\pi n = \text{Im}[\ln s]$$

Another important property of the analytic signal is its instantaneous frequency. This parameter (denoted by ψ) measures the rate of change of phase and from the previous expression can be written as

$$\psi = \frac{d\theta}{dx} = \text{Im}\left(\frac{d}{dx}\ln s\right) = \text{Im}\left(\frac{1}{s}\frac{ds}{dx}\right)$$

or alternatively (since $s = f + iq$)

$$\psi = \text{Im}\left(\frac{s^*}{|s|^2}\frac{ds}{dx}\right)$$

$$= \frac{1}{A^2}\left(f\frac{dq}{dx} - q\frac{df}{dx}\right)$$

The instantaneous frequency provides a quantitative estimate of the frequency of the real valued signal f at any instant in time. From this parameter, we may obtain another closely related description for the signal in terms of its frequency modulations which are given by $|\psi|$. Also, the phase θ can be obtained from ψ by integrating. Using the initial conditions

$$\int^x \psi(x')dx' = 0, \quad x = 0$$

and

$$\theta = \theta_0 \quad \text{when} \quad x = 0$$

we get

$$\theta(x) = \theta_0 + \int^x \psi(x')dx'$$

This phase function is called the unwrapped phase. It is not multivalued and therefore the problem of choosing a principal range to compute the phase does not occur. Collectively, the amplitude modulations, frequency modulations and the instantaneous phase are known as the attributes of the analytic signal. They all provide different but related information on the time history of a signal. Methods of imaging which are based on an operator viewing the amplitude modulations (AM), frequency modulations (FM) or phase in a collection of signals is referred to as AM, FM and phase imaging respectively. Analysis of coherent images is usually based on viewing the amplitiude modulations. This is due partly to convension but also because of the practical problems that arise in computing ψ and hence the unwrapped phase. These problems stem from the algebraic form for ψ which includes the quantity $1/A^2$. The nonlinear nature of this result means that ψ is sensitive to small errors in A and is singular when $A = 0$. Methods of data processing which overcome this problem are discussed and illustrated in Chapter 11 (section 5) which deals with solutions to the coherent phase imaging problem.

2.7 FILTERS

Any operation which changes the distribution of the Fourier components of a function (via a multiplicative process) may be defined as a filtering operation. Thus, in an operation of the form

$$S(k) = P(k)F(k)$$

P may be referred to as a filter and S can be considered to be a filtered version of F. In this sense, many of the operations already described can be thought of as just filtering operations. For example, we may consider the Hilbert transform to be just a special type of filter of the form

$$P(k) = -i\,\mathrm{sgn}(k)$$

Similarly, we may consider differentiation to be characterized by the filter

$$P(k) = ik$$

and integration to be characterized by the filter

$$P(k) = \frac{1}{ik}$$

39

In general, filters fall into one of three classes:

1. Lowpass filters

2. Highpass filters

3. Bandpass filters

A lowpass filter is one which suppresses or attenuates the high frequency components of a spectrum while 'passing' the low frequencies within a specified range. A highpass filter does exactly the opposite to a lowpass filter and a bandpass filter only allows those frequencies within a certain band to pass through. Hence, lowpass and highpass filters are just special types of bandpass filters. Nearly all signals can be modelled in terms of some bandpass filter modifying the distribution of the complex Fourier components associated with an information source. Data processing is then required to restore the out-of-band frequencies in order to recover the complex spectrum of the source. This requires a good estimate of the original bandpass filter.

2.8 THE FOURIER TRANSFORM IN 2D

Using vector notation, the 2D Fourier transform can be written as

$$F(\mathbf{k}) = \int_{-\infty}^{\infty} f(\mathbf{r}) \exp(-i\mathbf{k} \cdot \mathbf{r}) d^2\mathbf{r}$$

In Cartesian coordinates, the Fourier transform of a two-dimensional function $f(x, y)$ is given by

$$F(k_x, k_y) = \hat{F}_2 f(x, y) = \int_{-\infty}^{\infty} \int_{-\infty}^{\infty} f(x, y) \exp(-ik_x x) \exp(-ik_y y) dx dy$$

The parameters k_x and k_y are the spatial frequencies of the function (in cycles per metre). Observe, that in Cartesian co-ordinates, the Fourier transform of a two-dimensional function can be obtained by generating the one-dimensional transform in x and y separately

$$F(k_x, k_y) = \int_{-\infty}^{\infty} f(x, k_y) \exp(-ik_x x) dx = \int_{-\infty}^{\infty} f(k_x, y) \exp(-ik_y y) dy$$

Hence, if $f(x, y)$ is separable so that we can write

$$f(x, y) = f_1(x) f_2(y)$$

then the Fourier transform is also separable

$$F(k_x, k_y) = F_1(k_x) F_2(k_y)$$

The inverse Fourier transform in 2D can be derived in exactly the same way as the inverse Fourier transform in 1D. Thus, multiplying $F(\mathbf{k})$ by $\exp(i\mathbf{k} \cdot \mathbf{r}')$ and integrating over $\mathbf{k}$, we have

$$\int_{-\infty}^{\infty} F(\mathbf{k}) \exp(i\mathbf{k} \cdot \mathbf{r}') d^2\mathbf{k} = \int_{-\infty}^{\infty} d^2\mathbf{r} f(\mathbf{r}) \int_{-\infty}^{\infty} \exp[i\mathbf{k} \cdot (\mathbf{r}' - \mathbf{r})] d^2\mathbf{k}$$

$$= \int_{-\infty}^{\infty} d^2\mathbf{r} f(\mathbf{r}) (2\pi)^2 \delta^2 (\mathbf{r}' - \mathbf{r})$$

$$= (2\pi)^2 f(\mathbf{r}')$$

Hence,

$$f(\mathbf{r}) = \hat{F}_2^{-1} F(\mathbf{k}) = \frac{1}{(2\pi)^2} \int_{-\infty}^{\infty} F(\mathbf{k}) \exp(i\mathbf{k} \cdot \mathbf{r}) d^2\mathbf{k}$$

In Cartesian coordinates,

$$f(x, y) = \frac{1}{(2\pi)^2} \int_{-\infty}^{\infty} \int_{-\infty}^{\infty} F(k_x, k_y) \exp(ik_x x) \exp(ik_y y) dk_x dk_y$$

2D Convolution

The convolution theorem is the same in two dimensions. By using the symbol $\otimes\otimes$ to denote 2D convolution we can write

$$g(x, y) \otimes \otimes f(x, y) \iff G(k_x, k_y) F(k_x, k_y)$$

2.9 THE SAMPLING THEOREM AND SINC IN-TERPOLATION

Digital signals are usually obtained from analogue signals by converting them into a sequence of numbers (a digital signal) so that digital computers can be used to process them. This conversion is called digitization. When conversion takes place, it is essential that all the information in the original analogue signal is retained in the digital signal. To do this, the analogue signal must be sampled at the correct rate. So what is the correct rate? The answer to this question is provided by the sampling theorem. This theorem states that if a continuous function $f(x)$ is bandlimited and has a complex spectrum $F(k)$, $|k| \leq K$, then it is fully specified by values spaced at regular intervals

$$\delta x \leq \frac{\pi}{K}$$

apart. The parameter K/π is important and is given a special name - it is called the 'Nyquist frequency'. To convert an analogue signal into a digital signal with no loss of information one must choose a sampling rate that is at least equal to the Nyquist frequency of the signal. To show why this is the case, a function called the comb function must first be introduced.

The comb function

The comb function describes a train of unit impulse functions and is given by

$$\text{comb}(x) = \sum_{n=-\infty}^{\infty} \delta(x - nX)$$

where

$$\delta(x - nX) = \begin{cases} 1, & x = nX \\ 0, & x \neq nX \end{cases}$$

This function is a sequence of unit delta functions spaced apart by X. Sampling a function can be describe mathematically by multiplying it by this comb function. If $f(x)$ is the bandlimited function and g is the sampled function, then we can write

$$g(x) = \text{comb}(x)f(x)$$

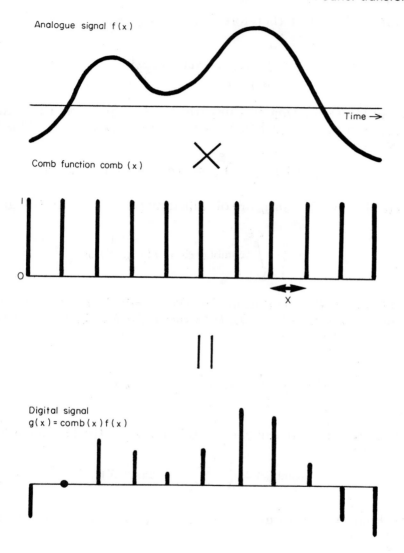

Figure 2.2 Sampling by multiplication with the comb function

This is illustrated in figure 2.2. The sampling theorem is obtain by analysing the spectrum of the sampled function $g(x)$. To do this the Fourier transform of the comb function must first be

43

obtained. We must therefore evaluate the integral

$$\int\limits_{-\infty}^{\infty} \text{comb}(x)\exp(-ikx)dx$$

The key to evaluating this integral lies in expressing the comb function in terms of a Fourier series (not a transform). This is given by

$$\text{comb}(x) = \sum_{n=-\infty}^{\infty} a_n \exp(i2\pi nx/X)$$

where the coefficients a_n are obtained by computing the integral

$$a_n = \frac{1}{X}\int\limits_{-X/2}^{X/2} \text{comb}(x)\exp(-i2\pi nx/X)dx$$

Substituting the definition for the comb function into the equation above and noting that $\text{comb}(x) = \delta(x)$ in the interval $[-X/2, X/2]$, we get

$$a_n = \frac{1}{X}\int\limits_{-X/2}^{X/2} \delta(x)\exp(-i2\pi nx/X)dx = \frac{1}{X}$$

Hence, we can represent the comb function by the Fourier series

$$\text{comb}(x) = \frac{1}{X}\sum_{n=-\infty}^{\infty} \exp(i2\pi nx/X)$$

The Fourier transform of the comb function can therefore be written as

$$\int\limits_{-\infty}^{\infty} \frac{1}{X}\sum_{n=-\infty}^{\infty} \exp(i2\pi nx/X)\exp(-ikx)dx$$

$$= \frac{1}{X}\sum_{n=-\infty}^{\infty}\int\limits_{-\infty}^{\infty} \exp[-ix(k-2\pi n/X)]dx$$

$$= \frac{2\pi}{X} \sum_{n=-\infty}^{\infty} \delta(k - 2\pi n/X)$$

Hence, we obtain the important result (crucial to the proof of the sampling theorem)

$$\sum_{n=-\infty}^{\infty} \delta(x - nX) \Longleftrightarrow \frac{2\pi}{X} \sum_{n=-\infty}^{\infty} \delta(k - 2\pi n/X)$$

Proof of the sampling theorem

Suppose we sample a function at regular intervals of δx. The sampled function g is then given by

$$g(x) = f(x) \sum_{n=-\infty}^{\infty} \delta(x - n\delta x)$$

Using the product theorem, in Fourier space, this equation becomes

$$G(k) = F(k) \otimes \frac{2\pi}{\delta x} \sum_{n=-\infty}^{\infty} \delta(k - 2\pi n/\delta x)$$

$$= \frac{2\pi}{\delta x} \sum_{n=-\infty}^{\infty} F(k - 2\pi n/\delta x)$$

This result demonstrates that sampling the function f, creates a new spectrum G which is a periodic replica of the spectrum F spaced at regular intervals $\pm 2\pi/\delta x, \pm 4\pi/\delta x, \pm 6\pi/\delta x$ and so on. This is illustrated in figure 2.3. The total width of the spectrum F is $K - (-K) = 2K$ and so if $2\pi/\delta x < 2K$, then the replicated spectra will overlap. This effect known as aliasing. To ensure that aliasing does not occur, we require that

$$\frac{\pi}{\delta x} \geq K$$

or a sampling rate where

$$\delta x \leq \frac{\pi}{K}$$

A digital signal that has been sampled according to the condition

$$\delta x = \frac{\pi}{K}$$

Quantitative coherent imaging

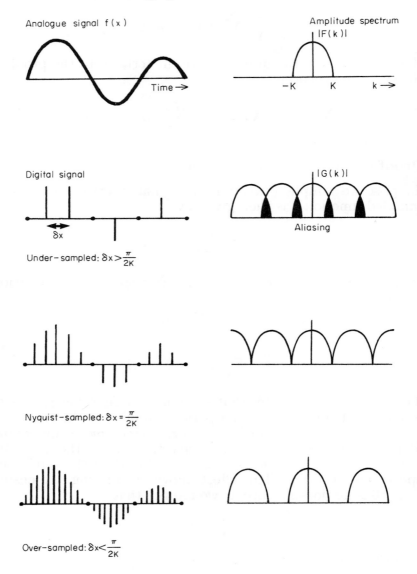

Analogue signal f(x)

Time →

Amplitude spectrum
|F(k)|

−K   K   k →

Digital signal

δx

Under−sampled: $\delta x > \dfrac{\pi}{2K}$

|G(k)|

Aliasing

Nyquist−sampled: $\delta x = \dfrac{\pi}{2K}$

Over−sampled: $\delta x < \dfrac{\pi}{2K}$

Figure 2.3 The sampling theorem. If an analogue signal is under sampled, then a digital signal is obtained which does not contain the same amount of information. This effect is known as aliasing. The information that is lost is associated with that part of the spectrum which overlaps (the shaded regions). Aliasing is eliminated by sampling the analogue signal at a rate equal to $1/2K$ where K is the highest frequency in the signal

is called a Nyquist sampled signal.

Sinc interpolation

If the condition given above provides the necessary sampling rate that is required to convert an analogue signal into a digital signal without loss of information, then one should be able to recover the analogue signal from the digital signal also without loss of information. Assuming that f has been sampled at the Nyquist frequency, the only difference between g and f is that the spectrum of g consists of F repeated at regular interval $2\pi n/\delta x; n = \pm 1, \pm 2, \pm 3, .., \pm \infty$. Hence, f can be obtained from g by retaining just the part of G for values of $\mid k \mid$ less than or equal to K and setting all other values in the spectrum to zero. In other words

$$F(k) = G(k)$$

provided we set

$$G(k) = 0 \forall \mid k \mid > K$$

We can describe this provision mathematically by multiplying G with the top hat function

$$H(k) = \begin{cases} 1, & \mid k \mid \leq K \\ 0, & \mid k \mid > 0 \end{cases}$$

Thus, F is related to G by the equation

$$F(k) = H(k)G(k)$$

Using the convolution theorem, we then obtain

$$f(x) = 2K \operatorname{sinc}(Kx) \otimes g(x)$$

The restoration of a continuous function from a sampled function is known generally as interpolation. The above result shows that a function can be interpolated by convolving it with the appropriate sinc function. This is known as sinc interpolation. In practice, it is equivalent to 'zero padding' the spectrum of the sampled function g. The use of a Fast Fourier Transform (FFT) for this purpose provides an efficient method of interpolation which is discussed further in section 2.12.

2.10 THE DISCRETE FOURIER TRANSFORM

Suppose we Nyquist sample an analogue signal $f(x)$ to get a digital signal $f(x_n)$ which consists of N numbers where $f(x_n)$ is a sample of $f(x)$ at x_n. If we want to compute the Fourier transform of $f(x_n)$, then we must evaluate the discrete Fourier transform. This transform and its corresponding inverse can be obtained from the complex Fourier series representation of a function. In the range $[-N/2, N/2]$, this series is given by

$$f(x) = \sum_{m=-\infty}^{\infty} F_m \exp(i2\pi mx/X)$$

where

$$F_m = \frac{1}{N} \int_{-N/2}^{N/2} f(x) \exp(-i2\pi mx/X)$$

If we now consider the case where we restrict the complex co-efficients F_m to the range $[-N/2, N/2]$ and let $f(x) \to f(x_n)$ then we can write

$$f_n = \sum_{m=-N/2}^{N/2} F_m \exp(i2\pi nm/N)$$

where

$$F_m = \frac{1}{N} \sum_{n=-N/2}^{N/2} f_n \exp(-i2\pi nm/N)$$

and

$$f_n \equiv f(x_n)$$

The last equation for F_m is called the discrete Fourier transform or DFT and the equation for f_n is the inverse DFT. The numbers f_n and F_m are samples of the signal $f(x)$ and spectrum $F(k)$ respectively. If we let Δx_n represent the interval between the samples x_n and Δk_m denote the interval between the samples k_m, then we can write

$$k_m x_n = m\Delta k_m n\Delta x_n$$

From this result it is clear that

$$\Delta k_m \Delta x_n = \frac{2\pi}{N}$$

In two dimensions, the DFT is given by

$$F_{pq} = \frac{1}{NM} \sum_{n=-N/2}^{N/2} \sum_{m=-M/2}^{M/2} f_{nm} \exp(-i2\pi pn/N) \exp(-i2\pi qm/M)$$

where $N \times M$ is the total number of samples. As in the one-dimensional case, the interval Δk_x between the numbers F_{pq} in the k_x direction is related to the interval Δx between the numbers f_{nm} in the x direction by

$$\Delta k_x = \frac{2\pi}{N\Delta x}$$

Similarly,

$$\Delta k_y = \frac{2\pi}{M\Delta y}$$

The DFT has many properties which are similar to the Fourier transform. The following list presents those properties which are used extensively in digital signal processing. In this list

$$\sum_n \equiv \sum_{n=-N/2}^{N/2}$$

1. Convolution theorem

$$f_n \otimes g_n \iff NF_m G_m$$

where $\otimes$ is used to denote the convolution sum, i.e.

$$f_n \otimes g_n = \sum_m f_{n-m} g_m$$

2. Shift theorem

$$f_{n-l} \iff \exp(-i2\pi ml/N) F_m$$

3. Product theorem

$$f_n g_n \iff \sum_m F_{n-m} G_m$$

49

4. Correlation theorem

$$f_n^* \odot g_n \iff N F_m^* G_m$$

5. Autocorrelation theorem

$$f_n^* \odot f_n \iff N \mid F_m \mid^2$$

6. DC level

$$\sum_n f_n = N F_0$$

7. Parseval's theorem

$$\sum_n f_n^* g_n \iff N \sum_m F_m^* G_m$$

8. Rayleigh's theorem

$$\sum_n \mid f_n \mid^2 \iff N \sum_m \mid F_m \mid^2$$

The results above also apply in two dimensions. For example, the 2D convolution theorem is

$$f_{nm} \otimes \otimes g_{nm} \iff N^2 F_{pq} G_{pq}$$

2.11 THE FAST FOURIER TRANSFORM

As the name suggests, the Fast Fourier Transform (FFT) is just a method of computing the DFT which is able to save on computer time. In other words, it is a fast way of computing a DFT. This is done by exploiting certain properties of the DFT to design a computer program which reduces the number of operations (i.e. multiplications and additions) required to compute the DFT. Fast Fourier transforms usually operate on arrays of size $N = 2^K$ where K is a positive integer. In this case, the number of operations is reduced from approximately N^2 to

$N \log_2 N$ giving a large saving in computer time. For example, if $N = 32$, then

$$\frac{N \log_2 N}{N^2} = \frac{\log_2 N}{N} \simeq 0.16$$

The saving in time is even greater when N is large. For $N = 1024$, the above ratio is $\simeq 0.01$.

A variety of FFT algorithms are available, and details on their individual design and performance can be found in a number of specialist textbooks (some of these a listed at the end of this chapter). Here, we shall concentrate on how the FFT may be used to perform a variety of operations which are important in imaging science.

The 1D FFT

The following FORTRAN program is a subroutine for computing the DFT in 1D. This program has been adapted from Gonzalez and Wintz, *Digital image processing*, Addison-Wesley, 1987.

```
        SUBROUTINE FFT1D(A,B,N,ISGN)
        REAL A(64),B(64)
        COMPLEX C(64),U,V,W,CMPLX
        PI=4.*ATAN(1.)
        P=FLOAT(N)
        Q=LOG(P)/LOG(2.)
        K=INT(Q)
        NH=N/2
        NM=N-1
        J=1
        DO 1 I=NH+1,N
        C(J)=CMPLX(A(I),B(I))
1       J=J+1
        DO 2 I=1,NH
        C(J)=CMPLX(A(I),B(I))
2       J=J+1
        J=1
        DO 3 I=1,NM
        IF(I.GE.J)GOTO 10
        V=C(J)
        C(J)=C(I)
        C(I)=V
```

```
10    JJ=NH
4     IF(JJ.GE.J)GOTO 3
      J=J-JJ
      JJ=JJ/2
      GOTO 4
3     J=J+JJ
      DO 6 L=1,K
      L1=2**L
      X=2.*PI*FLOAT(ISGN)/L1
      W=CMPLX(COS(X),SIN(X))
      L2=L1/2
      U=(1.,0.)
      DO 6 J=1,L2
      DO 5 I=J,N,L1
      II=I+L2
      V=C(II)*U
      C(II)=C(I)-V
5     C(I)=C(I)+V
6     U=U*W
      J=1
      DO 7 I=1,N
7     C(I)=C(I)/FLOAT(N)
      DO 8 I=NH+1,N
      A(J)=REAL(C(I))
      B(J)=AIMAG(C(I))
8     J=J+1
      DO 9 I=1,NH
      A(J)=REAL(C(I))
      B(J)=AIMAG(C(I))
9     J=J+1
      RETURN
      END
```

On input, A and B are the real and imaginary parts of the complex function whose DFT is required. On output A and B are the real and imaginary parts of the DFT. The parameter N, defines the size of the arrays which must be an integer power of 2 and ISGN specifies whether the forward (ISGN=-1) or inverse (ISGN=1) DFT is required. Observe, that the size of the arrays A, B and C in this program have been set at 64. Hence, as it stands, this program may only be used to process

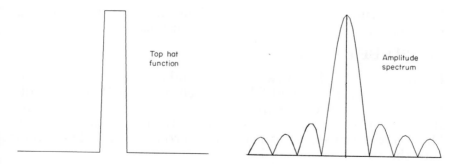

Figure 2.4 One-dimensional DFT of a top hat function using subroutine FFT1D

arrays of size

$$N(= 2^K) \le 64; \quad K = 1, 2, ..$$

Larger arrays may of course by used by providing A, B and C with sufficient work space. Note, that the DC level of the output spectrum occurs at N/2+1. Also note, that if the DFT of a real valued function is required, then the imaginary component B must be set to zero before calling FFT1D.

A simple demonstration of subroutine FFT1D is provided in figure 2.4. This shows the amplitude spectrum of a top hat function generated by FFT1D using an array size of 128 ($N = 2^7$). This is a fast numerical computation of the transform

$$F(k) = \int_{-\infty}^{\infty} f(x) \exp(-ikx) dx$$

where

$$f(x) = \begin{cases} 1, & |x| \le a \\ 0, & |x| > a \end{cases}$$

and $2a$ is the width of the the top hat function. The analytical result is

$$F(k) = 2a \operatorname{sinc}(ka)$$

and the amplitude spectrum is given by

$$A(k) = |F(k)| = 2a |\operatorname{sinc}(ka)|$$

53

The amplitude spectrum given in figure 2.4 is therefore just a graphical representation of the function $|\operatorname{sinc}(ka)|$.

The 2D FFT

To obtain the DFT of a two-dimensional array, we simply compute the one-dimensional DFT of each row and then each column. This result follows from the fact that in Cartesian coordinates, the two- dimensional Fourier transform is separable. The following program utilizes the subroutine FFT1D to compute the two-dimensional DFT:

```
SUBROUTINE FFT2D(A,B,N,ISGN)
DIMENSION A(64,64),B(64,64),C(64,64),D(64,64)
DIMENSION AA(64),BB(64),CC(64),DD(64)
DO J=1,N
DO I=1,N
AA(I)=A(I,J)
BB(I)=B(I,J)
ENDDO
CALL FFT1D(AA,BB,N,ISGN)
DO I=1,N
C(I,J)=AA(I)
D(I,J)=BB(I)
ENDDO
ENDDO
DO I=1,N
DO J=1,N
CC(J)=C(I,J)
DD(J)=D(I,J)
ENDDO
CALL FFT1D(CC,DD,N,ISGN)
DO J=1,N
A(I,J)=CC(J)
B(I,J)=DD(J)
ENDDO
ENDDO
RETURN
END
```

As before, on input, A and B contain the real and imaginary arrays and on output contain the real and imaginary parts of the two-dimensional DFT respectively. The DC level occurs at

(N/2+1,N/2+1).

Subroutine FFT2D is demonstrated in figure 2.5, which shows an image of the power spectrum of a circular disc. This spectrum is circularly symmetric and is composed of a central lobe surrounded by a sequence of concentric rings (N.B. for display purposes, this spectrum has been histogram equalized to reveal its full structure. Histogram equalization is discussed in chapter 11). This is a fast numerical computation of the two- dimensional Fourier transform

$$F(k_x, k_y) = \int\limits_{-\infty}^{\infty} \int\limits_{-\infty}^{\infty} \exp(-ik_x x)\exp(-ik_y y) f(x,y) dx dy$$

where

$$f(x,y) = \begin{cases} 1, & \sqrt{x^2 + y^2} \le a \\ \\ 0, & \sqrt{x^2 + y^2} > a \end{cases}$$

and a is the radius of the disc. This transform can be computed analytically. The result is

$$F(k_x, k_y) = 2\pi a \frac{J_1\left(a\sqrt{k_x^2 + k_y^2}\right)}{\sqrt{k_x^2 + k_y^2}}$$

where J_1 is the first-order Bessel function. This is a well known result of Fraunhofer diffraction theory. The square modulus of the right hand side of the above equation describes the intensity pattern produced by the diffraction of light at a circular aperture (under the assumption that the thickness of the aperture is much smaller than the wavelength of light) - a result that was first derived by the Astronomer Royal, George Airy, in 1835. In this sense, figure 2.5 is just a numerical simulation of the characteristic diffraction pattern produced by a circular aperture. It is a grey level map of the function

$$4\pi^2 a^2 \frac{\mid J_1\left(a\sqrt{k_x^2 + k_y^2}\right)\mid^2}{k_y^2 + k_y^2}$$

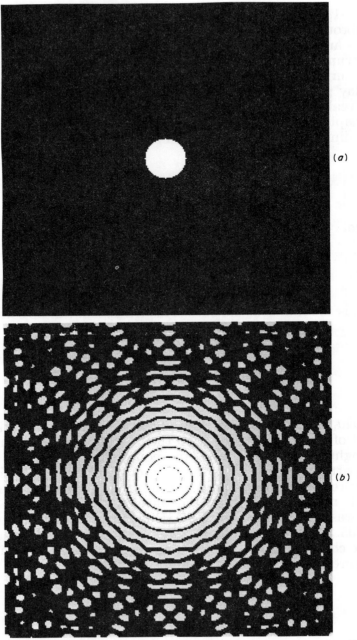

Figure 2.5 Two-dimensional DFT of a circular disc using subroutine FFT2D. (*a*) disc; (*b*) power spectrum

2.12 SOME IMPORTANT PROPERTIES OF THE FFT

Convolution

The convolution of two functions can be obtained by multiplying their complex spectra together and taking the inverse Fourier transform of the complex function that is produced by this operation. The FFT allows this to be done with minimal effort as shown in the following program which convolves two real arrays A and B of size N using the convolution theorem and FFT1D:

```
        SUBROUTINE CONVOL(A,B,C,N)
C
C FUNCTION: THIS SUBROUTINE USES A FFT (FFT1D) AND THE
C           CONVOLUTION THEOREM TO CONVOLVE TWO, ONE
C           DIMENSIONAL ARRAYS (A AND B) OF SIZE N.
C           THE RESULT IS STORED IN ARRAY C.
C
        DIMENSION A(64),B(64),C(64)
        DIMENSION AA(64),BB(64),CC(64)
C
C INITILIZE IMAGINIARY ARRAYS AA, BB AND CC.
C
        DO I=1,N
        AA(I)=0.
        BB(I)=0.
        CC(I)=0.
        ENDDO
C
C TAKE FOURIER TRANSFORMS OF A AND B.
C
        CALL FFT1D(A,AA,N,-1)
        CALL FFT1D(B,BB,N,-1)
C
C DO COMPLEX MULTIPLICATION.
C
        DO I=1,N
        C(I)=A(I)*B(I)-AA(I)*BB(I)  !REAL PART
        CC(I)=A(I)*BB(I)+AA(I)*B(I) !IMAGINARY PART
        ENDDO
```

```
C
C INVERSE FOURIER TRANSFORM.
C
      CALL FFT1D(C,CC,N,1)
C
      RETURN
      END
```

On output C is the result of convolving A with B. The program required to convolve two real 2D arrays is of the same form except that the one-dimensional arrays are replaced by two-dimensional arrays, single DO loops are replaced by double DO loops and FFT1D is replaced by FFT2D.

The analytic signal

Recall that if $f(x)$ is a real function with Fourier transform $F(k)$, then the spectrum of the analytic signal $S(k)$ is given by

$$S(k) = \begin{cases} 0, & k < 0 \\ 2F(k), & k > 0 \end{cases}$$

This result can be used to compute the analytic signal using FFT1D. A subroutine to do this is given below.

```
      SUBROUTINE ANASIG(F,Q,N)
C
C FUNCTION: THIS SUBROUTINE COMPUTES THE ANALYTIC SIGNAL
C           OF A REAL FUNCTION USING FFT1D.
C
      DIMENSION F(64),Q(64)
      NH=N/2
C
C INITIALIZE IMAGINARY ARRAY Q.
C
      DO I=1,N
      Q(I)=0.
      ENDDO
C
C FOURIER TRANSFORM.
C
      CALL FFT1D(F,Q,N,-1)
C
```

```
C SET NEGATIVE HALF OF COMPLEX SPECTRUM TO ZERO.
C
      DO I=1,NH
      F(I)=0.
      Q(I)=0.
      ENDDO
C
C MULTIPLY POSITIVE HALF OF COMPLEX SPECTRUM BY 2.
C
      DO I=NH+1,N
      F(I)=2.*F(I)
      Q(I)=2.*Q(I)
      ENDDO
C
C INVERSE FOURIER TRANSFORM.
C
      CALL FFT1D(F,Q,N,1)
C
      RETURN
      END
```

On input, F is the real part of the analytic function (the original real valued signal). On output, F and Q are the real and imaginary parts of the analytic signal respectively. In other words, on output, F is the original real valued signal and Q is its Hilbert transform.

Sinc interpolation

The FFT can be used to interpolate a digital signal or image by employing sinc interpolation. The program below demonstrates how this can be done in one dimension using FFT1D. This program allows a signal of size N to be interpolated to a size M where both N and M are integer powers of 2 (i.e. arrays whose size is compatible with those required by FFT1D).

```
      SUBROUTINE INTERP(X,Y,N,M)
C
C FUNCTION:  THIS SUBROUTINE SINC INTERPOLATES A SIGNAL
C            BY ZERO PADDING ITS COMPLEX SPECTRUM
C            USING FFT1D.
C
      DIMENSION X(64),XR(64),XI(64)
```

```
      DIMENSION Y(64),YR(64),YI(64)
C
C X-INPUT; Y-OUTPUT.
C N-SIZE OF INPUT.
C M-SIZE OF INTERPOLATED DATA.
C BOTH N AND M MUST BE AN INTEGER POWER OF 2.
C
C FOURIER TRANSFORM.
C
      DO I=1,N
      XR(I)=X(I)
      XI(I)=0.
      ENDDO
      CALL FFT1D(XR,XI,N,-1)
C
C ZERO PAD XR AND XI.
C
      NH=N/2
      MH=M/2
      DO I=1,MH-NH
      YR(I)=0.
      YI(I)=0.
      ENDDO
      J=1
      DO I=MH-NH+1,MH+NH
      YR(I)=XR(J)
      YI(I)=XI(J)
      J=J+1
      ENDDO
      DO I=MH+NH+1,M
      YR(I)=0.
      YI(I)=0.
      ENDDO
C
C INVERSE FOURIER TRANSFORM.
C
      CALL FFT1D(YR,YI,M,1)
C
C WRITE OUTPUT.
C
      DO I=1,M
      Y(I)=YR(I)
```

```
      ENDDO
C
      RETURN
      END
```

SUMMARY OF IMPORTANT RESULTS

Delta function

$$\delta(x) = \frac{1}{2\pi} \int\limits_{-\infty}^{\infty} \exp(ikx)dk$$

Fourier transform

$$F(k) = \int\limits_{-\infty}^{\infty} f(x)\exp(-ikx)dx$$

Inverse Fourier transform

$$f(x) = \frac{1}{2\pi} \int\limits_{-\infty}^{\infty} F(k)\exp(ikx)dk$$

Convolution theorem

$$f(x) \otimes g(x) \Longleftrightarrow F(k)G(k)$$

Hilbert transform

$$q(x) = \frac{1}{\pi x} \otimes f(x)$$

Analytic signal

$$s(x) = f(x) + iq(x)$$

Sampling theorem

$$\text{sampling interval} \ \leq \frac{1}{\text{Nyquist frequency}}$$

DFT

$$F_m = \frac{1}{N} \sum_n f_n \exp(-2\pi i nm/N)$$

Inverse DFT

$$f_n = \sum_m F_m \exp(2\pi i nm/N)$$

FURTHER READING

1. Bracewell R N, *The Fourier Transform and its Applications*, McGraw-Hill, 1978. A fully comprehensive discussion of the Fourier transform is provided in this book - a standard text.

2. Bateman H, *Tables of Integral Transforms*, McGraw-Hill, 1954. Gives one of the most complete lists of Fourier transform pairs.

3. Gradshteyn I S and Ryzhik I M, *Tables of Integrals, Series and Products*, Academic Press, 1980. A useful table of Fourier transform pairs is given in chapter 17 (Fourier and Laplace transforms).

4. Gonzalez R C and Wintz P, *Digital Image Processing*, Addison-Wesley, 1987. Chapter 3 (section 4) discusses the FFT. The subroutine FFT1D given in section 2.11 has been adapted from the program provided in this book which uses a technique called the 'successive doubling method'.

5. Brigham E O, *The Fast Fourier Transform and its Applications*, Prentice-Hall, 1988. An excellent and fully comprehensive book on the FFT which includes a variety of sample programs written in both BASIC and PASCAL.

6. Press W H et al., *Numerical Recipes*, Cambridge University Press, 1986. Chapter 12 of this book discusses the Fast Fourier transform together and some of its applications. Two editions of this book are available, one edition presents code in FORTRAN, the other provides programs written in C.

3 Scattering theory

In this chapter the principal methods used to solve scattering problems associated with coherent imaging systems are presented. Only linear scattering theory is discussed. This involves the use of an approximation which is commonly referred to as the Born approximation after the German physicist Max Born, who was among the first to use it to solve scattering problems in quantum mechanics. The important feature about this approximation is that is provides a mathematical model for the scattered field that is linear and therefore consistent with the coherent imaging equation. The Born approximation therefore allows us to simplify the scattering problem associated with a coherent imaging system in such a way that we can obtain mathematical expressions for the object function in terms of the fluctuating material parameters of the scatterer. This provides results which are important in the interpretation of the object function after the data have been deconvolved.

3.1 GREEN'S FUNCTIONS

Green's functions are used in a wide range of physical problems. They are one of the most important functions in mathematical physics because of the way in which they allow partial differential equations to be solved. In this section only those

Green's functions that are used for scattering theory are discussed. Physically, these Green's functions represent the way in which a wave propagates from one point in space and time to another. For this reason, they are sometimes referred to as propagators.

The type of equations that we are forced to deal with in scattering problems and the analytical techniques that have been developed to cope with them, nearly always originate in some way from the properties of the Green's function that is used. A concrete understanding of these functions is therefore required if the basic elements of coherent imaging theory are to be understood.

Notation

A Green's functions is synonymous with the source-receiver system illustrated in figure 3.1. If the position of the source is denoted by $\mathbf{r}_0$ and the position of the observer by $\mathbf{r}$, then the Green's function is written as a function of $|\mathbf{r} - \mathbf{r}_0|$ where in Cartesian coordinates,

$$|\mathbf{r} - \mathbf{r}_0| = \sqrt{(x - x_0)^2 + (y - y_0)^2 + (z - z_0)^2}$$

The Green's function is denoted by the letter g or G as a reminder of its name. When the functional dependence of g is declared, instead of writing $g(|\mathbf{r} - \mathbf{r}_0|)$, which is messy, it is more convenient to write $g(\mathbf{r}, \mathbf{r}_0)$ or $g(\mathbf{r} \mid \mathbf{r}_0)$. In this book, the latter notation shall be used throughout, so remember,

$$g(\mathbf{r} \mid \mathbf{r}_0) \equiv g(|\mathbf{r} - \mathbf{r}_0|)$$

Homogeneous wave equations

As an introduction to Green's functions, let us first consider the case where we have a source of radiation a long distance away from an observer at $\mathbf{r}$. In this case, the scalar wavefield Φ as a function of space $\mathbf{r}$ and time t is described by the well known homogeneous equation

$$\left(\nabla^2 + \frac{1}{c^2}\frac{\partial^2}{\partial t^2}\right)\Phi(\mathbf{r}, t) = 0 \tag{3.1.1}$$

where c is the velocity at which the radiation propagates from the source to the observer. This equation is known as the homogeneous wave equation.

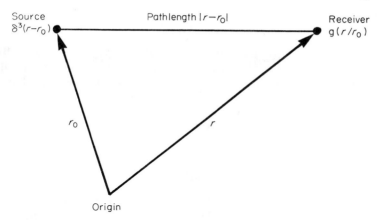

Figure 3.1 Source-receiver geometry used to define the Green's function

CW sources

Let us assume that the source emits a continuous wave which oscillates at a fixed frequency. In this case, the source is known as a continuous wave (CW) or monochromatic source. The time dependence of the radiation field is described by the complex exponential function $\exp(i\omega t)$ where ω is the angular frequency $(= 2\pi \times \text{frequency})$. The time dependent field Φ can therefore be written as

$$\Phi(\mathbf{r}, t) = \phi(\mathbf{r}, \omega) \exp(i\omega t) \tag{3.1.2}$$

Substituting this expression into equation (3.1.1), we obtain

$$(\nabla^2 + k^2)\phi(\mathbf{r}, k) = 0$$

where

$$k = \frac{\omega}{c} = \frac{2\pi}{\lambda}$$

The parameter k, is known as the wavenumber. The parameter λ is the wavelength of the wavefield described by the function Φ. The solution to this equation is well known. It is called the plane wave solution and is given by

$$\phi(\mathbf{r}, k) = \exp(i\mathbf{k} \cdot \mathbf{r})$$

65

where

$$\mathbf{k} = k\hat{\mathbf{n}}$$

and it is assumed that the amplitude of the wave is 1. The unit vector $\hat{\mathbf{n}}$ points along the direction in which the wave propagates. This solution can be combined with equation (3.1.2) so that the time dependent wavefield becomes

$$\Phi(\mathbf{r}, t) = \exp[i(\mathbf{k} \cdot \mathbf{r} + \omega t)]$$

An equally valid solution is

$$\Phi(\mathbf{r}, t) = \exp[i(\mathbf{k} \cdot \mathbf{r} - \omega t)]$$

which is obtained by using the $\exp(-i\omega t)$ to describe the time dependence of the wavefield. If we imagine a straight line along the direction of $\hat{\mathbf{n}}$, then the above solution represents a wave propagating to the right whereas the former solution represents a wave propagating to the left. The function

$$\exp[i(\mathbf{k} \cdot \mathbf{r} + \omega t)]$$

is said to describe a left-travelling wave and

$$\exp[i(\mathbf{k} \cdot \mathbf{r} - \omega t)]$$

is referred to as a right-travelling wave.

Pulsed sources

If the source emits a pulse of radiation, then the time dependent field can be written as the sum of many different monochromatic waves of different frequencies ω and amplitudes ϕ. If we consider all the different possible frequencies that can exist between $-\infty$ and ∞ then, $\Phi(\mathbf{r}, t)$ can be written in terms of the Fourier transform of ϕ,

$$\Phi(\mathbf{r}, t) = \frac{1}{2\pi} \int\limits_{-\infty}^{\infty} \phi(\mathbf{r}, \omega) \exp(i\omega t) d\omega$$

Here, Φ describes a left-travelling pulse. We can also consider a solution for a right-travelling pulse by writing

$$\Phi(\mathbf{r}, t) = \frac{1}{2\pi} \int\limits_{-\infty}^{\infty} \phi(\mathbf{r}, \omega) \exp(-i\omega t) d\omega$$

Substituting either of these expressions into equation (3.1.1), we obtain

$$(\nabla^2 + k^2)\phi(\mathbf{r}, k) = 0$$

where this time k is not fixed but can take on any value between $-\infty$ and ∞. The time dependent field produced by a left-travelling pulse is therefore

$$\Phi(\mathbf{r}, t) = \frac{1}{2\pi} \int\limits_{-\infty}^{\infty} \exp[i(\mathbf{k} \cdot \mathbf{r} + \omega t)]d\omega$$

If we now write $\mathbf{k} \cdot \mathbf{r}$ as $k\hat{\mathbf{n}} \cdot \mathbf{r} = (\omega/c)\hat{\mathbf{n}} \cdot \mathbf{r}$, then, using equation (2.1.1), the above equation can be written as

$$\Phi(\mathbf{r}, t) = \frac{1}{2\pi} \int\limits_{-\infty}^{\infty} \exp[i\omega(t + \hat{\mathbf{n}} \cdot \mathbf{r}/c)]d\omega = \delta(t + \hat{\mathbf{n}} \cdot \mathbf{r}/c)$$

The expression for a right-travelling pulse is given by

$$\Phi(\mathbf{r}, t) = \delta(t - \hat{\mathbf{n}} \cdot \mathbf{r}/c)$$

Basic equations for the Green's function

Let us now turn our attention to the case when the source is not at infinity but close to an observer at $\mathbf{r}$. To describe this situation mathematically, we introduce a source function $S(\mathbf{r}, t)$. The wavefield is then governed by the inhomogeneous equation

$$\left(\nabla^2 + \frac{1}{c^2}\frac{\partial^2}{\partial t^2}\right)\Phi(\mathbf{r}, t) = -S(\mathbf{r}, t)$$

Now, the Green's function describes the wavefield that is produced when a very special and unique type of source function is considered, namely, when the source function is a delta function, i.e. when

$$S(\mathbf{r}, t) = \delta^n(\mathbf{r} - \mathbf{r}_0)\delta(t - t_0)$$

where $n = 1, 2$ or 3 depending on whether we are considering a one-, two-, or three-dimensional wavefield respectively. Hence, the equation for the time dependent Green's function (which is usually denoted by G) is given by

$$\left(\nabla^2 + \frac{1}{c^2}\frac{\partial^2}{\partial t^2}\right)G(\mathbf{r} \mid \mathbf{r}_0, t \mid t_0) = -\delta^n(\mathbf{r} - \mathbf{r}_0)\delta(t - t_0) \tag{3.1.3}$$

where $\mathbf{r}_0$ is the position of the source and $t \mid t_0 \equiv t - t_0$. To obtain the equation for the time independent Green's function, we write G and $\delta(t - t_0)$ as Fourier transforms,

$$G(\mathbf{r} \mid \mathbf{r}_0, t \mid t_0) = \frac{1}{2\pi} \int_{-\infty}^{\infty} g(\mathbf{r} \mid \mathbf{r}_0, \omega) \exp[i\omega(t - t_0)]d\omega$$

and

$$\delta(t - t_0) = \frac{1}{2\pi} \int_{-\infty}^{\infty} \exp[i\omega(t - t_0)]d\omega$$

Substituting these equations into equation (3.1.3) we then get

$$(\nabla^2 + k^2)g(\mathbf{r} \mid \mathbf{r}_0, k) = -\delta^n(\mathbf{r} - \mathbf{r}_0) \qquad (3.1.4)$$

Note that once g has been obtained, the time dependent Green's function can be obtained by computing the Fourier integral given above. Physically, we may view the Green's function $g(\mathbf{r} \mid \mathbf{r}_0, k)$ as a spherically diverging wave with a wavenumber k, emanating from a source $\mathbf{r}_0$ and propagating to $\mathbf{r}$.

Time independent Green's functions

The time independent Green's function is obtained by solving equation (3.1.4).

One dimension (n=1)

In one dimension, the Green's function is given by the solution to

$$\left(\frac{\partial^2}{\partial x^2} + k^2\right) g(x \mid x_0, k) = -\delta(x - x_0) \qquad (3.1.5)$$

The solution to this equation is based on employing the properties of the Fourier transform. Writing $X = x - x_0$, we express g and δ as Fourier transforms

$$g(X, k) = \frac{1}{2\pi} \int_{-\infty}^{\infty} g(u, k) \exp(iuX)du \qquad (3.1.6)$$

and

$$\delta(X) = \frac{1}{2\pi} \int_{-\infty}^{\infty} \exp(iuX)du$$

Substituting these expressions into equation (3.1.5) and differentiating gives

$$\frac{1}{2\pi} \int_{-\infty}^{\infty} (-u^2 + k^2)g(u, k)\exp(iuX)du = -\frac{1}{2\pi} \int_{-\infty}^{\infty} \exp(iuX)du$$

from which it follows that

$$g(u, k) = \frac{1}{u^2 - k^2}$$

Substituting this result back into equation (3.1.6), we get

$$g(X, k) = \frac{1}{2\pi} \int_{-\infty}^{\infty} \frac{\exp(iuX)}{u^2 - k^2} du$$

$$= \frac{1}{2\pi} \int_{-\infty}^{\infty} \frac{\exp(iuX)}{(u - k)(u + k)} du$$

The problem is therefore reduced to that of evaluating the above integral. This can be done using Cauchy's integral formula, i.e.

$$\oint_C f(u)du = 2\pi i \times (\text{sum of the residues enclosed by } C)$$

where C is the contour defining the path of integration. In order to evaluate the integral explicitly using this formula, we must consider the singular nature or poles of the integrand at $u = -k$ and $u = k$. Without a prescription indicating how the path of integration along the contour C should be chosen, the Green's function cannot be properly defined. We therefore need to introduce a physical argument about the behaviour of g. Physically, we require an expression for a wave that originates from a point at x_0 and propagates away from this point. In other words, we should look for a solution that represents an outgoing wave. For this reason, the Green's function we require is known as the outgoing Green's function.

Since x and x_0 are points on a line, let us consider the case when the wave propagates away from x_0 by travelling in a direction that is to the left of x_0. In this case, only points along

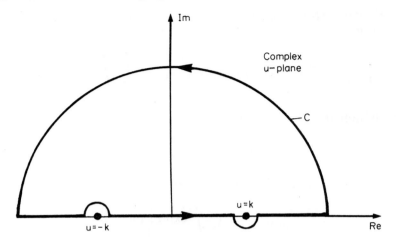

Figure 3.2 Contour of integration used to evaluate the Green's function for a left-travelling wave

x which are to the left and therefore less than x_0 will be disturbed by the wave. If we allow the poles at both $u = k$ and $u = -k$ to contribute, it is evident that the residues will contain factors of the form $\exp(ikX)$ and $\exp(-ikX)$ respectively. Now, a left-travelling wave is given by multiplying these expressions by $\exp(i\omega t)$ giving

$$\exp[i(kX + \omega t)] = \exp(-ikx_0)\exp[i(kx + \omega t)]$$

for $u = k$ or

$$\exp[-i(kX - \omega t)] = \exp(ikx_0)\exp[-i(kx - \omega t)]$$

for $u = -k$. The first expression corresponds to a wave travelling to the left and the second expression represents a wave travelling to the right. Hence, if the Green's function is to represent a left-travelling wave, then the latter function should be ignored. This corresponds to ignoring the pole at $u = -k$. The contour of integration will then only enclose one pole at $u = k$ as shown in figure 3.2 and the calculation is straightforward, the out going Green's function being given by

$$g(x \mid x_0, k) = 2\pi i \operatorname{Res} \left[\frac{1}{2\pi} \frac{\exp(iuX)}{(u+k)(u-k)} \right]_{u=k}$$

$$= \frac{i}{2k} \exp(ik \mid x - x_0 \mid), \quad x < x_0 \tag{3.1.7}$$

If we consider the alternative case where the wave travels to the right of the source, then the outgoing Green's function is given by

$$g(x \mid x_0, k) = \frac{i}{2k} \exp(-ik \mid x - x_0 \mid), \quad x > x_0$$

Two dimensions (n=2)

In two dimensions, the same method can be used to obtain the Green's function, i.e. to solve the equation

$$(\nabla^2 + k^2) g(\mathbf{r} \mid \mathbf{r}_0, k) = -\delta^2(\mathbf{r} - \mathbf{r}_0)$$

where

$$\mathbf{r} = \hat{x}x + \hat{y}y$$

and

$$\nabla^2 = \frac{\partial^2}{\partial x^2} + \frac{\partial^2}{\partial y^2}$$

Writing $\mathbf{R} = \mathbf{r} - \mathbf{r}_0$ and using the same technique as before (i.e. the one used to derive an integral representation of the one-dimensional Green's function) we obtain

$$g(R, k) = \frac{1}{(2\pi)^2} \int\limits_{-\infty}^{\infty} \frac{\exp(i\mathbf{u} \cdot \mathbf{R})}{u^2 - k^2} d^2\mathbf{u}$$

In Cartesian coordinates, where

$$\mathbf{u} = \hat{x}u_x + \hat{y}u_y$$

and

$$d^2\mathbf{u} = du_x du_y$$

this result becomes

$$g(R,k) = \frac{1}{(2\pi)^2} \int\limits_{-\infty}^{\infty} du_x \int\limits_{-\infty}^{\infty} du_y \frac{\exp(iu_x x)\exp(iu_y y)}{u_x^2 + u_y^2 - k^2}$$

Choosing to integrate over u_y first, we have

$$\frac{1}{2\pi} \int\limits_{-\infty}^{\infty} \frac{\exp(iu_y y)}{u_y^2 - (k^2 - u_x^2)} du_y$$

$$= \frac{i}{2\sqrt{k^2 - u_x^2}} \exp[i\sqrt{k^2 - u_x^2}\, y]$$

Once again, the contour of integration has been chosen to give an expression for the outgoing Green's function which can now be written in the form

$$g(R,k) = \frac{i}{4\pi} \int\limits_{-\infty}^{\infty} \frac{\exp[i(u_x x + \sqrt{k^2 - u_x^2}\, y)]}{\sqrt{k^2 - u_x^2}} du_x$$

The integral over u_x can be simplified by switching to polar coordinates

$$u_x = k\cos(\theta + \phi)$$

$$x = R\cos\phi$$

and

$$y = R\sin\phi$$

The Green's function is then given by

$$g(R,k) = \frac{i}{4\pi} \int\limits_{i\infty}^{-i\infty} \exp(ikR\cos\theta) d\theta$$

Writing the Green's function in this form allows us to employ the result

$$H_0^{(1)}(kR) = \frac{1}{\pi} \int\limits_{i\infty}^{-i\infty} \exp(ikR\cos\theta) d\theta$$

where $H_0^{(1)}$ is known as the Hankel function (of the first kind and of order zero). The two-dimensional Green's function may then be written as

$$g(\mathbf{r} \mid \mathbf{r}_0, k) = \frac{i}{4} H_0^{(1)}(k \mid \mathbf{r} - \mathbf{r}_0 \mid)$$

A useful approximation for this function can be obtained by employing the result

$$H_0^{(1)}(kR) \simeq \sqrt{\frac{2}{\pi}} \exp(i\pi/4) \frac{\exp(ikR)}{\sqrt{kR}}$$

which is valid when

$$kR \gg 1$$

This condition means that the wavelength of the radiation originating from $\mathbf{r}_0$ is very small compared to the distance between $\mathbf{r}_0$ and $\mathbf{r}$. In many coherent imaging systems this is a physically reasonable condition and so a two-dimensional Green's function of the following form can be used,

$$g(\mathbf{r} \mid \mathbf{r}_0, k) = \frac{1}{\sqrt{8\pi}} \exp(i\pi/4) \frac{\exp(ik \mid \mathbf{r} - \mathbf{r}_0 \mid)}{\sqrt{k \mid \mathbf{r} - \mathbf{r}_0 \mid}} \qquad (3.1.8)$$

Three dimensions (n=3)

In three dimensions, the Green's function is given by the solution to the equation

$$(\nabla^2 + k^2) g(\mathbf{r} \mid \mathbf{r}_0, k) = -\delta^3(\mathbf{r} - \mathbf{r}_0)$$

where

$$\mathbf{r} = \hat{\mathbf{x}} x + \hat{\mathbf{y}} y + \hat{\mathbf{z}} z$$

and

$$\nabla^2 = \frac{\partial^2}{\partial x^2} + \frac{\partial^2}{\partial y^2} + \frac{\partial^2}{\partial z^2}$$

In this case

$$g(R, k) = \frac{1}{(2\pi)^3} \int_{-\infty}^{\infty} \frac{\exp(i\mathbf{u} \cdot \mathbf{R})}{u^2 - k^2} d^3\mathbf{u}$$

73

It proves convenient to evaluate this integral using spherical polar coordinates which gives

$$g(R, k) = \frac{1}{(2\pi)^3} \int\limits_0^{2\pi} d\phi \int\limits_{-1}^{1} d(\cos\theta) \int\limits_0^{\infty} \frac{\exp(iuR\cos\theta)u^2}{u^2 - k^2} du$$

Integrating over ϕ and θ we then obtain

$$g(R, k) = \frac{1}{2\pi^2 R} \int\limits_0^{\infty} \frac{u\sin(uR)}{u^2 - k^2} du$$

Since the integrand is an even function we may extend the integration to include the interval $-\infty$ to 0 by writing

$$g(R, k) = \frac{1}{4\pi^2 R} \int\limits_{-\infty}^{\infty} \frac{u\sin(uR)}{u^2 - k^2} du$$

This is done in anticipation of using Cauchy's integral formula to evaluate the final integral. Using the result

$$\sin(uR) = \frac{\exp(iuR) - \exp(-iuR)}{2i}$$

we can write this integral in the form

$$g(R, k) = \frac{1}{8\pi^2 iR} \int\limits_{-\infty}^{\infty} \frac{u\exp(iuR)}{(u + k)(u - k)} du - \frac{1}{8\pi^2 iR} \int\limits_{-\infty}^{\infty} \frac{u\exp(-iuR)}{(u + k)(u - k)} du$$

Once again, in order to evaluate the above integrals, the path of integration which encloses the relevant pole must be specified and so we again choose the pole which leads to an expression for the outgoing Green's function. The first integral is then given by

$$2\pi i \operatorname{Res}\left[\frac{u\exp(iuR)}{(u + k)(u - k)}\right]_{u=k} = 2\pi i \frac{k\exp(ikR)}{2k} = i\pi \exp(ikR)$$

and the second integral is given by

$$-2\pi i \operatorname{Res}\left[\frac{u\exp(-iuR)}{(u + k)(u - k)}\right]_{u=-k} = -i\pi \exp(ikR)$$

The outgoing Green's function is therefore given by

$$g(\mathbf{r} \mid \mathbf{r}_0, k) = \frac{1}{4\pi \mid \mathbf{r} - \mathbf{r}_0 \mid} \exp(ik \mid \mathbf{r} - \mathbf{r}_0 \mid) \qquad (3.1.9)$$

Observe, that in all three dimensions the Green's function is singular. The precise nature of the singularity changes from one dimension to the next. In three dimensions, the Green's function is spatially singular when $\mathbf{r} = \mathbf{r}_0$ whereas in one dimension the singularity is temporal (i.e. the singularity occurs when $k = 0$). In two dimensions, the Green's function is a Hankel function whose argument is $k \mid \mathbf{r} - \mathbf{r}_0 \mid$ and has both a temporal and spatial singularity (i.e. it is singular when either $k = 0$ or $\mathbf{r} = \mathbf{r}_0$).

Time dependent Green's functions

The time dependent Green's function can be obtained by evaluating the Fourier integral

$$G(\mathbf{r} \mid \mathbf{r}_0, t \mid t_0) = \frac{1}{2\pi} \int\limits_{-\infty}^{\infty} g(\mathbf{r} \mid \mathbf{r}_0, k) \exp[i\omega(t - t_0)]d\omega \qquad (3.1.10)$$

In three dimensions, the time dependent Green's function is easy to compute. It is given by

$$G(\mathbf{r} \mid \mathbf{r}_0, t \mid t_0) = \frac{1}{2\pi} \int\limits_{-\infty}^{\infty} \frac{1}{4\pi \mid \mathbf{r} - \mathbf{r}_0 \mid} \exp(ik \mid \mathbf{r} - \mathbf{r}_0 \mid) \exp[i\omega(t - t_0)]d\omega$$

$$= \frac{1}{4\pi \mid \mathbf{r} - \mathbf{r}_0 \mid} \delta(t - t_0 + \mid \mathbf{r} - \mathbf{r}_0 \mid /c), \quad t - t_0 \geq \mid \mathbf{r} - \mathbf{r}_0 \mid /c$$

In two dimensions, the point source (which depends on x and y), can be treated as a line source, i.e. a uniform source extending from $z_0 = -\infty$ to $z_0 = \infty$ along a line parallel to the z axis and passing through the point (x_0, y_0). The two-dimensional Green's function can therefore be obtained by integrating the three-dimensional Green's function from $z_0 = -\infty$ to $z_0 = \infty$, i.e.

$$G(\mathbf{s} \mid \mathbf{s}_0, t \mid t_0) = \int\limits_{-\infty}^{\infty} \frac{\delta(t - t_0 + \mid \mathbf{r} - \mathbf{r}_0 \mid /c)}{4\pi \mid \mathbf{r} - \mathbf{r}_0 \mid} dz_0 \qquad (3.1.11)$$

where
$$\mathbf{s} = \hat{\mathbf{x}}x + \hat{\mathbf{y}}y$$

and
$$\mathbf{s_0} = \hat{\mathbf{x}}x_0 + \hat{\mathbf{y}}y_0$$

Writing $\tau = (t - t_0)c, \xi = z_0 - z, S = \mid \mathbf{s} - \mathbf{s_0} \mid$ and $R = \mid \mathbf{r} - \mathbf{r_0} \mid$ we have
$$R^2 = \xi^2 + S^2$$

and
$$\frac{dR}{dz_0} = \frac{\xi}{R}$$

Equation (3.1.11) can then be written in the form

$$G(S, \tau) = \frac{1}{4\pi} \int\limits_{-\infty}^{\infty} \frac{\delta(\tau + R)}{\sqrt{R^2 - S^2}} dR$$

$$= \frac{1}{4\pi} \frac{1}{\sqrt{\tau^2 - S^2}}, \quad \tau > S$$

In one dimension, the time dependent Green's function can be calculated by integrating the three dimensional Green's function over z_0 and y_0. Alternatively, we can substitute the expression for $g(x \mid x_0, k)$ into equation (3.1.10) giving

$$G(x \mid x_0, t \mid t_0) = \frac{1}{2\pi} \int\limits_{-\infty}^{\infty} \frac{i}{2k} \exp(ik \mid x - x_0 \mid) \exp[i\omega(t - t_0)]d\omega$$

This equation is the inverse Fourier transform of the product of two spectra, namely $i/2k$ and $\exp(ik \mid x - x_0 \mid)$. Thus, using the convolution theorem and noting that

$$\frac{1}{2\pi} \int\limits_{-\infty}^{\infty} \frac{i}{2k} \exp[i\omega(t - t_0)]d\omega = \frac{c}{4} \operatorname{sgn}(t - t_0)$$

and

$$\frac{1}{2\pi} \int\limits_{-\infty}^{\infty} \exp(ik \mid x - x_0 \mid) \exp[i\omega(t - t_0)]d\omega = \delta(t - t_0 + \mid x - x_0 \mid /c)$$

we obtain

$$G(x \mid x_0, t \mid t_0) = \frac{c}{4} \operatorname{sgn}(t - t_0) \otimes \delta(t - t_0 + \mid x - x_0 \mid /c)$$

$$= \frac{c}{4} \operatorname{sgn}[t - t_0 + (x - x_0)/c], \quad t - t_0 \geq \mid x - x_0 \mid /c$$

Discussion

There is a striking difference between the time dependent Green's functions derived above. In three dimensions, the effect of an impulse after a time $t - t_0$ is found concentrated on a sphere of radius $c(t - t_0)$ whose centre is the source point. The effect of the impulse can therefore only be experience by an observer at one location over an infinitely short period of time. After the pulse has passed by an observer, the disturbance ceases. In two dimensions, the disturbance is spread over the entire plane $\mid \mathbf{s} - \mathbf{s}_0 \mid$. At $\mid \mathbf{s} - \mathbf{s}_0 \mid = c(t - t_0)$, there is a singularity which defines the position of the two dimensional wave front as it propagates outwards from the source point $\mathbf{s}_0$. For $\mid \mathbf{s} - \mathbf{s}_0 \mid < c(t - t_0)$, the Green's function is still finite and therefore, unlike the three-dimensional case, the disturbance is still felt after the wave front has passed by the observer. In one dimension, the disturbance is uniformly distributed over all points of observation through which the wave front has passed, i.e. for $(x - x_0) < c(t - t_0)$, the Green's function is $c/4$.

Compared with the Green's function in one and two dimensions, the three-dimensional Green's function possesses the strongest singularity. Compared to the delta function, the singularity of the two-dimensional Green's function at $\mid \mathbf{s} - \mathbf{s}_0 \mid = c(t - t_0)$ is very weak. In one dimension, the time dependent Green's function is not singular but discontinuous at $(x - x_0) = c(t - t_0)$. Illustrations of all three time dependent Green's functions are shown in figure 3.3.

Approximations of the Green's function

Although Green's functions are fundamental to coherent imaging problems, it is rarely necessary to use them in the forms already given. This is because the geometry of many coherent imaging systems justifies an approximation.

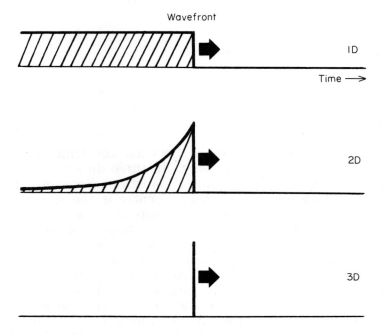

Figure 3.3 Time history of the Green's function in one, two and three dimensions

The Fraunhofer approximation

Approximations to the Green's functions are based on considering the case where the source at r_0 is moved further and further away from the observer at r. Ultimately, we may consider the source to be at infinity. This provides an asymptotic approximation to the Green's function. Physically, we refer to the source as being a long distance away from the observer.

In one dimension, the asymptotic form of the Green's function can be established by writing

$$| x - x_0 | = \sqrt{(x - x_0)^2} = \sqrt{x^2 - 2xx_0 + x_0^2}$$

$$= x_0 \left(1 - \frac{2x}{x_0} + \frac{x^2}{x_0^2} \right)^{\frac{1}{2}}$$

Now, if the source at x_0 is along way from the observer at x, then $| x | / x_0 \ll 1$ and so the square of this term can be neglected when it is compared with 1. A binomial expansion of the above result therefore gives,

$$| x - x_0 | \simeq x_0 - x$$

and the Green's function for a left-travelling wave can be written as

$$g(x \mid x_0, k) = \frac{i}{2k} \exp(ikx_0) \exp(-ikx)$$

For a right-travelling wave,

$$g(x \mid x_0, k) = \frac{i}{2k} \exp(-ikx_0) \exp(ikx)$$

A similar procedure can be adopted in two and three dimensions by studying the behaviour of the Green's function as the source moves away from the observer. In this case, we expand the path length between the source and observer in terms of their respective coordinates. To start with, let us look at the result in two dimensions. In this case, we can write

$$| \mathbf{r} - \mathbf{r}_0 | = \sqrt{r_0^2 + r^2 - 2\mathbf{r} \cdot \mathbf{r}_0}$$

$$= r_0 \left(1 - \frac{2\mathbf{r} \cdot \mathbf{r}_0}{r_0^2} + \frac{r^2}{r_0^2}\right)^{\frac{1}{2}}$$

where $\mathbf{r} = \hat{\mathbf{x}}x + \hat{\mathbf{y}}y$, $r = | \mathbf{r} |$ and $r_0 = | \mathbf{r}_0 |$. A binomial expansion of this result gives

$$| \mathbf{r} - \mathbf{r}_0 | = r_0 \left(1 - \frac{\mathbf{r} \cdot \mathbf{r}_0}{r_0^2} + \frac{r^2}{2r_0^2} + ...\right) \tag{3.1.12}$$

which under the condition

$$\frac{r}{r_0} << 1$$

reduces to

$$| \mathbf{r} - \mathbf{r}_0 | \simeq r_0 - \hat{\mathbf{n}}_0 \cdot \mathbf{r}$$

where

$$\hat{\mathbf{n}}_0 = \frac{\mathbf{r}_0}{r_0}$$

79

It is sufficient to let

$$\frac{1}{\mid \mathbf{r} - \mathbf{r}_0 \mid} \simeq \frac{1}{r_0}, \quad r_0 >> r$$

because small changes in $\hat{\mathbf{n}} \cdot \mathbf{r}$ compared to r_0 are not significant in expressions of this type. However, with the exponential function

$$\exp[ik(r_0 - \hat{\mathbf{n}}_0 \cdot \mathbf{r})]$$

a relatively small change in the value of $r_0 - \hat{\mathbf{n}}_0 \cdot \mathbf{r}$ compared to r_0 will still cause this term to oscillate rapidly, particularly if the value of k is large. We therefore write

$$\exp(ik \mid \mathbf{r} - \mathbf{r}_0 \mid) = \exp(ikr_0) \exp(-ik\hat{\mathbf{n}}_0 \cdot \mathbf{r})$$

The asymptotic form of the two dimensional Green's function is then given by

$$g(\mathbf{r} \mid \mathbf{r}_0, k) = \frac{\exp(i\pi/4)}{\sqrt{8\pi}} \frac{1}{\sqrt{kr_0}} \exp(ikr_0) \exp(-ik\hat{\mathbf{n}}_0 \cdot \mathbf{r})$$

In three dimensions, the result is

$$g(\mathbf{r} \mid \mathbf{r}_0, k) = \frac{1}{4\pi r_0} \exp(ikr_0) \exp(-ik\hat{\mathbf{n}}_0 \cdot \mathbf{r})$$

where

$$\mathbf{r} = \hat{\mathbf{x}}x + \hat{\mathbf{y}}y + \hat{\mathbf{z}}z$$

Notice that when we observe the field described by a Green's function at infinity (i.e. the field generated by a point source a long distance away), it behaves like a plane wave. Approximating the Green's function in this way provides a description for the wave in what is commonly referred to as the Fraunhofer zone or far field. In this zone, the wave front which reaches the observer is a plane wave front because the divergence of the field is so small. This is illustrated in figure 3.4. Observations of a scattered field in this zone are said to be in the Fourier plane. This is the basis for Fraunhofer diffraction theory. This theory is used in Chapter 6 to derive algorithms which can provide information on the structure and material composition of objects by the way in which they diffract acoustic and electromagnetic radiation.

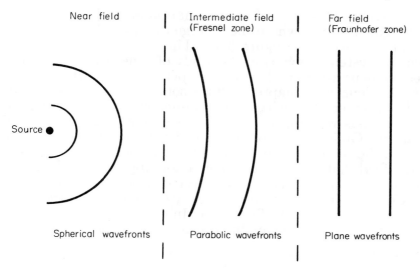

Figure 3.4 Characteristic wavefronts in the near, intermediate and far fields

The Fresnel approximation

When the source is brought closer to the observer, the wavefront ceases to be a plane wavefront. In this case, the Fraunhofer approximation is inadequate and another approximation for the Green's function must be used. This is known as the Fresnel approximation and is based incorporating the next term in the binomial expansion of $|\mathbf{r} - \mathbf{r}_0|$ (i.e. the quadratic term $r^2/2r_0^2$ in equation (3.1.12)). In this case, it is assumed that $r^2/r_0^2 \ll 1$ rather than $r/r_0 \ll 1$ so that all the terms in the binomial expansion of $|\mathbf{r} - \mathbf{r}_0|$ that occur after the quadratic term can be neglected. As before, $|\mathbf{r} - \mathbf{r}_0|^{-1}$ is approximated by $1/r_0$ but the exponential term now possesses an additional feature - a quadratic phase factor. In this case, the two and three-dimensional Green's functions are given by

$$g(\mathbf{r} \mid \mathbf{r}_0, k) = \frac{\exp(i\pi/4)}{\sqrt{8\pi}} \frac{\exp(ikr_0)}{\sqrt{kr_0}} \exp(-ik\hat{\mathbf{n}}_0 \cdot \mathbf{r}) \exp(ir^2/2r_0)$$

and

$$g(\mathbf{r} \mid \mathbf{r}_0, k) = \frac{\exp(ikr_0)}{4\pi r_0} \exp(-ik\hat{\mathbf{n}}_0 \cdot \mathbf{r}) \exp(ir^2/2r_0)$$

81

respectively. This type of approximation is used in the study of imaging systems where the divergence of the field is a measurable quantity (see figure 3.4). This is important in many focusing systems such as in the study of zone plates which are used to focus x-rays and synthetic aperture radar which is discussed at length in Chapter 7. If the source is moved even closer to the observer then neither the Fraunhofer nor the Fresnel approximations will apply. In such cases, it is usually easier to retain the Green's function in full rather than consider another term in the binomial expansion of the path length. Analysis of a wavefield that is produced when a non-approximated form of the Green's function is used is referred to as near field analysis. Coherent imaging systems usually fall in to one of the three categories illustrated in figure 3.4. In other words, a coherent imaging system can be analysed using one of the following :

1. Near field analysis.

2. Intermediate field (Fresnel zone).

3. Far field (Fraunhofer zone).

In practice, the far field approximation is much easier to use. This is because it leads to solutions that can be written in terms of a Fourier transform which is a relatively easy transform to work with and invert. Using the Fresnel approximation leads to solutions which involve a class of integral known as the Fresnel integral. The nonlinear character of this integral (i.e. the quadratic phase factor) makes it more difficult to evaluate compared with the Fourier integral. There are relatively few applications in coherent imaging which in practice require a full near field analysis. This is fortunate, because near field analysis presents some formidable computational problems.

3.2 FIELDS GENERATED BY SOURCES

We have already dealt with two particular types of partial differential equations namely: the homogeneous wave equation for which the solution is trivial and an inhomogeneous wave equation where the source function is a delta function (the solution being given by the Green's function). In this section, we turn our attention to the more general problem of developing a solution for the field generated by an arbitrary and time independent source $s(\mathbf{r})$. Working in three dimensions, our aim is to solve the following equation

$$(\nabla^2 + k^2)\phi = -s \tag{3.2.1}$$

for ϕ. We start by writing the equation for a Green's function, i.e.

$$(\nabla^2 + k^2)g(\mathbf{r} \mid \mathbf{r}_0, k) = -\delta^3(\mathbf{r} - \mathbf{r}_0)$$

If we now multiply both sides of the first equation by g and both sides of the second equation by ϕ, then by subtracting the two results we obtain

$$g\nabla^2\phi - \phi\nabla^2 g = -gs + \phi\delta^3$$

We assume that the source is confined to a finite region of space with a finite volume V. Outside this region, it is assumed that the source function is zero. By integrating the last equation over V, we can exploit the result

$$\int_V \phi(\mathbf{r}, k)\delta^3(\mathbf{r} - \mathbf{r}_0)d^3\mathbf{r} = \phi(\mathbf{r}_0, k), \quad \mathbf{r}_0 \in V$$

and therefore write

$$\phi(\mathbf{r}_0, k) = \int_V s(\mathbf{r})g(\mathbf{r} \mid \mathbf{r}_0, k)d^3\mathbf{r}$$

$$+ \int_V [g(\mathbf{r} \mid \mathbf{r}_0, k)\nabla^2\phi(\mathbf{r}, k) - \phi(\mathbf{r}, k)\nabla^2 g(\mathbf{r} \mid \mathbf{r}_0, k)]d^3\mathbf{r}$$

Observe, that this expression is not a proper solution for ϕ because this function occurs in both the left and right hand sides. What we require, is a solution for ϕ in terms of known quantities on the right hand side of the above equation. To this end, we can simplify the second term by using a result which is known as Green's theorem and given by

$$\int_V (g\nabla^2\phi - \phi\nabla^2 g)d^3\mathbf{r} = \oint_S (g\nabla\phi - \phi\nabla g) \cdot \hat{\mathbf{n}}dS$$

Here, S defines the surface enclosing the volume V and dS is an element of this surface. The unit vector $\hat{\mathbf{n}}$ points out of the source and is perpendicular to the surface element dS. This theorem allows us to write the field ϕ at $\mathbf{r}_0$ as

$$\phi = \int_V sg d^3\mathbf{r} + \oint_S (g\nabla\phi - \phi\nabla g) \cdot \hat{\mathbf{n}} dS \qquad (3.2.2)$$

Although Green's theorem allows us to simplify the solution for ϕ (in the sense that we now have a two dimensional instead of a three-dimensional integral), we still do not have a proper solution for ϕ. However, as a result of applying Green's theorem we now only need to specify ϕ and $\nabla\phi$ on the surface S. Therefore, if we know, *a priori*, the behaviour of ϕ and $\nabla\phi$ on S we can compute ϕ at any other observation point $\mathbf{r}_0$ from equation (3.2.2). Clearly, some sought of statement about the behaviour of ϕ and $\nabla\phi$ on S is required. Statements of this kind are known as boundary conditions. In general, the type of conditions that may be applied depends on the physics that is involved. In practice, two types of boundary conditions are used. The first one is known as the homogeneous Derichlet boundary condition which states that ϕ is zero on S and the second one is known as the homogeneous Neumann condition which states that $\nabla\phi$ is zero on S. When ϕ satisfies both types of boundary conditions, then the solution for ϕ is given by

$$\phi(\mathbf{r}_0, k) = \int_V s(\mathbf{r}) g(\mathbf{r} \mid \mathbf{r}_0, k) d^3\mathbf{r} \qquad (3.2.3)$$

because

$$\oint_S (g\nabla\phi - \phi\nabla g) \cdot \hat{\mathbf{n}} dS = 0$$

If the field generated by a source is measured a long distance away from the location of the source, then by using the far field approximation for the Green's function we have (in three dimensions)

$$\phi(\hat{\mathbf{n}}_0, k) = \frac{1}{4\pi r_0} \exp(ikr_0) \int_V s(\mathbf{r}) \exp(-ik\hat{\mathbf{n}}_0 \cdot \mathbf{r}) d^3\mathbf{r}$$

In this case, the field generated by the source is given by the Fourier transform of the source function s. By measuring the

84

radiation pattern produced by a source in the near field, the structure or spatial distribution of the source may be recovered by solving equation (3.2.3) for $s(\mathbf{r})$. In the far field, the source function can be recovered by taking the inverse Fourier transform of the observed field. These are examples of solutions to a class of problems known as inverse source problems.

3.3 FIELDS GENERATED BY BORN SCATTER-ERS

Unlike the field generated by a source, a scattered wavefield depends on both the nature of the scatterer and the type of radiation scattered by it. These properties are described by a characteristic inhomogeneous partial differential equation called the wave equation.

Basic equations

The simplest and one of the most widely studied types of wave equation occurs in a field of physics called quantum mechanics. In this case, waves - which are known as deBroglie waves - are scattered by an atomic or nuclear potential $V(\mathbf{r})$. If the potential is an elastic scatterer and the deBroglie waves describe non-relativistic particles, then, the appropriate wave equation is

$$(\nabla^2 + k^2)\phi = V\phi$$

This wave equation is known as the Schrödinger equation. Comparing this equation with equation (3.2.1), it is clear that the equation for a deBroglie wavefield is produced by replacing the source function s with $-V\phi$. In coherent imaging, one of the most basic type of wave equation is obtained by replacing the source function s with $k^2\gamma$, where γ is the scattering function. The wave equation is given by

$$(\nabla^2 + k^2)\phi = -k^2\gamma\phi$$

and is known as the Helmholtz equation. In quantitative coherent imaging, we are required to employ physical models which are more complete (i.e. models which describe a greater number of physical effects). In this case, the source function is replaced by $\hat{L}\phi$ where $\hat{L}$ is an inhomogeneous differential operator. Hence, the type of wave equations that are used to study the principles of quantitative coherent imaging are of the form

$$(\nabla^2 + k^2)\phi = -\hat{L}\phi$$

For example, if an acoustic scatterer is composed of variations in the compressibility γ_κ and density γ_ρ, then $\hat{L}\phi$ is given by

$$\hat{L}\phi = k^2 \gamma_\kappa \phi - \nabla \cdot (\gamma_\rho \nabla \phi)$$

Details of this equation and other wave equations which are important in the theory of coherent imaging and used later in this book are presented in section 5 of this chapter.

Basic solution

The same Green's function method that has already been presented in section 3.2 can be used to solve equations of the type given above. The basic solution is

$$\phi = \int_V g\hat{L}\phi d^3\mathbf{r} + \oint_S (g\nabla\phi - \phi\nabla g) \cdot \hat{\mathbf{n}} dS$$

Once again, to compute the surface integral, a condition for the behaviour of ϕ on the surface S of the scatterer must be chosen. Consider the case where we illuminate the scatterer with an incident field ϕ_i which is a simple plane wave

$$\exp(i\mathbf{k} \cdot \mathbf{r})$$

satisfying the homogeneous wave equation

$$(\nabla^2 + k^2)\phi_i(\mathbf{r}, k) = 0$$

By choosing the condition, $\phi(\mathbf{r}, k) = \phi_i(\mathbf{r}, k)$ on the surface of the scatterer, we obtain

$$\phi = \int_V g\hat{L}\phi d^3\mathbf{r} + \oint_S (g\nabla\phi_i - \phi_i\nabla g) \cdot \hat{\mathbf{n}} dS$$

Now, using Green's theorem to convert the surface integral back into a volume integral, we have

$$\oint_S (g\nabla\phi_i - \phi_i\nabla g) \cdot \hat{\mathbf{n}} dS = \int_V (g\nabla^2\phi_i - \phi_i\nabla^2 g) d^3\mathbf{r}$$

Noting that

$$\nabla^2 \phi_i = -k^2 \phi_i$$

and

$$\nabla^2 g = -\delta^3 - k^2 g$$

we get

$$\int_V (g\nabla^2\phi_i - \phi_i\nabla^2 g)d^3\mathbf{r} = \int_V \delta^3\phi_i d^3\mathbf{r} = \phi_i$$

Hence, by choosing the field ϕ to be equal to the incident field ϕ_i on the surface of the scatterer, we obtain the solution

$$\phi = \phi_i + \phi_s$$

where

$$\phi_s = \int_V g\hat{L}\phi d^3\mathbf{r}$$

The wavefield ϕ_s is called the scattered field.

The Born approximation

From the last result it is clear that in order to compute the scattered field ϕ_s, we must define ϕ inside the volume integral. Unlike the surface integral in equation (3.2.2), a boundary condition will not help here because it is not sufficient to specify the behaviour of ϕ at a boundary. In this case, the behaviour of ϕ throughout V needs to be known. In general, it is not possible to do this and we are forced to choose a model for ϕ inside V that is compatible with a particular physical problem in the same way that an appropriate set of boundary conditions are required to evaluate the surface integral. The simplest model for the internal field is based on assuming that ϕ behaves like ϕ_i for $\mathbf{r} \in V$. The scattered field is then given by

$$\phi_s(\mathbf{r}_0, k) = \int_V g(\mathbf{r} \mid \mathbf{r}_0, k)\hat{L}\phi_i(\mathbf{r}, k)d^3\mathbf{r}$$

This assumption provides an approximate solution for the scattered field which is linear and known as the Born approximation.

There is another way of deriving this result that is instructive and will be used later on. We start with the general scalar wave equation

$$(\nabla^2 + k^2)\phi = -\hat{L}\phi$$

and write ϕ in terms of a sum of the incident and scattered fields, i.e.

$$\phi = \phi_i + \phi_s$$

The wave equation then becomes

$$(\nabla^2 + k^2)\phi_s + (\nabla^2 + k^2)\phi_i = -\hat{L}(\phi_i + \phi_s)$$

If the incident field satisfies

$$(\nabla^2 + k^2)\phi_i = 0$$

then

$$(\nabla^2 + k^2)\phi_s = -\hat{L}(\phi_i + \phi_s)$$

Assuming that

$$\phi_i + \phi_s \simeq \phi_i, \quad \mathbf{r} \in V$$

we obtain

$$(\nabla^2 + k^2)\phi_s \simeq -\hat{L}\phi_i$$

Solving for ϕ_s and using the boundary conditions, $\phi_s = 0$ on S and $\nabla\phi_s = 0$ on S, we get

$$\phi_s = \oint_S (g(\nabla\phi_s - \phi_s\nabla g) \cdot \hat{\mathbf{n}}dS + \int_V g\hat{L}\phi_i d^3\mathbf{r}$$

$$= \int_V g\hat{L}\phi_i d^3\mathbf{r}$$

Conditions for the validity of the Born approximation

In general, the Born approximation requires that ϕ_s is 'small' compared to ϕ_i. The question is: what do we really mean by the term 'small' and how can we quantify it? One way to answer this question is to compute an appropriate statistical parameter for both the incident and scattered fields and compare the two results. Consider the case where we compute the root mean square modulus of each field. We then require

$$\left(\int_V | \phi_s(\mathbf{r}_0, k) |^2 \, d^3\mathbf{r}_0 \right)^{1/2} << \left(\int_V | \phi_i(\mathbf{r}_0, k) |^2 \, d^3\mathbf{r}_0 \right)^{1/2}$$

or

$$\frac{\|\phi_s\|}{\|\phi_i\|} << 1 \qquad (3.3.1)$$

Essentially, this condition means that the average intensity of the scattered field in V is small compared to the average intensity of the incident field in V. Let us look in more detail at the nature of this condition. Ideally, what we want is a version of this condition in terms of a set of experimental parameters (such as the wavelength and the size of scatterer). To do this, we must introduce a specific form for the operator $\hat{L}$. Let us consider the case when

$$\hat{L}\phi_i = k^2 \gamma \phi_i$$

which is common to both electromagnetic and acoustic scalar wave theory. In this case, the Born scattered field at $\mathbf{r}_0$ is given by

$$\phi_s(\mathbf{r}_0, k) = k^2 \int_V g(\mathbf{r} \mid \mathbf{r}_0, k)\gamma(\mathbf{r})\phi_i(\mathbf{r}, k)d^3\mathbf{r}$$

By taking the norm of this equation we can write

$$\|\phi_s(\mathbf{r}_0, k)\| = \|k^2 \int_V g(\mathbf{r} \mid \mathbf{r}_0, k)\gamma(\mathbf{r})\phi_i(\mathbf{r}, k)d^3\mathbf{r}\|$$

$$\leq k^2 \|\phi_i(\mathbf{r}_0, k)\| \times \| \int_V g(\mathbf{r} \mid \mathbf{r}_0, k)\gamma(\mathbf{r})d^3\mathbf{r}\|$$

Using this result, the condition required for the Born approximation to hold (i.e. condition 3.3.1) can be written as

$$k^2 \| \int_V g(\mathbf{r} \mid \mathbf{r}_0, k)\gamma(\mathbf{r})d^3\mathbf{r}\| << 1, \quad \mathbf{r}_0 \in V \qquad (3.3.2)$$

Here, the norm involves integration over the spatial variable $\mathbf{r}_0$ in the scattering volume V. To emphasize this we write $\mathbf{r}_0 \in V$.

Although (3.3.2) provides a technically correct condition for the Born approximation, it is not, in itself, a particularly useful result. To achieve a more useful analytical expression in terms of an appropriate set of experimental variables, we resort to comparing just the modulus of the scattered and incident fields. In this case, we require that

$$\frac{|\phi_s|}{|\phi_i|} << 1, \quad \forall \mathbf{r}_0 \in V$$

Since

$$|\phi_s(\mathbf{r}_0, k)| = |k^2 \int_V g(\mathbf{r} \mid \mathbf{r}_0, k)\gamma(\mathbf{r})\phi_i(\mathbf{r}, k)d^3\mathbf{r}|$$

$$\leq k^2 |\phi_i(\mathbf{r}_0, k)| \times |\int_V g(\mathbf{r} \mid \mathbf{r}_0, k)\gamma(\mathbf{r})d^3\mathbf{r}|$$

we can write this condition in the form

$$I(\mathbf{r}_0) << 1$$

where

$$I(\mathbf{r}_0) = k^2 |\int_V g(\mathbf{r} \mid \mathbf{r}_0, k)\gamma(\mathbf{r})d^3\mathbf{r}|$$

$$\leq k^2 \left(\int_V |g(\mathbf{r} \mid \mathbf{r}_0, k)| \, d^3\mathbf{r} \int_V |\gamma(\mathbf{r})|^2 \, d^3\mathbf{r}\right)^{\frac{1}{2}}$$

Substituting the expression for the three-dimensional Green's function (equation 3.1.9) into the above expression, we have

$$I(\mathbf{r}_0) \leq k^2 \left(\frac{1}{16\pi^2} \int_V \frac{1}{|\mathbf{r} - \mathbf{r}_0|^2}d^3\mathbf{r} \int_V |\gamma(\mathbf{r})|^2 \, d^3\mathbf{r}\right)^{\frac{1}{2}}$$

A relatively simple calculation can now be performed if we consider the scatterer to be a sphere of volume V and radius R. However, even in this case, it is still difficult to evaluate the first integral over $\mathbf{r}$ for all values of $\mathbf{r}_0$. We therefore resort to calculating its least upper bound which occurs when $r_0 = 0$. Changing to polar coordinates, we have

$$\sup \int_V \frac{1}{|\mathbf{r} - \mathbf{r}_0|^2} d^3\mathbf{r} = \int_V \frac{1}{r^2} d^3\mathbf{r} = \int_0^{2\pi} \int_{-1}^{1} \int_0^R dr \, d(\cos\theta) d\phi$$

$$= 4\pi R$$

where sup stands for the 'least upper bound' (the **sup**erior value). Using this result, we can write

$$\sup I(\mathbf{r}_0) \leq k^2 \left(\frac{R}{4\pi} \int_V |\gamma(\mathbf{r})|^2 d^3\mathbf{r} \right)^{\frac{1}{2}}$$

and noting that

$$V = \int_V d^3\mathbf{r} = \frac{4}{3}\pi R^3$$

we get

$$\sup I(\mathbf{r}_0) \leq \frac{1}{\sqrt{3}} k^2 R^2 \sqrt{<\gamma^2>}$$

where

$$<\gamma^2> = \frac{\int |\gamma|^2 d^3\mathbf{r}}{\int d^3\mathbf{r}}$$

Hence, the condition for the Born approximation to apply becomes (ignoring $\sqrt{3}$)

$$k^2 R^2 \sqrt{<\gamma^2>} << 1$$

or

$$\sqrt{<\gamma^2>} << \frac{1}{k^2 R^2}$$

This condition demonstrates that in principle large values of the scattering function γ can occur so long as its root mean square value over the scattering volume V is small compared to $1/k^2 R^2$. The scatterer is said to be a weak scatterer. Note that when k or R approach zero, this condition is easy to satisfy and that Born scattering is more likely to occur in situations where

$$\frac{\lambda}{R} >> 1$$

If

$$\frac{\lambda}{R} \sim 1$$

then the value of $\sqrt{<\gamma^2>}$ must be small for Born scattering to occur.

By repeating the method given above, it is easy to show that in two dimensions the condition required for the Born approximation to apply is given by

$$\sqrt{<\gamma^2>} << \frac{1}{(kR)^{3/2}}$$

where R is the radius of a disc of area A. In one dimension, the result is

$$\sqrt{<\gamma^2>} << \frac{1}{kL}$$

where L is the length of the scatterer. In each case, we are assuming that the scattered field is, on average, weak compared to the incident field. We may consider the term 'weak', to imply that the total energy of the scattered field inside the scatterer is small compared to the incident field inside the scatterer.

Born scattering in the far field

By measuring the scattered field ϕ_s we can attempt to invert the relevent integral equation and hence recover or reconstruct the scattering function. This type of problem is known as the inverse scattering problem, and solutions to this problem are called inverse scattering solutions. The simplest type of inverse scattering problem occurs when Born scattered waves are measured in the far field or Fraunhofer zone. When the incident field is a plane wave

$$\phi_i = \exp(ik\hat{\mathbf{n}}_i \cdot \mathbf{r})$$

where $\hat{\mathbf{n}}_i$ points in the direction of the incident field, the scattered field observed at $\mathbf{r}_s$ becomes (working in 3D)

$$\phi_s(\hat{\mathbf{n}}_s, \hat{\mathbf{n}}_i, k) = \frac{k^2}{4\pi r_s} \exp(ikr_s) \int_V \exp[-ik(\hat{\mathbf{n}}_s - \hat{\mathbf{n}}_i) \cdot \mathbf{r}]\gamma(\mathbf{r})d^3\mathbf{r} \qquad (3.3.3)$$

where $\hat{\mathbf{n}}_s(= \mathbf{r}_s/r_s)$ denotes the direction of the scattered field. From this result, it is clear, that the scattering function γ can be recovered from ϕ_s by three-dimensional Fourier inversion. The scattered field produced by a two-dimensional Born scatterer in the far field is given by

$$\phi_s(\hat{\mathbf{n}}_i, \hat{\mathbf{n}}_s, k) = \frac{\exp(i\pi/4)}{\sqrt{8\pi}} \frac{k^2}{\sqrt{kr_s}} \exp(ikr_s) \int_A \exp[-ik(\hat{\mathbf{n}}_s - \hat{\mathbf{n}}_i) \cdot \mathbf{r}]\gamma(\mathbf{r})d^2\mathbf{r}$$

In one dimension, the equivalent result is

$$\phi_s(x_s, k) = \frac{ik}{2} \exp(ikx_s) \int_L \gamma(x)dx$$

Notice that when $\hat{\mathbf{n}}_s = \hat{\mathbf{n}}_i$, equation (3.3.3) becomes

$$\phi_s = \frac{k^2}{4\pi r_0} \exp(ikr_0) \int_V \gamma(\mathbf{r})d^3\mathbf{r}$$

This is called the forward-scattered field and is obtained by integrating the scattering function over V. In terms of Fourier analysis, this represents the DC level of the spectrum of γ. Another special case arises when $\hat{\mathbf{n}}_s = -\hat{\mathbf{n}}_i$. The scattered field that is produced in this case is called the back-scattered field and in three dimensions is given by

$$\phi_s(\hat{\mathbf{n}}_s, k) = \frac{k^2}{4\pi r_s} \int_V \exp(-2ik\hat{\mathbf{n}}_s \cdot \mathbf{r})\gamma(\mathbf{r})d^3\mathbf{r}$$

In one dimension, the result is

$$\phi_s(k) = \frac{ik}{2} \exp(ikx_s) \int_L \exp(-2ikx)\gamma(x)dx$$

Observe, that in one dimension, the scattering function can only be recovered (via Fourier inversion) by measuring the back-scattered spectrum whereas in two and three dimensions, the scattering function can be recovered by either keeping k fixed or varying k. The choice available in two and three dimensions means that we can either use a CW source or a pulsed source to recover the scattering function. Both methods are presented in Chapter 6 which discusses quantitative diffraction tomography using CW and pulsed sources.

3.4 EXAMPLES OF BORN SCATTERING

By way of a short introduction to the applications and uses of the Born approximation, some well known examples are presented in this section. Here, the approximation is used to derive expressions for the differential cross-section associated with a variety of scattering phenomena.

Rutherford's scattering experiment

In this famous experiment (which dates from 1910), alpha particles were scattered by gold leaf. The differential cross-section $d\sigma/d\Omega$ (the number of particles scattered into a solid angle $d\Omega$ per unit time divided by the number of particles incident per unit area per unit time) was then measured at different scattering angles θ. By treating the α-particles as classical Newtonian particles, Rutherford showed that if the scattering potential (i.e. the nucleus of the atoms in the gold leaf) is a repulsive Coulomb potential, then

$$\frac{d\sigma}{d\Omega} \propto \frac{1}{\sin^4(\theta/2)}$$

This was before the development of quantum mechanics and the emergence of Schrödinger's equation. In quantum mechanics, elementary particles of matter appear (to the human observer) to behave like waves called deBroglie waves. The mechanics becomes that of wave motion and wave functions are used to describe the behaviour of quantum systems. The square modulus of the wave function is taken to represents the probability of a particle existing at a given point in space. For this reason, the wave functions are sometimes called probability waves. In terms of quantum mechanics we can consider Rutherford's scattering experiment to consist of a source of plane waves (i.e. the deBroglie or probability waves associated with the α-particles), a scattering function (the potential associated with the nucleus of the atoms which make up the gold leaf) and a measuring device which allows us to record the intensity of the scattered radiation at different angles to the incident beam. From Schrödinger's equation, the Born scattered wave in the far field due to a scattering potential V which is influential over all space is given by

$$\phi_s(\hat{\mathbf{n}}_s, \hat{\mathbf{n}}_i, k) = -\frac{\exp(ikr_s)}{4\pi r_s} \int\limits_{-\infty}^{\infty} \exp[-ik(\hat{\mathbf{n}}_s - \hat{\mathbf{n}}_i) \cdot \mathbf{r}]V(\mathbf{r})d^3\mathbf{r} \qquad (3.4.1)$$

For fixed k and r_s (the distance at which the scattered field is measured from the scatterer), the measured intensity of the scattered wave is given by

$$I = \phi_s\phi_s^* = \frac{1}{16\pi^2 r_s^2} \mid A \mid^2$$

where A is the scattering amplitude,

$$A(\hat{\mathbf{n}}_s, \hat{\mathbf{n}}_i, k) = \hat{F}_3 V = \int\limits_{-\infty}^{\infty} \exp[-ik(\hat{\mathbf{n}}_s - \hat{\mathbf{n}}_i) \cdot \mathbf{r}]V(\mathbf{r})d^3\mathbf{r}$$

The differential cross section measures the flux of particles through a given area in specific period of time. It is essentially a measure of the intensity and it can be shown that

$$\frac{d\sigma}{d\Omega} = \mid A \mid^2$$

Hence, using quantum mechanics (i.e. Schrödinger's equation), the differential cross-section for Rutherford's scattering experiment can be obtained by evaluating the Fourier transform of the potential V. For a radially symmetric potential $V(r)$, the scattering amplitude becomes (switching to spherical polar coordinates r, ψ, ϕ)

$$A(\hat{\mathbf{n}}_s, \hat{\mathbf{n}}_i) = \int\limits_{0}^{2\pi} d\phi \int\limits_{-1}^{1} d(\cos\psi) \int\limits_{0}^{\infty} dr r^2 \exp(-ik \mid \hat{\mathbf{n}}_s - \hat{\mathbf{n}}_i \mid r \cos\psi)V(r)$$

The modulus of $\hat{\mathbf{n}}_s - \hat{\mathbf{n}}_i$ is given by

$$\mid \hat{\mathbf{n}}_s - \hat{\mathbf{n}}_i \mid = \sqrt{(\hat{\mathbf{n}}_s - \hat{\mathbf{n}}_i) \cdot (\hat{\mathbf{n}}_s - \hat{\mathbf{n}}_i)} = \sqrt{2(1 - \cos\theta)}$$

where

$$\cos\theta = \hat{\mathbf{n}}_s \cdot \hat{\mathbf{n}}_i$$

and θ is the scattering angle (the angle between the incident and scattered fields). Using the half angle formula,

$$1 - \cos\theta = 2\sin^2(\theta/2)$$

we can write

$$|\hat{\mathbf{n}}_s - \hat{\mathbf{n}}_i| = 2\sin(\theta/2)$$

and integrating over ϕ and ψ the scattering amplitude as a function θ can be written as

$$A(\theta) = \frac{2\pi}{k\sin(\theta/2)} \int_0^\infty \sin[2kr\sin(\theta/2)]V(r)r\,dr \qquad (3.4.2)$$

All we need to do now is compute the remaining integral over r. If we use a simple Coulomb potential where $V(r) \propto 1/r$, then we run in to a problem because the integrand does not converge as $r \to \infty$. For this reason, another radially symmetric potential is introduced which is given by

$$V(r) = a\frac{\exp(-br)}{r} \qquad (3.4.3)$$

where a and $b > 0$ are both constants. This type of potential is known as a screened Coulomb potential. The parameter b determines the range over which the potential is influential. This distance is about $1/b$ and is called the range of the potential. Equation (3.4.3) allows us to evaluate the scattering amplitude analytically. We can then observe the behaviour of $|A|^2$ for a Coulomb potential by letting b approach zero. Substituting equation (3.4.3) into equation (3.4.2), the scattering amplitude becomes

$$A(\theta) = \frac{2\pi a}{k\sin(\theta/2)} \int_0^\infty \sin[2kr\sin(\theta/2)]\exp(-br)\,dr$$

This integral is given by

$$\frac{2k\sin(\theta/2)}{b^2 + [2k\sin(\theta/2)]^2}$$

and we can write

$$A(\theta) = \frac{\pi a}{k^2\sin^2(\theta/2)}\left(1 + \frac{b^2}{[2k\sin(\theta/2)]^2}\right)^{-1}$$

Hence, as b approaches zero, we obtain

$$A(\theta) \simeq \frac{\pi a}{k^2 \sin^2(\theta/2)}$$

The scattered intensity is therefore given by

$$|A(\theta)|^2 = \frac{d\sigma}{d\Omega} \propto \frac{1}{\sin^4(\theta/2)}$$

One may think of Rutherford's scattering experiment as an inverse scattering problem in the sense that he deduced the potential of the nucleus by recording the way in which it scattered alpha particles. However, he did not actually solve the inverse problem directly because he assumed that the scattering potential acted like a repulsive Coulomb potential *a priori* and justified this hypothesis later by showing that the theoretical and experimental results were compatible.

Rayleigh scattering

Rayleigh scattering is the scattering of electromagnetic radiation by small dielectric scatterers. If we consider a scalar electromagnetic wave theory, then we can take an equation of the form

$$(\nabla^2 + k^2)\phi = -k^2\gamma\phi, \quad \gamma = \epsilon_r - 1$$

to describe the behaviour of the electric field ϕ where ϵ_r is the relative permittivity. This is of course a highly idealized case, but it helps to provide another demonstration of Born scattering in a form that is pertinent to coherent imaging. In the context of electromagnetic scattering problems, the Born approximation is sometimes referred to as the Rayleigh-Gan approximation - just a different name for an identical mathematical technique. Using this approximation, the scattered electric field in the Fraunhofer zone is given by

$$\phi_s(\hat{\mathbf{n}}_s, \hat{\mathbf{n}}_i, k) = \frac{k^2}{4\pi r_s} \exp(ikr_s) \int_V \exp[-ik(\hat{\mathbf{n}}_s - \hat{\mathbf{n}}_i) \cdot \mathbf{r}]\gamma(\mathbf{r})d^3\mathbf{r}$$

There are two important differences between this equation and its counterpart in quantum mechanics (i.e. equation (3.4.1)). First, the coefficient in front of the integral possesses a factor

k^2. Secondly, the integral itself is over a finite volume of space V which is determined by the extent of the scatterer whereas in equation (3.4.1) the influence of the potential is felt over all space so that the integral is over the interval $[-\infty, \infty]$. This is an important distinction between scattering problems in quantum mechanics which involve asymptotic potentials (i.e. potentials which go to zero at infinity) and classical scattering problems. In the latter case, the scatterer has a finite spatial extent.

Consider a model where a plane electromagnetic wave is incident on a homogeneous spherical dielectric object of radius R and relative permittivity ϵ_{ro}. The theory which describes this type of scattering (i.e. scattering of light from uniform spheres) is called Mie theory. In this case, the Born scattered amplitude is given by

$$A(\theta) = \frac{2\pi k \gamma_0}{\sin(\theta/2)} \int_0^R \sin[2kr\sin(\theta/2)] r \, dr \qquad (3.4.4)$$

where

$$\gamma_0 = \epsilon_{r0} - 1$$

If the dimensions of the scatterer are small compared to the wavelength, then

$$kR << 1$$

and

$$\sin[2kr\sin(\theta/2)] \simeq 2kr\sin(\theta/2), \quad 0 \le r \le R$$

The scattering amplitude is then given by

$$A(\theta) \simeq 4\pi k^2 \gamma_0 \int_0^R r^2 \, dr = k^2 \gamma_0 V$$

where $V = 4\pi R^3/3$ is the volume of the scatterer. In this case, the scattering is entirely isotropic (i.e. the scattering amplitude is independent of the scattering angle) and the differential cross-section is proportional to k^4 or

$$\frac{d\sigma}{d\Omega} \propto \frac{1}{\lambda^4}$$

Note, the large inverse depedance on the wavelength. This result is characteristic of Rayleigh scattering and of the spectra

produced by light scattering from small sub-wavelength structures. In the visible part of the spectrum, the cross section is
greatest for blue light (the colour associated with the smallest
wavelength of the visible spectrum). This is why the sky is blue
- sunlight being scattered by small sub-wavelength particles in
the upper atmosphere.

When $kR \sim 1$, the scattering amplitude is obtained by evaluating the integral in equation (3.4.4). This is easy to do, the
scattering amplitude being given by

$$A(\theta) = 3V\gamma_0 k^2 \frac{j_1[2kR\sin(\theta/2)]}{2kR\sin(\theta/2)}$$

where j_1 is the spherical Bessel function

$$j_1(x) = \frac{\sin(x)}{x^2} - \frac{\cos(x)}{x}$$

In this case, the scattering is not isotropic but strongly dependent on the scattering angle. This is an example of Fraunhofer
diffraction.

3.5 FIELD EQUATIONS AND WAVE EQUATIONS

The field equations determine the physical characteristics and
behaviour of a particular type of field. Two types of fields are
important in coherent imaging: the electromagnetic field and
the acoustic field. The purpose of this section is primarily to
introduce and discuss the electromagnetic and acoustic fields
equations which are employed in later chapters. From these
results, we derive equations which describe the propagation of
different wavefields through various types of materials.

Electromagnetic field equations (Maxwell's equations)

These equations were first derived by James Clerk Maxwell and
can be written in the form

$$\nabla \cdot \epsilon\mathbf{E} = \rho \tag{3.5.1}$$

$$\nabla \cdot \mu\mathbf{H} = 0 \tag{3.5.2}$$

$$\nabla \wedge \mathbf{E} = -\mu\frac{\partial \mathbf{H}}{\partial t} \tag{3.5.3}$$

and

$$\nabla \wedge \mathbf{H} = \epsilon \frac{\partial \mathbf{E}}{\partial t} + \mathbf{J} \qquad (3.5.4)$$

The symbols are defined as follows:

$\mathbf{E}(\mathbf{r}, t)$ - Electric field (volts/metre)

$\mathbf{H}(\mathbf{r}, t)$ - Magnetic field (amperes/metre)

$\mathbf{J}(\mathbf{r}, t)$ - Current density (amperes/metre^2)

$\rho(\mathbf{r}, t)$ - Charge density (charge/metre^2)

$\epsilon(\mathbf{r})$ - Permittivity (farads/metre)

$\mu(\mathbf{r})$ - Permeability (henries/metre)

t - time

$\mathbf{r}$ - position vector

In general, ϵ, μ and σ may be anisotropic and vary with time. Here, it is assumed that these material parameters are both isotropic and time invariant. The values of ϵ and μ in a vacuum (denoted by ϵ_0 and μ_0 respectively) are:

$$\epsilon_0 = 8.854 \times 10^{-12} \text{ farads/metre}$$

and

$$\mu_0 = 4\pi \times 10^{-7} \text{ henries/metre}$$

In electromagnetic scattering problems there are two important physical models:

1. Scattering from nonconductive dielectrics

In this case, it is assumed that the conductivity of the scattering object is negligible and no current can flow. As a consequence of this, the charge density is zero. Hence, we have

$$\mathbf{J} = 0$$

and

$$\rho = 0$$

Equation (3.5.1) then becomes

$$\nabla \cdot \epsilon \mathbf{E} = 0$$

and equation (3.5.4) is just

$$\nabla \wedge \mathbf{H} = \epsilon \frac{\partial \mathbf{E}}{\partial t}$$

2. Scattering from good conductors

In this case, the scatterer is assumed to be a good conductor. A current is induced which depends on the magnitude of the electric field and the conductivity σ (seimens/metre) of the material from which the scatterer is composed. The relationship between the electric field and the current density is given by Ohm's law

$$\mathbf{J} = \sigma \mathbf{E} \tag{3.5.5}$$

A good conductor is one where σ is large. By taking the divergence of equation (3.5.4) and noting that

$$\nabla \cdot (\nabla \wedge \mathbf{H}) = 0$$

we obtain (using equation (3.5.1) for constant ϵ)

$$\frac{\partial \rho}{\partial t} + \frac{\sigma}{\epsilon} \rho = 0$$

The solution to this equation is

$$\rho(t) = \rho_0 \exp(-\sigma t/\epsilon), \quad \rho_0 = \rho(t = 0)$$

This solution shows that the charge decays exponentially. Typical values of ϵ are $\sim 10^{-12} - 10^{-10}$ farads/metre. Hence, provided σ is not to small, the dissipation of charge is very rapid. It is therefore physically reasonable to set the charge density to zero. Thus, for problems involving the scattering of electromagnetic waves from good conductors, equation (3.5.1) can be approximated by

$$\nabla \cdot \epsilon \mathbf{E} = 0 \tag{3.5.6}$$

and equation (3.5.4) reduces to

$$\nabla \wedge \mathbf{H} = \epsilon \frac{\partial \mathbf{E}}{\partial t} + \sigma \mathbf{E}$$

Electromagnetic wave equation

In most electromagnetic imaging systems, the field that is measured is the electric field. It is therefore appropriate to use a wave equation which describes the behaviour of the electric field. This can be obtained by decoupling Maxwell's equations for the magnetic field $\mathbf{H}$. Starting with equation (3.5.3), we divide through by μ and take the curl of the resulting equation. This gives

$$\nabla \wedge \left(\frac{1}{\mu} \nabla \wedge \mathbf{E} \right) = -\frac{\partial}{\partial t} \nabla \wedge \mathbf{H}$$

By taking the derivative with respect to time t of equation (3.5.4) and using Ohm's law (equation (3.5.5)), we obtain

$$\frac{\partial}{\partial t} (\nabla \wedge \mathbf{H}) = \epsilon \frac{\partial^2 \mathbf{E}}{\partial t^2} + \sigma \frac{\partial \mathbf{E}}{\partial t}$$

From the previous equation we can then write

$$\nabla \wedge \left(\frac{1}{\mu} \nabla \wedge \mathbf{E} \right) = -\epsilon \frac{\partial^2 \mathbf{E}}{\partial t^2} - \sigma \frac{\partial \mathbf{E}}{\partial t} \tag{3.5.7}$$

Expanding the first term, multiplying through by μ and noting that

$$\mu \nabla \left(\frac{1}{\mu} \right) = -\nabla \ln \mu$$

we get

$$\nabla \wedge \nabla \wedge \mathbf{E} + \epsilon \mu \frac{\partial^2 \mathbf{E}}{\partial t^2} + \sigma \mu \frac{\partial \mathbf{E}}{\partial t} = (\nabla \ln \mu) \wedge \nabla \wedge \mathbf{E}$$

Expanding equation (3.5.6) we have

$$\epsilon \nabla \cdot \mathbf{E} + \mathbf{E} \cdot \nabla \epsilon = 0$$

or

$$\nabla \cdot \mathbf{E} = -\mathbf{E} \cdot \nabla \ln \epsilon$$

Hence, using the well known vector identity

$$\nabla \wedge \nabla \wedge \mathbf{E} = -\nabla^2 \mathbf{E} + \nabla (\nabla \cdot \mathbf{E})$$

we obtain the following wave equation for the electric field

$$\nabla^2 \mathbf{E} - \epsilon\mu\frac{\partial^2 \mathbf{E}}{\partial t^2} - \sigma\mu\frac{\partial \mathbf{E}}{\partial t} = -\nabla(\mathbf{E}\cdot\nabla\ln\epsilon) - (\nabla\ln\mu)\wedge\nabla\wedge\mathbf{E}$$

This equation is inhomogeneous in ϵ, μ and σ. Solutions to this equation provide information on the behaviour of the electric field in a fluctuating dielectric environment. In electromagnetic scattering problems, interest focuses on the behaviour of the scattered field generated by variations in ϵ, μ and σ. In this context, ϵ, μ and σ are referred to as the electromagnetic scatter generating parameters or just the material parameters. In quantitative electromagnetic imaging, the problem is to reconstruct these parameters by measuring certain properties of the scattered electric field. This is a three parameter reconstruction problem.

Acoustic field equations

The acoustic field equations are obtained by linearizing the hydrodynamic equations of motion and may be written in the form

$$\nabla\cdot\mathbf{v} = \kappa\frac{\partial p}{\partial t} \tag{3.5.8}$$

$$\nabla p = \rho\frac{\partial \mathbf{v}}{\partial t} - \nabla\cdot\mathbf{T} \tag{3.5.9}$$

$\mathbf{v}(\mathbf{r}, t)$ - Velocity field (length/time)

$p(\mathbf{r}, t)$ - Pressure field (force/area)

$\mathbf{T}(\mathbf{r}, t)$ - Material stress tensor (force/volume)

$\rho(\mathbf{r})$ - Density (mass/volume)

$\kappa(\mathbf{r})$ - Compressibility (area/force)

Here, it is assumed that the material to which these equations comply is adiabatic. The first equation comes from the law of conservation of mass and the second equation is a consequence of the law of conservation of momentum. The material stress tensor is determined by two parameters known as the first and second elastic Lamé parameters (α and β respectively), whose dimensions are force×time/volume. For compressional waves alone, this tensor is given by

$$\mathbf{T} = \mathbf{I}\alpha\nabla\cdot\mathbf{v} + 2\beta\nabla\mathbf{v}$$

where $\mathbf{I}(= \hat{\mathbf{x}}\hat{\mathbf{x}} + \hat{\mathbf{y}}\hat{\mathbf{y}} + \hat{\mathbf{z}}\hat{\mathbf{z}})$ is the unit dyad. Here, it is assumed that the shear wave (the rotational component of the velocity field) is zero, i.e.

$$\nabla \wedge \mathbf{v} = 0$$

The parameters α and β are related to the bulk ζ and shear η viscosities of a material by the equations

$$\alpha = \zeta - \frac{2}{3}\eta$$

and

$$\beta = \eta$$

When the viscosity is zero (i.e. when $\zeta = \eta = 0$) we are left with the following acoustic field equations:

$$\nabla \cdot \mathbf{v} = \kappa \frac{\partial p}{\partial t} \tag{3.5.10}$$

$$\nabla p = \rho \frac{\partial \mathbf{v}}{\partial t} \tag{3.5.11}$$

As in the electromagnetic case, it is assumed that ρ, κ, α and β are both isotropic and time invariant.

Acoustic wave equation

By decoupling the field equations (3.5.10) and (3.5.11) for $\mathbf{v}$, a scalar wave equation for the pressure p can be obtained. This is done by dividing equation (3.5.11) by ρ and taking the divergence of each term giving

$$\frac{\partial}{\partial t}\nabla \cdot \mathbf{v} = \nabla \cdot \left(\frac{1}{\rho}\nabla p\right)$$

Differentiating equation (3.5.10) with respect to time t then gives

$$\frac{\partial}{\partial t}\nabla \cdot \mathbf{v} = \kappa \frac{\partial^2 p}{\partial t^2}$$

Hence, we can write

$$\nabla \cdot \left(\frac{1}{\rho}\nabla p\right) - \kappa \frac{\partial^2 p}{\partial t^2} = 0 \tag{3.5.12}$$

or, after expanding the first term,

$$\nabla^2 p - \kappa\rho\frac{\partial^2 p}{\partial t^2} = \nabla\ln\rho\cdot\nabla p$$

This wave equation is based on a physical model where it is assumed that scattering is only due to variations in the compressibility and density. When fluctuations in the bulk and shear viscosity are present an additional source of scattering occurs. In this case, the appropriate wave equation is obtained by decoupling equations (3.5.8) and (3.5.9) for p giving

$$\nabla\left(\frac{1}{\kappa}\nabla\cdot\mathbf{v}\right) = \rho\frac{\partial^2\mathbf{v}}{\partial t^2} - \frac{\partial}{\partial t}\left(\nabla(\alpha\nabla\cdot\mathbf{v}) + 2\nabla\cdot(\beta\nabla\mathbf{v})\right) \tag{3.5.13}$$

Inhomogeneous wave equations

In order to use the appropriate Green's functions to solve any of the wave equations already discussed, they must be re-written in the form

$$(\nabla^2 + k^2)\phi = -\hat{L}\phi \tag{3.5.14}$$

where $\hat{L}$ is some inhomogeneous differential operator. Consider the electromagnetic case first. Starting with equation (3.5.7), by adding

$$\epsilon_0\frac{\partial^2\mathbf{E}}{\partial t^2} - \frac{1}{\mu_0}\nabla\wedge\nabla\wedge\mathbf{E}$$

to both sides of this equation and re-arranging, we can write

$$\nabla\wedge\nabla\wedge\mathbf{E} + \epsilon_0\mu_0\frac{\partial^2\mathbf{E}}{\partial t^2} = -\epsilon_0\mu_0\gamma_\epsilon\frac{\partial^2\mathbf{E}}{\partial t^2} - \mu_0\sigma\frac{\partial\mathbf{E}}{\partial t} + \nabla\wedge(\gamma_\mu\nabla\wedge\mathbf{E})$$

where

$$\gamma_\epsilon = \frac{\epsilon - \epsilon_0}{\epsilon_0}$$

$$\gamma_\mu = \frac{\mu - \mu_0}{\mu}$$

We can then use the result (valid for $\rho \sim 0$)

$$\nabla\wedge\nabla\wedge\mathbf{E} = -\nabla^2\mathbf{E} + \nabla(\nabla\cdot\mathbf{E})$$

$$= -\nabla^2\mathbf{E} - \nabla(\mathbf{E}\cdot\nabla\ln\epsilon)$$

so that the above wave equation can be written as

$$\nabla^2 \mathbf{E} - \epsilon_0 \mu_0 \frac{\partial \mathbf{E}}{\partial t^2} = \mu_0 \epsilon_0 \gamma_\epsilon \frac{\partial^2 \mathbf{E}}{\partial t^2}$$

$$+ \mu_0 \sigma \frac{\partial \mathbf{E}}{\partial t} - \nabla(\mathbf{E} \cdot \nabla \ln \epsilon) - \nabla \wedge (\gamma_\mu \nabla \wedge \mathbf{E})$$

Finally, introducing the Fourier transform

$$\mathbf{E}(\mathbf{r}, t) = \frac{1}{2\pi} \int\limits_{-\infty}^{\infty} \widetilde{\mathbf{E}}(\mathbf{r}, \omega) \exp(i\omega t) d\omega$$

we can write the above wave equation in the time independent form

$$(\nabla^2 + k^2)\widetilde{\mathbf{E}} = -k^2 \gamma_\epsilon \widetilde{\mathbf{E}} + ikz_0\sigma\widetilde{\mathbf{E}} - \nabla(\widetilde{\mathbf{E}} \cdot \nabla \ln \epsilon) - \nabla \wedge (\gamma_\mu \nabla \wedge \widetilde{\mathbf{E}}) \quad (3.5.15)$$

where

$$k = \frac{\omega}{c_0}$$

$$c_0 = \frac{1}{\sqrt{\epsilon_0 \mu_0}}$$

and

$$z_0 = \mu_0 c_0$$

The parameter z_0 is known as the free space wave impedance and is approximately equal to 376.6 ohms. The constant c_0 is the velocity at which electromagnetic waves propagate in a vacuum which is approximately equal to 3×10^8 ms^{-1}.

In acoustics, we use the same basic technique to write the wave equation in the form of equation (3.5.14). Consider the case when the viscosity of the material is zero. By adding

$$\kappa_0 \frac{\partial^2 p}{\partial t^2} - \frac{1}{\rho_0} \nabla \cdot \nabla p$$

to both sides of equation (3.5.12) we can write

$$\nabla^2 p - \frac{1}{c_0^2} \frac{\partial^2 p}{\partial t^2} = \gamma_\kappa \frac{1}{c_0^2} \frac{\partial^2 p}{\partial t^2} + \nabla \cdot (\gamma_\rho \nabla p)$$

where

$$\gamma_\kappa = \frac{\kappa - \kappa_0}{\kappa_0}$$

$$\gamma_\rho = \frac{\rho - \rho_0}{\rho}$$

$$c_0 = \frac{1}{\sqrt{\rho_0 \kappa_0}}$$

Here, c_0 is the velocity at which acoustic waves propagate in a homogeneous material with a density ρ_0 and compressibility κ_0. If we then introduce the Fourier transform

$$p(\mathbf{r}, t) = \frac{1}{2\pi} \int\limits_{-\infty}^{\infty} P(\mathbf{r}, \omega) \exp(i\omega t) dt$$

then the above wave equation becomes

$$(\nabla^2 + k^2)P = -k^2 \gamma_\kappa P + \nabla \cdot (\gamma_\rho \nabla P)$$

The quantitative inverse scattering problem posed by this equation involves reconstructing γ_κ and γ_ρ by measuring certain properties of the scattered pressure field. This is a two parameter reconstruction problem and is discussed further in Chapter 6.

The problem becomes a little more complicated when we consider an inhomogeneous viscous material. In this case, by adding

$$\frac{\partial}{\partial t}\left(\nabla(\alpha_0 \nabla \cdot \mathbf{v}) + 2\nabla \cdot (\beta_0 \nabla \mathbf{v})\right) - \rho_0 \frac{\partial^2 \mathbf{v}}{\partial t^2} - \nabla\left(\frac{1}{\kappa_0}\nabla \cdot \mathbf{v}\right)$$

to both sides of equation (3.5.13) and noting that (no shear waves)

$$\nabla\nabla \cdot \mathbf{v} = \nabla^2 \mathbf{v}, \quad \nabla \wedge \mathbf{v} = 0$$

we obtain the wave equation

$$\left(1 + \tau_0 \frac{\partial}{\partial t}\right)\nabla^2 \mathbf{v} - \frac{1}{c_0^2}\frac{\partial^2 \mathbf{v}}{\partial t^2} = \gamma_\rho \frac{1}{c_0^2}\frac{\partial^2 \mathbf{v}}{\partial t^2}$$

$$+ \nabla(\gamma_\kappa \nabla \cdot \mathbf{v}) - \tau\frac{\partial}{\partial t}\left(\nabla(\gamma_\alpha \nabla \cdot \mathbf{v}) + 2\nabla \cdot (\gamma_\beta \nabla \mathbf{v})\right) \tag{3.5.16}$$

where

$$\gamma_\kappa = \frac{\kappa - \kappa_0}{\kappa}$$

$$\gamma_\rho = \frac{\rho - \rho_0}{\rho_0}$$

$$\gamma_\alpha = \frac{\alpha - \alpha_0}{\alpha_0 + 2\beta_0}$$

$$\gamma_\beta = \frac{\beta - \beta_0}{\alpha_0 + 2\beta_0}$$

$$c_0 = \frac{1}{\sqrt{\rho_0 \kappa_0}}$$

and

$$\tau_0 = \kappa_0(\alpha_0 + 2\beta_0)$$

The parameter τ_0 is known as the relaxation time and may be written in the form

$$\tau_0 = \frac{\alpha_0 + 2\beta_0}{\rho_0 c_0^2}$$

The quantity

$$\alpha_0 + 2\beta_0 = \zeta_0 + \frac{4}{3}\eta_0$$

is known as the compressional viscosity. Introducing the Fourier transform

$$\mathbf{v}(\mathbf{r}, t) = \frac{1}{2\pi} \int\limits_{-\infty}^{\infty} \mathbf{V}(\mathbf{r}, \omega) \exp(i\omega t) dt,$$

equation (3.5.16) can be written as

$$(1 + i\omega\tau)\nabla^2\mathbf{V} + k^2\mathbf{V} = -k^2\gamma_\rho\mathbf{V} + \nabla(\gamma_\kappa\nabla \cdot \mathbf{V})$$

$$-i\omega\tau[\nabla(\gamma_\lambda\nabla \cdot \mathbf{V}) + 2\nabla \cdot (\gamma_\beta\nabla\mathbf{V})]$$

If we then use the relationship

$$\omega\tau = k\ell$$

where ℓ is the relaxation length $(= \tau/c_0)$ and divide through by $1 + ik\ell$, we obtain

$$(\nabla^2 + \xi^2)\mathbf{V} = -\xi^2\gamma_\rho\mathbf{V} + \frac{1}{1 + ik\ell}\nabla(\gamma_\kappa\nabla \cdot \mathbf{V})$$

$$-\frac{ik\ell}{1 + ik\ell}\Big(\nabla(\gamma_\lambda \nabla \cdot \mathbf{V}) + 2\nabla \cdot (\gamma_\beta \nabla \mathbf{V})\Big) \qquad (3.5.16)$$

where

$$\xi = \frac{k}{\sqrt{1 + ik\ell}}$$

Finally, we can obtain a scalar wave equation by writing $\mathbf{V}$ as

$$\mathbf{V} = \nabla\phi$$

where ϕ is called the longitudinal velocity potential. Substituting this expression into equtaion (3.5.16) and taking the divergence of each term, equation (3.5.16) can be written in the form

$$(\nabla^2 + \xi^2)\Phi = -\hat{L}\phi$$

where

$$\hat{L}\phi = \xi^2 \nabla \cdot (\gamma_\rho \nabla\phi) - \frac{1}{1 + ik\ell}\nabla^2(\gamma_\kappa \nabla^2\phi)$$

$$+\frac{ik\ell}{1 + ik\ell}\Big(\nabla^2(\gamma_\alpha \nabla^2\phi) + 2\nabla \cdot [\nabla \cdot (\gamma_\beta \nabla\nabla\phi)]\Big)$$

and

$$\Phi = \nabla^2\phi$$

The field Φ is known as the acoustic dilatation. It represents the fractional change in the volume of a material due to the disturbance of an acoustic wave. The quantitative coherent imaging problem posed by the wave equation above involves finding inverse solutions for the four acoustic scatter generating parameters $\gamma_\rho, \gamma_\kappa, \gamma_\alpha$ and γ_β. This is a four-parameter reconstruction problem.

SUMMARY OF IMPORTANT RESULTS

Green's functions

The time independent Green's function g is the solution to the equation

$$(\nabla^2 + k^2)g(\mathbf{r} \mid \mathbf{r}_0, k) = -\delta^n(\mathbf{r} - \mathbf{r}_0)$$

and is given by:

Quantitative coherent imaging

n=1

$$g(x \mid x_0, k) = \frac{i}{2k} \exp(ik \mid x - x_0 \mid), \quad x_0 > x$$

$$g(x \mid x_0, k) = \frac{i}{2k} \exp(-ik \mid x - x_0 \mid), \quad x_0 < x$$

n=2

$$g(\mathbf{r} \mid \mathbf{r}_0, k) = \frac{i}{4} H_0(k \mid \mathbf{r} - \mathbf{r}_0 \mid)$$

$$\simeq \frac{1}{\sqrt{8\pi}} \exp(i\pi/4) \frac{\exp(ik \mid \mathbf{r} - \mathbf{r}_0 \mid)}{\sqrt{k \mid \mathbf{r} - \mathbf{r}_0 \mid}}, \quad k \mid \mathbf{r} - \mathbf{r}_0 \mid \gg 1$$

n=3

$$g(\mathbf{r} \mid \mathbf{r}_0, k) = \frac{1}{4\pi \mid \mathbf{r} - \mathbf{r}_0 \mid} \exp(ik \mid \mathbf{r} - \mathbf{r}_0 \mid)$$

Fresnel and Fraunhofer approximations

Fresnel approximation

$$\exp(ik \mid \mathbf{r} - \mathbf{r}_0 \mid) \simeq \exp(ikr_0) \exp(-ik\hat{\mathbf{n}}_0 \cdot \mathbf{r}) \exp(ir^2/2r_0), \quad \hat{\mathbf{n}}_0 = \mathbf{r}_0/r_0$$

Fraunhofer approximation

$$\exp(ik \mid \mathbf{r} - \mathbf{r}_0 \mid) \simeq \exp(ikr_0) \exp(-ik\hat{\mathbf{n}}_0 \cdot \mathbf{r})$$

Born scattering theory

The solution to the inhomogeneous equation

$$(\nabla^2 + k^2)\phi(\mathbf{r}, k) = -\hat{L}\phi(\mathbf{r}, k)$$

is given by

$$\phi = \phi_i + \phi_s$$

where

$$\phi_s(\mathbf{r}_0, k) = \int g(\mathbf{r} \mid \mathbf{r}_0, k)\hat{L}\phi_i(\mathbf{r}, k)d^3\mathbf{r}$$

provided

$$\|\phi_s(\mathbf{r}, k)\| \ll \|\phi_i(\mathbf{r}, k)\| \quad \text{Born approximation}$$

ϕ_i - Incident field

ϕ_s - Scattered field

$\hat{L}$ - Inhomogenous differential operator

Inhomogeneous wave equations

Electromagnetic waves in a conductive dielectric

$$(\nabla^2 + k^2)\widetilde{\mathbf{E}} = -\hat{L}\widetilde{\mathbf{E}}$$

where

$$\hat{L}\widetilde{\mathbf{E}} = k^2\gamma_\epsilon\widetilde{\mathbf{E}} - ikz_0\sigma\widetilde{\mathbf{E}} + \nabla(\widetilde{\mathbf{E}} \cdot \nabla \ln \epsilon) + \nabla \wedge (\gamma_\mu\nabla \wedge \widetilde{\mathbf{E}})$$

$$\gamma_\epsilon = \frac{\epsilon - \epsilon_0}{\epsilon_0}$$

$$\gamma_\mu = \frac{\mu - \mu_0}{\mu}$$

$\widetilde{\mathbf{E}}$ - Electric field (Fourier transform of)

ϵ - Permittivity

μ - Permeability

σ - Conductivity

Acoustic waves in a nonviscous medium

$$(\nabla^2 + k^2)P = -\hat{L}P$$

where

$$\hat{L}P = k^2\gamma_\kappa P - \nabla \cdot (\gamma_\rho\nabla P)$$

$$\gamma_\kappa = \frac{\kappa - \kappa_0}{\kappa_0}$$

$$\gamma_\rho = \frac{\rho - \rho_0}{\rho}$$

P - Pressure field (Fourier transform of)

κ - Compressibility

ρ - Density

Acoustic waves in a viscous medium

$$(\nabla^2 + \xi^2)\Phi = -\hat{L}\phi$$

where

$$\hat{L}\phi = \xi^2 \nabla \cdot (\gamma_\rho \nabla \phi) - \frac{1}{1 + ik\ell} \nabla^2 (\gamma_\kappa \nabla^2 \phi)$$

$$\frac{ik\ell}{1 + ik\ell} \left(\nabla^2(\gamma_\alpha \nabla^2 \phi) + 2\nabla \cdot [\nabla \cdot (\nabla \gamma_\beta \nabla \nabla \phi)] \right)$$

$$\gamma_\kappa = \frac{\kappa - \kappa_0}{\kappa}; \gamma_\rho = \frac{\rho - \rho_0}{\rho_0}$$

$$\gamma_\alpha = \frac{\alpha - \alpha_0}{\alpha_0 + 2\beta_0}; \gamma_\beta = \frac{\beta - \beta_0}{\alpha_0 + 2\beta_0}$$

$$\xi = \frac{k}{\sqrt{1 + ik\ell}}$$

ϕ - Longitudinal velocity potential (Fourier transform of)

$\Phi = \nabla^2 \phi$ - Dilatation

α, β - First and second Lamé parameters respectively

FURTHER READING

1. Butkov E, *Mathematical physics*, Addison-Wesley, 1973. A good introduction to Green's functions is provided in chapter 12.

2. Taylor J G, *Quantum Mechanics (An Introduction)*, George Allen and Unwin, 1970. Chapter 6 provides a good introduction to quantum scattering theory using the Born approximation.

3. Morse P M and Feshbach H, *Methods of Theoretical Physics*, 1953, McGraw-Hill. This book provides an in-depth discussion of Green's functions in part 1 (chapter 7). Part 2 covers integral equations for scattering and the Born approximation (chapter 9).

4. Morse P M and Ingard K U, *Theoretical Acoustics*, McGraw-Hill, 1968. A comprehensive study of the propagation and

scattering of acoustic radiation. The wave equation that is used in acoustic scattering problems is derived in chapter 8.

5. Economou E N, *Green's Functions in Quantum Physics*, Springer-Verlag, 1979. This book is primarily concerned with the use of Green's functions for solving problems in solid state physics. However, a useful discussion of Green's functions in mathematical physics is provided in part 1.

6. Roach G F, *Green's Functions (Introductory Theory with Applications)*, Van Nostrand Reinhold, 1970. A good introductory text to the theory and applications of the Green's function which focuses attention on their application to boundary value problems associated with both ordinary and partial differential equations.

7. Newton R G, *Scattering Theory of Wave and Particles*, Springer-Verlag, 1966. This book gives a fully comprehensive account of the mathematical techniques used to study the scattering of electromagnetic radiation. It also covers the scattering of classical particles and quantum scattering theory.

PART TWO

Coherent Imaging Techniques

4 Quantitative imaging of layered media

Many coherent imaging methods are based on the assumption that the scattering body is composed of layers. This is a highly idealized type of model and reduces the dimension of a scattering problem to one dimension. In some special cases this is consistent with the physical nature of the imaging system. A good example, is seismic imaging.

Seismic imaging

The propagation and reflection of seismic waves through the earth has been studied intensively in the context of exploration of oil, coal and natural gas. In this case, an image is generated of the interior structure of the ground. This provides information on the geology of regions which are usually stratified. Hence, seismic imaging is based on the theory of scattering from layered media. Seismic prospecting is conducted either on land or at sea. Seismic waves are generated by chemical explosions or vibrating impacts of short duration. By recording the time history of the reflected seismic waves, information on the nature and geological significance of the earths interior can be obtained.

An interesting example of a seismic image is given in figure 4.1. This type of image is produced by collecting together and displaying side by side the seismic signals which are produced

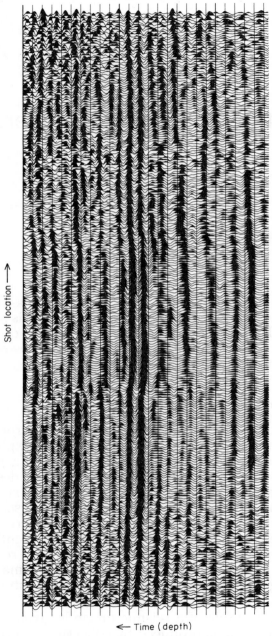

⟵ Time (depth)

Figure 4.1 Seismic image of a section of the South Yorkshire coal field in the UK

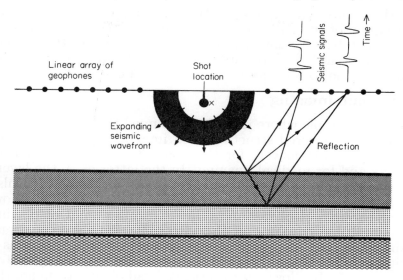

Figure 4.2 A small charge is placed below the surface of the earth at the point marked *X*. The explosion creates a seismic wave which travels through the earth and is reflected at interfaces between different rock strata. The seismic reflections travel back to the surface of the earth where they are recorded by a linear array of geophones. The signals are corrected for normal moveout and added together to form a single trace. By repeating this type of experiment for different shot locations, a seismic image can be built up of the type given in Figure 4.1

at different shot locations (the location of a small chemical explosion below the surface of the earth) as shown in figure 4.2. Each trace is the sum of all the signals that have been detected by a linear array of geophones extending either side of the shot location after they have been corrected for normal moveout (i.e. aligned to coincide with reflections from points at a common depth). This is called stacking. A seismic image of this type is therefore known as a common depth point (CDP) stack. It provides a set of seismic signals with an improved signal to noise ratio compared to the original pre-stacked data. It also reduces episodes in the data which are due to multiple scattering by enhancing the amplitude of the primary events. The example given in figure 4.1 shows a region of the South Yorkshire coal field. It is convention to shade in the area un-

119

der the positive lobes of each trace to emphasizes the lateral correlation of the data. This makes it easier for a geologist to distinguish between layers of geological interest. In this image, the main event (which occurs approximately half way down the image) is due to seismic reflections from a coal seam.

Ultrasonic imaging

Another example where it is often assumed that the scattering object has a layered structure is in imaging with ultrasound. This is used extensively for the nondestructive evaluation of objects and for medical imaging. In the latter case, the layers are of different tissue types. Reflections of an ultrasonic pulse are generated at the interface between these layers. By moving the source of ultrasound (the transducer) and displaying the amplitude envelope of the ultrasonic signals on a visual display unit, an image can be generated which is known as a 'brightness' or B-scan. This type of experiment is illustrated in figure 4.3. It allows an experienced radiologist to judge the pathological state of the tissues. In some cases, a dramatic difference can be observed between healthy and unhealthy tissues. A good example of this is provided in figure 4.4. This shows two transverse B-scans of the thigh for a normal patient (left) and a patient suffering from muscular dystrophy (right) where the muscle wastes away being replaced in part by fatty tissues. Figure 4.4 demonstrates that in healthy tissue, the B-scan illustrates bulk anatomical features such as the skin (S), fascia lata (FL) and bone (B) which are clearly defined. In the case of muscular dystrophy, the B-scan demonstrates the striking differences in intensity and diffuseness of the scattered ultrasonic field in the muscle compared with normal muscle and the absence of scattering from bone.

In addition to many other applications in acoustics a large number of electromagnetic phenomena are related to problems involving layered materials (e.g. the response of light, radio and microwaves to layered dielectric materials). Also problems that involve a certain degree of radial symmetry may often be reduced to a form where one-dimensional scattering theory can be employed. One-dimensional scattering models may also be used effectively in cases when the probe is a narrow collimated beam - a so-called pencil beam. Ideally, all coherent imaging theory should be fully three-dimensional. No arguments can then arise about the geometrical validity of the theory. How-

120

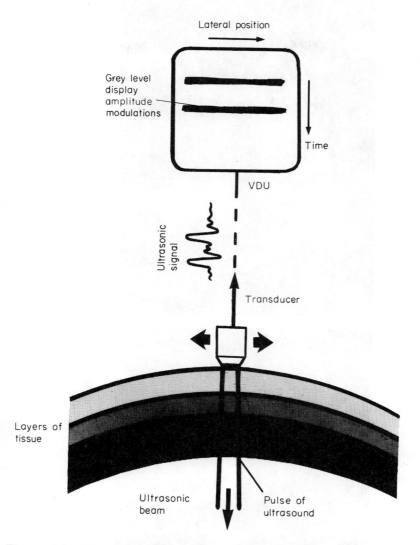

Figure 4.3 Medical imaging with ultrasound utilizes a short pulse which is emitted by a transducer. The pulse is reflected by the tissue layers. The characteristic signal is recorded and the amplitude modulations displayed on a visual display unit (VDU). Lateral movement of the transducer provides an ultrasonic image (a 'brightness' or B-scan)

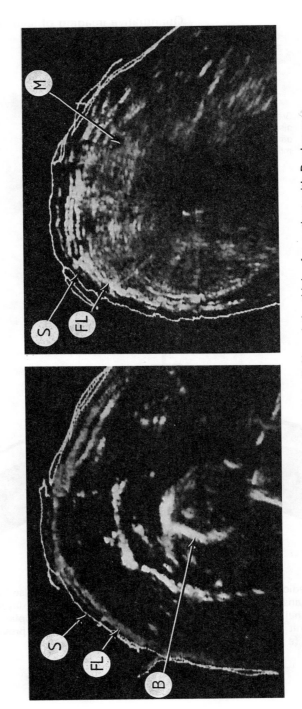

Figure 4.4 Transverse B-scans of healthy thigh (*left*) and the thigh of a patient with Duchenne dystrophy (*right*). S, skin; FL, fascia lata; B, bone; M, muscle

ever, it is often useful to reduce the dimension of a theoretical model for a physical problem when the opportunity arises. This chapter is concerned with some of the techniques that can be used when such opportunities arise.

4.1 PULSE-ECHO EXPERIMENTS

All the imaging methods that are discussed in this chapter can be classified as 'pulse-echo' experiments. This is where a short pulse of radiation is emitted from a source and the 'time history' of the scattered field is recorded by a receiver which is placed in the vicinity of the location of the source. By moving both the source and receiver and repeating this type of experiment, an image can be built up based on the nature of the reflected pulse at different source locations. The resolution that can be obtained with pulse-echo experiments of this type is determined by the length of the pulse that is used and the width of the beam. To obtain high resolution, a short pulse and narrow 'pencil beam' are required. In some cases, the lateral resolution can be synthesized. This type of imaging is known as synthetic aperture imaging and is discussed in Chapter 7.

In a pulse-echo experiment, the receiver monitors the time history of the reflected waves (the echo). After a short delay (which depends on the distance of the source from the scatterer and the speed at which the pulse propagates), the first reflections are received followed by a series or 'train' of other reflections from the interior of the material. This process continues until all the energy of the pulse has been dissipated. In each case, the receiver produces a voltage trace which is proportional to the variations in time of the reflected waves. For example, in seismic imaging, the pulse is often produced by detonating a small charge which is placed in the ground. Seismic reflections are monitored by an array of instruments called geophones.

A geophone consists of a thin wire coil which is free to move through a radial magnetic field induced by a bar magnet around which the coil is mounted. The geophone is weighted so that the coil moves in sympathy with the motion of the ground surface that is induced by the arrival of seismic reflections. The oscillation of the coil then produces a time varying voltage which can be amplified and recorded as an analogue or digital signal. Thus, a record of the time history of the seismic waves is obtained. In ultrasonic imaging, the pulse is produced by an instrument known as a transducer. This instrument translates an electrical impulse into a mechanical impulse or visa versa. The reflected ultrasonic pressure waves induce motion of the transducer face which consequently produces a time varying voltage. As before, the time varying signal can be amplified and digitized, providing data on the time history of the scattered field at a point in space. In electromagnetic imaging, the scattered electric field is measured by the way in which it induces a time varying voltage in an antenna.

Basic equation

The signal produced in a pulse-echo experiment is described by the equation

$$s(t) = p(t) \otimes f(t) \tag{4.1.1}$$

where p is the spike spread function and f is the object function. In pulse-echo experiments, p describes the profile in time of the pulse that is used to probe the material and f describes the response of the material to this probe. For this reason, f is called the impulse function. It represents the signal that would be produced in the hypothetical case when p is an infinitely short pulse (an impulse or delta function). In this case,

$$s(t) = \delta(t) \otimes f(t) = f(t)$$

The basic processing that is undertaken in pulse-echo imaging involves the reconstruction of f form s. This is known as deconvolution. The resolution that can be obtained in a pulse-echo experiment of this kind is determined by the length of the pulse. The shorter the pulse, the greater the resolution. In practice, the length of the pulse is limited by a number of physical constraints such as the amount of energy which is required to penetrate the material. This particular constraint is determined by the characteristic absorption of the material which tends to increase at higher frequencies in a manner that is invariably nonlinear. For example, in acoustic imaging, the absorption coefficient is proportional to the square of the frequency.

The spike spread function p depends upon the imaging system, whereas the impulse response is a description for the material that is being imaged. A pulse-echo imaging system attempts to find out as much about the nature of the impulse response function as possible. To generate quantitative images of a layered material, expressions for the impulse response function must be derived in terms of an appropriate set of material parameters. In the following sections, expressions for this function are derived for an electromagnetic and acoustic continuum with a layered structure. To do this we employ the Born approximation. This approximation leads to an expression for the reflected field which is the same as equation (4.1.1). Here, the principal assumption is that multiple scattering does not contribute to the information in the signal.

4.2 QUANTITATIVE ELECTROMAGNETIC IMAGING OF A LAYERED DIELECTRIC

From Maxwell's equations, the wave equation for an electric field in a material composed of variations in the permittivity ϵ permeability μ and conductivity σ is given by (using the results derived in section 3.5)

$$\nabla \wedge \nabla \wedge \mathbf{E} + \epsilon\mu\frac{\partial^2 \mathbf{E}}{\partial t^2} + \mu\sigma\frac{\partial \mathbf{E}}{\partial t} = (\nabla \ln \mu) \wedge \nabla \wedge \mathbf{E} \qquad (4.2.1)$$

We now introduce the following model:

1. A plane layered conductive dielectric

$$\epsilon = \epsilon(x); \mu = \mu(x); \sigma = \sigma(x) \qquad (4.2.2)$$

2. A plane polarized E-field

$$\mathbf{E} = \hat{\mathbf{z}}E_z(x, y, t) \qquad (4.2.3)$$

Our problem is to solve the quantitative inverse Born scattering problem posed by this model and hence, reconstruct ϵ, μ and σ.

Substituting equations (4.2.2) and (4.2.3) into equation (4.2.1) we obtain

$$\left(\frac{\partial^2}{\partial x^2} + \frac{\partial^2}{\partial y^2}\right)E_z - \epsilon\mu\frac{\partial^2 E_z}{\partial t^2} - \mu\sigma\frac{\partial E_z}{\partial t} = \frac{d\ln \mu}{dx}\frac{\partial E_z}{\partial x} \qquad (4.2.4)$$

125

By introducing the Fourier transform

$$E_z(x, y, t) = \frac{1}{2\pi} \int\limits_{-\infty}^{\infty} \tilde{E}_z(x, y, \omega) \exp(i\omega t)d\omega$$

equation (4.2.4) can be written in the form

$$\left(\frac{\partial^2}{\partial x^2} + \frac{\partial^2}{\partial y^2}\right)\tilde{E} + \omega^2 \epsilon\mu \left(1 - \frac{i}{\omega\tau}\right)\tilde{E}_z = \frac{d\ln\mu}{dx}\frac{\partial\tilde{E}_z}{\partial x}$$

where

$$\tau = \frac{\epsilon}{\sigma}$$

The parameter τ is called the relaxation time. For one-dimensional scattering problems of this kind, it is convenient to separate the electric field into two components. Since the material is homogeneous in the y direction, we can write the electric field as

$$\tilde{E}_z(x, y, \omega) = \phi(x, \omega)\exp(-iky\sin\theta), \quad k = \frac{\omega}{c_0}$$

where θ is the angle of incidence and c_0 is the velocity of the electromagnetic waves in a vacuum. Using this result, the wave equation above can be reduced to the form

$$\left[\frac{\partial^2}{\partial x^2} + \omega^2\epsilon\mu\left(1 - \frac{i}{\omega\tau}\right)\right]\phi = \frac{d\ln\mu}{dx}\frac{\partial\phi}{\partial x} + \phi\frac{\omega^2}{c_0^2}\sin^2\theta \qquad (4.2.5)$$

Notice, that this equation is inhomogeneous on both the left and right hand sides. The next thing to do is to write this equation in a form that enables us to use the appropriate Green's function to solve it. In one-dimensional problems we can do this by introducing the transform

$$\frac{dx}{d\xi} = c(\xi) \qquad (4.2.6)$$

This is known as the travel time transformation. The parameter ξ is the travel time and c is the velocity profile of the inhomogeneous dielectric given by

$$c = \frac{1}{\sqrt{\epsilon\mu}}$$

Using the chain rule together and equation (4.2.6) we can write

$$\frac{\partial^2 \phi}{\partial x^2} = \frac{1}{c^2} \frac{\partial^2 \phi}{\partial \xi^2} - \frac{1}{c^3} \frac{dc}{d\xi} \frac{\partial \phi}{\partial \xi}$$

and

$$\frac{d\ln \mu}{dx} \frac{\partial \phi}{\partial x} = \frac{1}{c^2} \frac{d\ln \mu}{d\xi} \frac{\partial \phi}{\partial \xi}$$

Noting that

$$\frac{1}{c} \frac{dc}{d\xi} = \frac{d\ln c}{d\xi}$$

equation (4.2.5) then becomes

$$\left(\frac{d^2}{d\xi^2} + \omega^2 \right) \phi = -\hat{L}\phi$$

where

$$\hat{L}\phi = -\frac{d\ln Z}{d\xi} \frac{\partial \phi}{\partial \xi} - \frac{i\omega}{\tau} \phi - \omega^2 \frac{c^2}{c_0^2} \sin^2 \theta$$

and

$$Z = \mu c$$

The parameter Z is called the impedance. Using the Born approximation, the equation for the scattered field ϕ_s becomes

$$\left(\frac{\partial^2}{\partial \xi^2} + \omega^2 \right) \phi_s = -\hat{L}\phi_i$$

where ϕ_i is the incident field. In a pulse-echo experiment, ϕ_s is the reflected or back-scattered field that is produced by the emission of a pulse $p(t)$ with a spectrum $P(\omega)$ where

$$p(t) = \frac{1}{2\pi} \int\limits_{-\infty}^{\infty} P(\omega) \exp(i\omega t) d\omega$$

Consider a pulse-echo experiment which utilizes a right travelling pulse. In this case

$$\phi_i = P \exp(-i\omega\xi) \tag{4.2.7}$$

and so

$$\hat{L}\phi_i = i\omega P \exp(-i\omega\xi)\frac{d}{d\xi}\ln Z - \frac{i\omega}{\tau}P\exp(-i\omega\xi) - \omega^2 P\exp(-i\omega\xi)\frac{c^2}{c_0^2}\sin^2\theta$$

$$(4.2.8)$$

The reflected field travels in the opposite direction to the incident field. Hence, in this case, we must use the Green's function which represents a left-travelling wave, i.e.

$$g(\xi \mid \xi_0, \omega) = \frac{i}{2\omega}\exp(i\omega \mid \xi - \xi_0 \mid)$$

The back-scattered field at ξ_0 is then given by

$$\phi_s(\xi_0, \omega) = \frac{i}{2\omega}\int_{-\infty}^{\infty}\exp(i\omega \mid \xi - \xi_0 \mid)\hat{L}\phi_i d\xi$$

In the far field when $\xi_0 \gg \xi$ and $\mid \xi - \xi_0 \mid = \xi_0 - \xi$,

$$\phi_s(\xi_0, \omega) = \exp(i\omega\xi_0)S(\omega)$$

where S is the reflection coefficient given by

$$S(\omega) = \frac{i}{2\omega}\int_{-\infty}^{\infty}\exp(-i\omega\xi)\hat{L}\phi_i d\xi \qquad (4.2.9)$$

Substituting equation (4.2.8) into equation (4.2.9) we obtain

$$S(\omega) = \frac{P}{2}\int_{-\infty}^{\infty}\left(-\frac{d}{dt}\ln Z + \frac{1}{2\tau}\right)\exp(-i\omega t)dt$$

$$-\frac{i\omega P\sin^2\theta}{4c_0^2}\int_{-\infty}^{\infty}c^2\exp(-i\omega t)dt$$

where $t = 2\xi$ (the two-way travel time). By taking the inverse Fourier transform of this equation, noting that

$$i\omega c^2 \Longleftrightarrow \frac{dc^2}{dt}$$

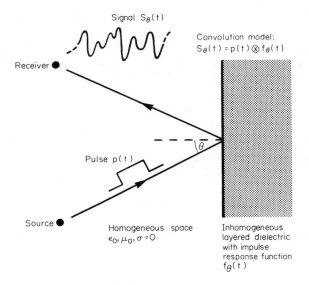

Figure 4.5 The type of experiment used for quantitatively imaging an inhomogeneous layered dielectric. The parameters ϵ, μ and σ are the permittivity, permeability and conductivity respectively

and using the convolution theorem, we get

$$s_\theta(t) = p(t) \otimes f_\theta(t) \qquad (4.2.10)$$

where

$$f_\theta = -\frac{1}{2}\frac{d}{dt}\ln Z + \frac{1}{4\tau} - \frac{\sin^2\theta}{4c_0^2}\frac{dc^2}{dt}$$

The function $s_\theta(t)$ represents the time varying signal that is measured in an experiment of the type illustrated in figure 4.5. In this example, the electromagnetic pulse is a right-travelling pulse. It travels through a homogeneous medium where the velocity of the wave is constant and the relaxation time is infinitely long (i.e. the conductivity is zero). The pulse is incident on the inhomogeneous region at an angle θ to the normal and the scattered field is observed at an angle 2θ to the path of the incident pulse. The receiver converts variations in the electric field as a function of the two-way travel time t into

129

a voltage trace. The function $s_\theta(t)$ is taken to describe this voltage trace.

Equation (4.2.10) is based on a solution for a right-travelling incident pulse. To indicate this we write s_θ and f_θ with the superscript $^-$. Equation (4.2.10) then becomes

$$s_\theta^-(t) = p(t) \otimes f_\theta^-(t)$$

An equally valid solution can be constructed by considering the case when a left travelling pulse is incident on the material. In this case, equation (4.2.7) is replaced by

$$\phi_i = P \exp(i\omega\xi)$$

and we must use the Green's function which represents a right-travelling wave, i.e.,

$$g(\xi \mid \xi_0, \omega) = \frac{i}{2\omega} \exp(-i\omega \mid \xi - \xi_0 \mid)$$

$$= \frac{i}{2\omega} \exp(i\omega\xi) \exp(-i\omega\xi_0); \xi_0 \gg \xi$$

In this case, the reflection coefficient becomes

$$S(\omega) = \frac{i}{2\omega} \int_{-\infty}^{\infty} \exp(i\omega\xi)\hat{L}\phi_i d\xi$$

where

$$\hat{L}\phi_i = -i\omega P \exp(i\omega\xi)\frac{d}{d\xi}\ln Z - \frac{i\omega}{\tau}P\exp(i\omega\xi) - \omega^2 P \exp(i\omega\xi)\frac{c^2}{c_0^2}\sin^2\theta$$

Evaluating this integral and taking the inverse Fourier transform, we then obtain an expression for the signal produced by a left-travelling incident pulse. This is given by

$$s_\theta^+(t) = p(t) \otimes f_\theta^+(t)$$

where

$$f_\theta^+ = \frac{1}{2}\frac{d}{dt}\ln Z + \frac{1}{4\tau} + \frac{\sin^2\theta}{4c_0^2}\frac{dc^2}{dt}$$

Hence, we can write the general solution for a left $(+)$ or right $(-)$ travelling pulse as

$$s_\theta^\pm = p(t) \otimes f_\theta^\pm(t)$$

where

$$f_\theta^\pm(t) = \pm\frac{1}{2}\frac{d}{dt}\ln Z + \frac{1}{4\tau} - \frac{\sin^2\theta}{4c_0^2}\frac{dc^2}{dt} \qquad (4.2.11)$$

The calculations given above, provide us with expressions for the signal where the impulse response function is defined in terms of the material parameters ϵ, μ and σ. In addition to this, we know that a change in the direction of the incident pulse only effects the polarity of one term in the impulse response functions, namely $\frac{1}{2}d_t\ln Z$. This result allows us to obtain a quantitative solution to the three- parameter problem (ϵ, μ, σ). By generating the data

$$s_0^+ = p \otimes f_0^+$$

$$s_0^- = p \otimes f_0^-$$

and

$$s_\theta^+ = p \otimes f_\theta^+$$

and deconvolving each signal, we can construct the simultaneous equations

$$f_0^+ = \frac{1}{2}\frac{d}{dt}\ln Z + \frac{1}{4\tau}$$

$$f_0^- = -\frac{1}{2}\frac{d}{dt}\ln Z + \frac{1}{4\tau}$$

$$f_\theta^+ = \frac{1}{2}\frac{d}{dt}\ln Z + \frac{1}{4\tau} - \frac{\sin^2\theta}{4c_0^2}\frac{dc^2}{dt}$$

Defining the functions

$$f_1 = f_0^+ - f_0^-$$

$$f_2 = f_0^+ + f_0^-$$

$$f_3 = f_0^+ - f_\theta^+$$

the following equations are obtained,

$$f_1 = \frac{d}{dt}\ln Z$$

$$f_2 = \frac{1}{2\tau}$$

$$f_3 = \frac{\sin^2 \theta}{4c_0^2} \frac{dc^2}{dt}$$

It is then a simple matter to solve each of these equations. Using the initial conditions,

$$Z(t) = Z_0, \quad t = 0$$

$$c(t) = c_0, \quad t = 0$$

$$\int^t f_1(t')dt' = 0, \quad t = 0$$

and

$$\int^t f_3(t')dt' = 0, \quad t = 0$$

we obtain

$$Z(t) = Z_0 \exp\left(\int^t f_1(t')dt'\right)$$

$$\tau(t) = \frac{1}{2f_2(t)}$$

and

$$c(t) = c_0 \left(1 + \frac{4}{\sin^2 \theta} \int^t f_3(t')dt'\right)^{\frac{1}{2}}$$

Using the definitions for Z, c and τ, the required set of parameters are given by

$$\epsilon = \frac{1}{Zc}$$

$$\mu = \frac{Z}{c}$$

and

$$\sigma = \frac{1}{Zc\tau}$$

These solutions can be written as a function of the displacement x by inverting the travel time transform (equation (4.2.6)). This gives

$$x(\xi) = \int^{\xi} c(\xi')d\xi'$$

4.3 QUANTITATIVE ACOUSTIC IMAGING OF A LAYERED MEDIUM

The same method that was used in section 4.2 can be employed to study the reflection of an acoustic pulse from a layered acoustic continuum. The basic aim of the calculation is the same. However, because the wave equation for an acoustic field is more complicated, the calculations are a little more involved.

It has been shown in section 3.5 that the basic wave equation for the compressional velocity field $\mathbf{v}$ is given by

$$\rho\frac{\partial^2}{\partial t^2}\mathbf{v} = \nabla\left(\frac{1}{\kappa}\nabla\cdot\mathbf{v}\right) + \frac{\partial}{\partial t}\nabla\cdot(\alpha\,\mathbf{I}\,\nabla\cdot\mathbf{v} + 2\beta\nabla\mathbf{v}) \qquad (4.3.1)$$

assuming that the shear wave (the rotational component of the velocity field) is zero, or

$$\nabla\wedge\mathbf{v} = 0$$

We now consider the following models:

1. A layered viscous continuum

$$\rho = \rho(x); \kappa = \kappa(x); \alpha = \alpha(x); \beta = \beta(x) \qquad (4.3.2)$$

2. A longitudinal velocity field

$$\mathbf{v} = \hat{\mathbf{x}}v_x(x, y, t) \qquad (4.3.3)$$

Our problem is to solve the inverse acoustic Born scattering problem posed by this model.

Using the well known vector identity

$$\nabla\wedge\nabla\wedge\mathbf{v} = -\nabla^2\mathbf{v} + \nabla\nabla\cdot\mathbf{v}$$

we note, that if $\nabla \wedge \mathbf{v} = 0$, then

$$\nabla^2 \mathbf{v} = \nabla \nabla \cdot \mathbf{v}$$

Using this result, equation (4.3.1) becomes

$$\rho \frac{\partial^2}{\partial t^2} \mathbf{v} = \frac{1}{\kappa} \nabla^2 \mathbf{v} - \frac{1}{\kappa^2} (\nabla \kappa) \nabla \cdot \mathbf{v}$$

$$+ (\alpha + 2\beta) \frac{\partial}{\partial t} \nabla^2 \mathbf{v} + \frac{\partial}{\partial t} (\nabla \alpha) \nabla \cdot \mathbf{v} + 2 \frac{\partial}{\partial t} (\nabla \beta) \cdot \nabla \mathbf{v}$$

Substituting equations (4.3.2) and (4.3.3) into this equation and rearranging, we then obtain

$$\left(1 + \tau \frac{\partial}{\partial t}\right) \left(\frac{\partial^2}{\partial x^2} + \frac{\partial^2}{\partial y^2}\right) v_x - \kappa \rho \frac{\partial^2 v_x}{\partial t^2} = \frac{1}{\kappa} \frac{d\kappa}{dx} \frac{\partial v_x}{\partial x}$$

$$- \kappa \frac{d}{dx} (\alpha + 2\beta) \frac{\partial^2 v_x}{\partial x \partial t}$$

where τ is the relaxation time of the acoustic material given by

$$\tau = \kappa (\alpha + 2\beta)$$

Introducing the Fourier transform,

$$v_x(x, y, t) = \frac{1}{2\pi} \int\limits_{-\infty}^{\infty} V_x(x, y, \omega) \exp(i\omega t)$$

this equation becomes

$$(1 + i\omega\tau) \left(\frac{\partial^2}{\partial x^2} + \frac{\partial^2}{\partial y^2}\right) V_x + \kappa \rho \omega^2 V_x$$

$$= \frac{1 + i\omega\tau}{\kappa} \frac{d\kappa}{dx} \frac{\partial V_x}{\partial x} - i\omega \frac{d\tau}{dx} \frac{\partial V_x}{\partial x} \tag{4.3.4}$$

In this case, our problem is to reconstruct the density ρ, the compressibility κ and the bulk viscosity $\alpha + 2\beta$. To do this, exactly the same procedure as before can be used. Thus, we write

$$V_x(x, y, \omega) = \phi(x, \omega) \exp(-iky \sin \theta), \quad k = \frac{\omega}{c_0}$$

and introduce the travel time transformation

$$\frac{dx}{d\xi} = c(\xi)$$

where c is the acoustic velocity given by

$$c = \frac{1}{\sqrt{\rho\kappa}}$$

From equation (4.3.4) we then obtain

$$\left(\frac{d^2}{d\xi^2} + \omega^2\right)\phi = -(1 + i\omega\tau)\frac{d}{d\xi}\ln Z\frac{\partial\phi}{\partial\xi}$$

$$-i\omega\frac{d\tau}{d\xi}\frac{\partial\phi}{\partial\xi} - i\omega\tau\frac{\partial^2\phi}{\partial\xi^2} + \phi(1 + i\omega\tau)\omega^2\frac{c^2}{c_0^2}\sin^2\theta$$

where Z is the acoustic impedance given by

$$Z = \rho c = \sqrt{\rho/\kappa}$$

Using the Born approximation and repeating the same type of calculation that was performed in section 4.2, it can be shown that the signal produced by a right-travelling pulse is given by

$$s_\theta^-(t) = p(t) \otimes f_\theta^-(t)$$

where

$$f_\theta^- = \frac{1}{2}\frac{d}{dt}\ln Z + \frac{1}{2}\frac{d}{dt}\left(\tau\frac{d}{dt}\ln Z\right) + \frac{3}{4}\frac{d^2\tau}{dt^2} + \frac{\sin^2\theta}{4c_0^2}\frac{d}{dt}\left(c^2 + \frac{d}{dt}(\tau c^2)\right)$$

and for a left-travelling pulse, is given by

$$s_\theta^+(t) = p(t) \otimes f_\theta^+(t)$$

where

$$f_\theta^+ = -\frac{1}{2}\frac{d}{dt}\ln Z + \frac{1}{2}\frac{d}{dt}\left(\tau\frac{d}{dt}\ln Z\right) + \frac{3}{4}\frac{d^2\tau}{dt^2} + \frac{\sin^2\theta}{4c_0^2}\frac{d}{dt}\left(c^2 + \frac{d}{dt}(\tau c^2)\right)$$

At this stage, it is interesting to compare the acoustic impulse response function with the electromagnetic impulse response function derived in section 4.2. First of all, notice that when $\theta = 0$ and $\tau = 0$, the impulse response functions for both the electromagnetic and acoustic models are the same. In this case, reflections are induced by variations in the impedance Z alone. The major difference between the two models occurs when variations in the relaxation time τ are present. Notice that the strength of the reflection of an electromagnetic wave induced by variations in τ is determined by the magnitude of $1/\tau$ which is proportional to the conductivity of the material. However, the strength of the reflection of an acoustic wave is determined by both the first and second derivatives of τ. This means that even if the average viscosity of the material is small, a sudden change in this parameter can still generate strong reflections of an acoustic wave.

By recording the signals s_0^+, s_0^- and s_θ^+ and deconvolving, we can generate the data

$$f_0^+ = -\frac{1}{2}\frac{d}{dt}\ln Z + \frac{1}{2}\frac{d}{dt}\left(\tau\frac{d}{dt}\ln Z\right) + \frac{3}{4}\frac{d^2\tau}{dt^2}$$

$$f_0^- = \frac{1}{2}\frac{d}{dt}\ln Z + \frac{1}{2}\frac{d}{dt}\left(\tau\frac{d}{dt}\ln Z\right) + \frac{3}{4}\frac{d^2\tau}{dt^2}$$

and

$$f_\theta^+ = -\frac{1}{2}\frac{d}{dt}\ln Z + \frac{1}{2}\frac{d}{dt}\left(\tau\frac{d}{dt}\ln Z\right) + \frac{3}{4}\frac{d^2\tau}{dt^2} + \frac{\sin^2\theta}{4c_0^2}\frac{d}{dt}\left(c^2 + \frac{d(\tau c^2)}{dt}\right)$$

We are then faced with the problem of solving these three simultaneous equations for the functions Z, τ and c. To do this we generate the data

$$f_1 = f_0^+ - f_0^-$$

$$f_2 = f_0^+ + f_0^-$$

and

$$f_3 = f_\theta^+ - f_0^+$$

so that we can write

$$f_1 = -\frac{d}{dt}\ln Z \tag{4.3.5}$$

$$f_2 = \frac{d}{dt}\left(\tau\frac{d}{dt}\ln Z\right) + \frac{3}{2}\frac{d^2\tau}{dt^2} \tag{4.3.6}$$

and

$$f_3 = \frac{\sin^2 \theta}{4c_0^2} \frac{d}{dt} \left(c^2 + \frac{d(\tau c^2)}{dt} \right) \tag{4.3.7}$$

Compared to the electromagnetic case (see section 4.2), these equations are not as easy to solve except for equation (4.3.5) whose solution is

$$Z(t) = Z_0 \exp \left(- \int^t f_1(t')dt' \right)$$

provided that

$$Z = Z_0, \quad t = 0$$

and

$$\int^t f_1(t')dt' = 0, \quad t = 0$$

This solution is often used in acoustic imaging when the angle of incidence of the pulse is zero ($\theta = 0$) under the assumption that the viscosity of the material is also zero ($\tau = 0$). The reconstruction of the impedance from a signal by deconvolution and application of the above formula is known as impediography. This is discussed in more detail in the following section.

Solution to equation (4.3.6)

Using the initial conditions

$$\frac{dZ}{dt} = 0, \quad t = 0$$

$$\frac{d\tau}{dt} = 0, \quad t = 0$$

and

$$\int^t f_2(t')dt' = 0, \quad t = 0$$

the solution to equation (4.3.6) can be obtained by first integrating directly to get

$$\tau \frac{d}{dt} \ln Z + \frac{3}{2} \frac{d\tau}{dt} = \int^t f_2(t')dt'$$

137

Multiplying through by 2/3 and noting that

$$\frac{2}{3} \ln Z = \ln Z^{2/3}$$

and

$$\frac{d}{dt} \ln Z^{2/3} = \frac{1}{Z^{2/3}} \frac{d}{dt} Z^{2/3}$$

we can write

$$\frac{1}{Z^{2/3}} \frac{d}{dt} (\tau Z^{2/3}) = \frac{2}{3} \int^t f_2(t') dt'$$

Multiplying through by $Z^{2/3}$, integrating again and then using the initial conditions

$$Z = Z_0, \quad t = 0$$

$$\tau = \tau_0, \quad t = 0$$

and

$$\int^t dt' Z^{2/3}(t') \int^{t'} f_2(t'') dt'' = 0, \quad t = 0$$

we get,

$$\tau(t) = \tau_0 \left(\frac{Z_0}{Z(t)} \right)^{\frac{2}{3}} \left(1 + \frac{2}{3\tau_0 Z_0^{2/3}} \int^t dt' Z^{2/3}(t') \int^{t'} f_2(t'') dt'' \right)$$

Solution to equation (4.3.7)

Writing equation (4.3.7) as

$$\frac{d}{dt} \left(c^2 + \frac{d(\tau c^2)}{dt} \right) = \frac{4c_0^2 f_3}{\sin^2 \theta}$$

and introducing the initial conditions

$$c = c_0, \quad t = 0$$

$$\tau = \tau_0, \quad t = 0$$

$$\frac{dc}{dt} = 0, \quad t = 0$$

$$\frac{d\tau}{dt} = 0, \quad t = 0$$

we can integrate directly to obtain

$$\frac{d}{dt}(\tau c^2) + c^2 = c_0^2 \left(1 + \frac{4}{\sin^2 \theta} \int^t f_3(t')dt'\right)$$

We then use the relationship

$$\frac{d}{dt}(\tau c^2) + c^2 = \frac{d}{dt}\left[c^2\tau \exp\left(\int^t \frac{dt'}{\tau}\right)\right] \exp\left(-\int^t \frac{dt'}{\tau}\right)$$

so that we can write

$$\frac{d}{dt}\left[c^2\tau \exp\left(\int^t \frac{dt'}{\tau}\right)\right] = c_0^2\left(1 + \frac{4}{\sin^2 \theta}\int^t f_3 dt'\right)\exp\left(\int^t \frac{dt'}{\tau}\right)$$

Integrating this equation then yields the expression

$$c^2\tau \exp\left(\int^t \frac{dt'}{\tau}\right) = \tau_0 c_0^2 + c_0^2 \int^t dt' \exp\left(\int^{t'} \frac{dt''}{\tau}\right)\left(1 + \frac{4}{\sin^2 \theta}\int^{t'} f_3 dt''\right)$$

where, in addition to the initial conditions given above, we have chosen that

$$\int^t \frac{dt'}{\tau} = 0, \quad t = 0$$

and

$$\int^t dt' \exp\left(\int^{t'} \frac{dt''}{\tau}\right)\left(1 + \frac{4}{\sin^2 \theta}\int^{t'} f_3 dt''\right) = 0, \quad t = 0$$

The solution for the acoustic velocity can then be written in the form

$$c(t) = c_0 \left(\frac{\tau_0}{\tau(t)}\right)^{\frac{1}{2}} \exp\left(-\frac{1}{2}\int_0^t \frac{dt'}{\tau(t')}\right)$$

$$\times \left[1 + \frac{1}{\tau_0}\int^t dt' \exp\left(\int^{t'} \frac{dt''}{\tau(t'')}\right)\left(1 + \frac{4}{\sin^2 \theta}\int^{t'} f_3(t'')dt''\right)\right]^{\frac{1}{2}}$$

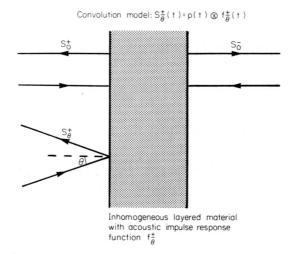

Convolution model: $S_\theta^\pm(t) = p(t) \otimes f_\theta^\pm(t)$

S_0^+ S_0^-

S_θ^+

θ

Inhomogeneous layered material
with acoustic impulse response
function $f_\theta^\pm$

Figure 4.6 The type of experiment required to recover the density ρ, compressibility κ and the viscosity $\alpha + 2\beta$ of a layered inhomogeneous material using acoustic radiation

Hence, using the definition for the impedance Z, velocity c and relaxation time τ of an acoustic material, we arrive at the quantitative solutions

$$\kappa = \frac{1}{Zc}$$

$$\rho = \frac{Z}{c}$$

and

$$\alpha + 2\beta = Zc\tau$$

An illustration of the type of experiment that is required to obtain the relevant data is shown in figure 4.6. Here, a left travelling acoustic pulse is emitted at normal incidence to the material and at an angle θ to the normal. This provides the data s_0^+ and s_θ^+ respectively. Another experiment is then required where the material is interrogated by a right travelling pulse to provide the data s_0^-. By deconvolving these data to recover the impulse response functions, the density, compressibility and viscosity profiles of the layered material can be reconstructed using the formulae given above.

4.4 SOME APPLICATIONS

The synthesis and analysis of signals and images using convolution models of the type presented in previous sections is a well established technique. In this section, some examples are discussed.

Synthesis of acoustic signals

Theoretical modelling of the propagation and interaction of acoustic radiation with different materials provides a vital input into the understanding of established acoustic imaging techniques and the development of new procedures. The synthesis of acoustic signals is important in a wide range of applications, especially when access to information on the relevant properties of the material is available. For example, in seismology it is common to have access to data which provide information on the vertical changes in the lithology of the ground. This data is obtained from a borehole and may includes a log of the fluctuations in the density and acoustic velocity of the ground. From this information, a detailed account of the changes in impedance of the material as a function of depth can be obtained. From the velocity log, a time-dependent impedance log can be generated. Assuming that the viscosity of the material is negligible, the relaxation time can be set to zero. A single seismic trace can then be written as (after stacking)

$$s(t) = p(t) \otimes f(t)$$

where

$$f(t) = \frac{1}{2} \frac{d}{dt} \ln Z(t) \qquad (4.4.1)$$

From the impedance log, the impulse response function for the ground can be computed from equation (4.4.1) (at the location of the bore hole). This result can be used to generate a synthetic seismic trace by convolving it with an appropriate wavelet $p(t)$. A detailed account of the precise nature of a seismic wavelet is difficult to obtain experimentally. It is therefore common practice to utilize appropriate models for the wavelet. A well known model used extensively in seismology is the Ricker wavelet (after N H Ricker, *Transient waves in Visco-elastic Media*; Developments in solid earth geophysics

141

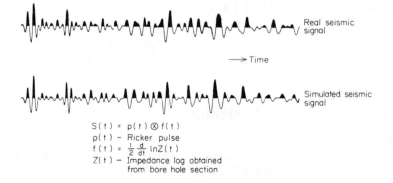

Figure 4.7 Comparison between a real seismic trace and a synthetic trace generated from the corresponding impedance log

10, Elsevier, 1976). This is given by

$$p(t) = \sqrt{\frac{\pi}{2}} \left(u^2 - \frac{1}{2} \right) \exp(-u^2)$$

where

$$u = \frac{\omega_0 t}{2}$$

Here, ω_0 is the centre carrier frequency of the wavelet. By convolving the impulse response function with a suitable Ricker wavelet (i.e. a Ricker wavelet with an appropriate carrier frequency) a synthetic seismic trace can be obtained. An example of this is given in figure 4.7. This figure compares a real seismic signal near to the location of the impedance log with a simulated signal which has been generated from the impedance log using a 200 Hz Ricker wavelet.

Impediography

Impediography is an inverse technique which seeks to reverse the process of deriving a synthetic signal from an impedance log. In other words, impediography attempts to reproduce the impedance variations (usually as a function of time) from a suitably processed signal. This technique is used in a wide variety of low frequency acoustic and ultrasonic imaging techniques. Its success depends on the quality of the deconvolved signal. In seismology, the impedance profile can be compared with real impedance logs. Done on a trace-by-trace basis, this effectively replaces a seismic image made up from a stack of seismic traces, with a seismic section made up of derived or pseudo impedance profiles. The wider the bandwidth of the original seismic trace, the more closely the derived impedance profile will match the real impedance log. This provides a technique which utilizes the processes inherent in broadband data to study in detail, lateral and vertical changes in lithology. At normal incidence, impediography assumes that the relaxation time is zero. After deconvolution, we can then employ the equation

$$\frac{1}{2}\frac{d}{dt}\ln Z(t) = f(t) \tag{4.4.2}$$

where $f(t)$ is the deconvolved data (the impulse response function). The analytical solution for the impedance is

$$Z(t) = Z_0 \exp\left(\int^t f\, dt\right)$$

This inverse process is essentially integration which amplifies the low frequency components of the deconvolved data. Numerically, the integration can be be performed using a variety of techniques. One of the simplest methods utilized for fast display purposes is based on writing equation (4.4.2) as a difference equation. Noting that

$$\frac{d}{dt}\ln Z = \frac{1}{Z}\frac{dZ}{dt}$$

we have

$$\frac{dZ}{dt} = 2Zf$$

Differencing this equation we obtain the simple iterative process

$$Z_{n+1} = Z_n(1 + 2\Delta t f_n) \tag{4.4.3}$$

Once the impedance of the first layer Z_0 is known, the others follow from application of this formula.

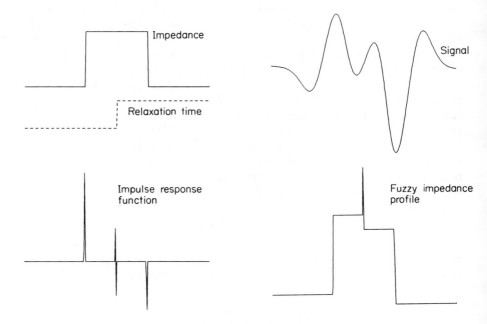

Figure 4.8 Fuzzy impedance profiles are obtained when features in the signal are due to variations in the relaxation time as well as the impedance

Fuzzy impediography

Conventional acoustic impediography assumes that a signal has been produced by single scattering from an inhomogeneous material with fluctuations in the impedance alone. When variations in the viscosity of the material are present, impediography can give rise to 'fuzzy images' of the impedance. A fuzzy image is an image which attempts to describe a single property of a material but fails to achieve this because the data are corrupted by some other interaction not included in the original model for the signal (i.e. the model for the impulse response function). This is a consequence of the fact that the reconstruction algorithm used to generate an image is ultimately determined by the type of wave equation which is used to describe the scattered field. A simple demonstration of this is given in figure 4.8. Here, a hypothetical layered material is considered which consists of a simple impedance profile and a single mismatch in the relaxation time. If we consider the interaction of this material with an acoustic pulse $p(t)$ at normal incidence, then the reflected signal is given by (for a right-travelling wave)

$$s(t) = p(t) \otimes f(t)$$

where

$$f(t) = \frac{1}{2}\frac{d}{dt}\ln Z + \frac{1}{2}\frac{d}{dt}\left(\tau\frac{d}{dt}\ln Z\right) + \frac{3}{4}\frac{d^2\tau}{dt^2} \qquad (4.4.4)$$

In figure 4.8, the signal has been computed by forward differencing equation (4.4.4) and convolving the result with a Ricker wavelet. Deconvolution recovers the impulse response function. If it is then assumed that the original signal does not contain features that are due to changes in the relaxation time, then the impulse response function is given by equation (4.4.2) rather than equation (4.4.4). Integration then gives a fuzzy reconstruction because the impediography algorithm (which in this example is given by equation (4.4.3) interprets the second echo (which arises from a mismatch in the relaxation time) as arising from an impedance mismatch.

To avoid the production of fuzzy acoustic impedance profiles and therefore errors in the interpretation of the distribution of impedance, one must resort to normal incidence reflection experiments of the type illustrated in figure 4.6. This requires access to both sides of the layered material which rules out a number applications such as seismic imaging where access is only available from the ground surface. In applications where the material can be scanned with an ultrasonic pulse from both sides, quantitative impediography may be utilized. This is illustrated in figure 4.9. Each transducer emits a pulse and records the echo obtained at different lateral positions. Both signals are deconvolved and used to construct the functions given by equations (4.3.5) and (4.3.6). These equations are then solved to provide $Z(t)$ and $\tau(t)$ respectively. Ultrasonic inspection of this type provides two images, one of the impedance of the material and another of the relaxation time.

Quantitative coherent imaging

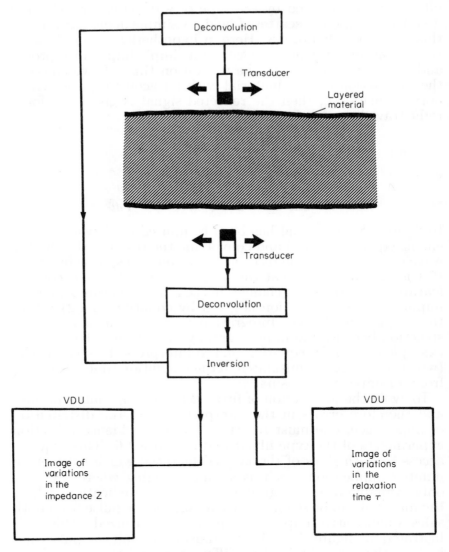

Figure 4.9 Quantitative ultrasonic impediography utilizes two transducers which provide data on the echoes generated from a material when it is insonified by a left- and right-travelling pulse. Deconvolution and inversion allow ultrasonic images of the variations in impedance and relaxation time of the material to be observed

Structural determination of the ionosphere

The ionosphere is a weakly ionized gas which exists between the earth's atmosphere and the magnetosphere. At long wavelengths the ionosphere behaves like a layered dielectric, and its ability to reflect radio waves is well known. By observing the way in which radio waves are reflected we can determine the structure and dielectric properties of the ionosphere using the methods discussed in section 4.2. In order to apply this method we are required to make some reasonable assumptions about the properties of ionospheric transport.

To a good approximation, the ionosphere is a three-component gas made up of ions, electrons and neutrals embedded in a magnetic field of uniform magnitude across its vertical extent (i.e. the earth's magnetic field). If the component x is vertical, then the gyrofrequencies (the frequencies at which a charged particle gyrate about a magnetic field line) of ions and electrons (Ω_i, Ω_e) are roughly constant in x. However, the collision frequencies of ions, electrons and neutrals (ν_i, ν_e, ν_n) can change by five orders of magnitude as a function of x due to the change in density as a function of altitude. As a consequence of this, transport at low altitudes is dominated by collisions $(\nu/\Omega \gg 1)$ whereas at high altitudes, the magnetic field is more important $(\nu/\Omega \ll 1)$, the collision frequencies being reduced by the low number densities that occur at high altitudes. In this type of model, it is assumed that thermal and viscous transport can be neglected. This is a reasonable assumption for a 'quiet' ionosphere where changes in its state are not abrupt but take place smoothly and over relatively long periods of time. If an electric field is applied perpendicular to the earth's magnetic field $\mathbf{H}$, current will flow in a parallel, intermediate and perpendicular direction for ν/Ω going from very large to very small values. The magnitude of the currents is a function of the anisotropic electrical conductivity. The conductivity is additionally anisotropic for electric field components parallel to $\mathbf{H}$. For the ionosphere, the current density $\mathbf{J}$ is related to the electric field $\mathbf{E}$ by the equation

$$\mathbf{J} = \sigma_1 \mathbf{E}_{\parallel} + \sigma_2 \mathbf{E}_{\perp} + \sigma_3 \mathbf{H} \wedge \mathbf{E} \qquad (4.4.1)$$

where $\parallel$ and $\perp$ indicate the electric field components parallel and perpendicular to $\hat{\mathbf{h}} = \mathbf{H}/ \mid \mathbf{H} \mid$ and $\mathbf{J}$ is the current density. Here, it is assumed that the conductivity is anisotropic

147

in three different senses. The first term in equation (4.4.1) describes the current that is generated parallel to the magnetic field, namely the direct current with an associated conductivity σ_1. The second term identifies the current that is induced due to an electric field perpendicular to the magnetic field which represents the Ohmic current with an associated conductivity σ_2. Finally, there will exist a current known as the Hall current which is perpendicular to both the electric and magnetic fields and is described by the third term of equation (4.4.1). This term arises from the differential motion between the ions and electrons as a result of an $\mathbf{E} \wedge \mathbf{H}$ drift. The conductivity components σ_1, σ_2 and σ_3 are known as the direct, Pederson and Hall conductivities respectively.

If we now consider the ionosphere to be a continuum composed of different layers so that $\epsilon = \epsilon(x)$, $\mu = \mu(x)$ and $\sigma_i = \sigma_i(x); i = 1, 2, 3$, then, from Maxwell's equations, our basic time-dependent wave equation for the electric field $\mathbf{E}$ becomes

$$\nabla \wedge \nabla \wedge \mathbf{E} - \epsilon\mu\frac{\partial^2 \mathbf{E}}{\partial t^2} - \mu\frac{\partial \mathbf{J}}{\partial t} = \hat{\mathbf{x}}\frac{d}{dx}\ln\mu \wedge \nabla \wedge \mathbf{E}$$

where $\hat{\mathbf{x}}$ is the unit vector in the x direction. Considerable simplification can be achieved by modelling the ionosphere at the equator where $\hat{\mathbf{h}}$ is to a good approximation, horizontal over the extent of the ionosphere as shown in figure 4.10. At the equator (where $\hat{\mathbf{h}} = \hat{\mathbf{y}}$ and $\hat{\mathbf{h}}\wedge\mathbf{E} = \hat{\mathbf{x}}E_z - \hat{\mathbf{z}}E_x$), the components of the current density are (from equation (4.4.1)):

$$J_x = \sigma_2 E_x + \sigma_3 E_z$$

$$J_y = \sigma_1 E_y$$

and

$$J_z = \sigma_2 E_z - \sigma_3 E_x$$

Using these results, the wave equation for the polarized electric field

$$\mathbf{E} = \hat{\mathbf{y}}E_y(x, y, t)$$

reduces to

$$\left(\frac{\partial^2}{\partial x^2} + \frac{\partial^2}{\partial y^2}\right)E_y - \epsilon\mu\frac{\partial^2 E_y}{\partial t^2} - \mu\sigma_1\frac{\partial E_y}{\partial t} = \frac{d}{dx}\ln\mu\frac{\partial}{\partial x}E_y \qquad (4.4.4)$$

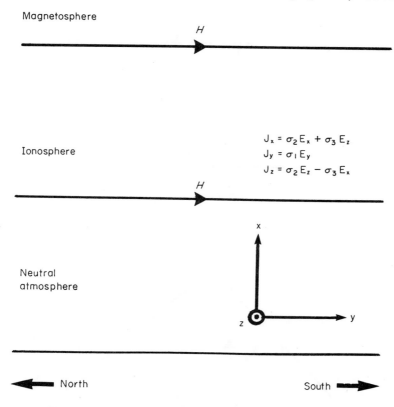

Figure 4.10 Model for the ionosphere at the Equator

When a polarized electric field of the form

$$\mathbf{E} = \hat{z}E_z(x, y, t)$$

is used, the wave equation reduces to

$$\left(\frac{\partial^2}{\partial x^2} + \frac{\partial^2}{\partial y^2}\right)E_z - \epsilon\mu\frac{\partial^2 E_z}{\partial t^2} - \mu\sigma_2\frac{\partial E_z}{\partial t} = \frac{d}{dx}\ln\mu\frac{\partial}{\partial x}E_z \qquad (4.4.5)$$

Both equations (4.4.4) and (4.4.5) are of the same form as equation (4.2.4) and thus, by repeating the method presented

149

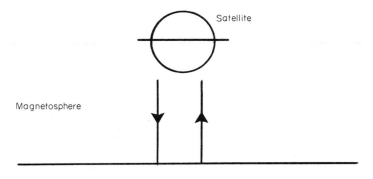

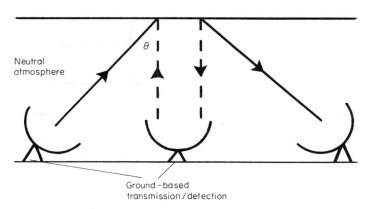

Figure 4.11 Illustration of the experiment required to recover the permittivity, permeability and conductivity of the ionosphere at the Equator

in section 4.2, we can obtain reconstructions for ϵ, μ and σ_1 using equation (4.4.4) and ϵ, μ and σ_2 using equation (4.4.5).

An illustration of the type of experiment required to reconstruct parameters ϵ, μ, σ_1 and σ_2 at the equator is shown in figure 4.11. A ground-based emitter-detector sends out a known pulse of radio waves with known polarization. The signal produced by the reflected electric field at normal incidence is then recorded. A second emitter generates another and preferably identical pulse of radio waves at some known angle θ to the normal vertical component. The signal produced by the reflected electric field is then recorded as shown. These records are then deconvolved to recover the impulse response functions. A further experiment is then required to obtain information about the reflection of radio waves from the top of the ionosphere. These data may be obtained by a low altitude satellite in a geostationary orbit.

By changing the polarization of the incident electric vector, reconstructions for two different types of conductivity can be obtained. This provides quantitative information about the anisotropic conductivity of the ionosphere.

SUMMARY OF IMPORTANT RESULTS

The signal $s(t)$ generated by the reflection of a pulse $p(t)$ from a layered inhomogeneous medium with an impulse response function $f(t)$ is given by

$$s(t) = p(t) \otimes f(t)$$

where t is the two way travel time.

EM imaging

$$f(t) = \frac{1}{2}\frac{d}{dt}\ln Z(t) + \frac{1}{4\tau} - \frac{\sin^2\theta}{4c_0^2}\frac{d}{dt}c^2$$

Z - EM impedance $= \mu c$

c - EM wave velocity$= 1/\sqrt{\epsilon\mu}$

τ - Relaxation time $= \epsilon/\sigma$

θ - Angle of incidence

ϵ, μ and σ are the permittivity, permeability and conductivity respectively.

Acoustic imaging

$$f(t) = \frac{1}{2}\frac{d}{dt}\ln Z + \frac{1}{2}\frac{d}{dt}\left(\tau\frac{d}{dt}\ln Z\right) + \frac{3}{4}\frac{d^2\tau}{dt^2}$$

151

$$+\frac{\sin^2\theta}{4c_0^2}\frac{d}{dt}\left(c^2+\frac{d}{dt}(\tau c^2)\right)$$

Z - Acoustic impedance $=\rho c$

c - Acoustic wave velocity $=1/\sqrt{\rho\kappa}$

τ - Relaxation time $=\kappa(\alpha+2\beta)$

κ, ρ and $\alpha+2\beta$ are the compressibility, density and bulk viscosity respectively.

FURTHER READING

1. Ricker N H, *Transient Waves in Visco-elestic Media*, Developments in Solid Earth Geophysics 10, Elsevier, 1976. Mathematical models for the propagation of seismic waves are presented including the Ricker wavelet.

2. Aki K and Richards P, *Quantitative Seismology (Theory and Methods)*, Freeman and Company, 1980. This work provides a detailed and up-to-date account of the theory and methods that are used to process and interpret seismic signals. Volume I concentrates on the theory of seismic wave propagation and volume II summarizes recent progress that has been made in seismology.

3. Wells P N T (editor), *Scientific Basis of Medical Imaging*, Churchill-Livingstone, 1982. Chapter 4 provides a useful introduction to ultrasonic imaging in medicine.

5 Projection tomography

Projection tomography is an imaging method which uses probes with a wavelength λ which are, in general, much smaller than the characteristic dimensions D of the scatterer, i.e.

$$\frac{\lambda}{D} << 1$$

In this sense, projection tomography is analogous to geometric optics and like geometric optics is based on assuming that the radiation field is composed of rays which can be described mathematically using geometric relationships.

In this chapter, the principles and theoretical basis for projection tomography are discussed. This is for two reasons. First, projection tomography is one of the most widely used methods for quantitatively imaging inhomogeneous materials. Secondly, although projection tomography is not a coherent imaging technique, its theoretical basis is important in other coherent imaging systems. For example, it is used in diffraction tomography (which is discussed in Chapter 6). It is starting to play an increasingly important role in image processing. Computer vision and artificial intelligence are also areas where the same theory has started to be applied (see for example Sanz et al. *Radon and Projection Transform-Based Computer Vision*, Springer-Verlag 1988).

5.1 BASIC PRINCIPLES

The history of projection tomography is interesting in two respects. First, it is a good example of a scientific development where advances in technology (particularly in digital computer power) aided theoretical progress in the subject. Secondly, a large number of early investigators were entirely unaware of former contributions that had been made. Indeed, the theoretical basis for projection tomography was 're-discovered' many times before it was realized in the early 1970s that the German mathematician Johannes Radon had studied the problem as early as 1917. It is now accepted that the theoretical basis for projection tomography is compounded in the analytical properties of the 'Radon transform'.

Although projection tomography now has a wide range of applications in many diverse subjects, it originated as a problem in medical diagnosis using X-rays. It is therefore appropriate to introduce projection tomography in terms of an X-ray imaging technique.

X-rays have been used for many years in medical diagnosis. This involves recording the intensity of X-rays on a photographic plate as they emerge from a three-dimensional object after having been attenuated by an amount that is determined by the path followed by a particular ray through the object. This gives an image known as an X-ray radiograph. Each grey level of this type of image is determined by the combined effect of all the absorbing elements that lie along the path of an individual ray.

We can consider a three-dimensional object to be composed of a number of two-dimensional slices stacked one on top of the other. Instead of looking at the absorption of X-rays over a composite stack of these slices, we can choose to study the absorption of X-rays as they pass through an individual slice. To do this we must assume that the absorption properties over the finite thickness of the slice are constant. The type of image produced by looking at the material composition and properties of a slice is known as a tomogram. The absorption of X-rays, as they pass through a slice provides a single profile of the X-ray intensity. This profile is characteristic of the distribution of material in the slice. This is illustrated in figure 5.1. A single profile of the X-ray intensity associated with a particular slice only provides a qualitative account of the distribution of ma-

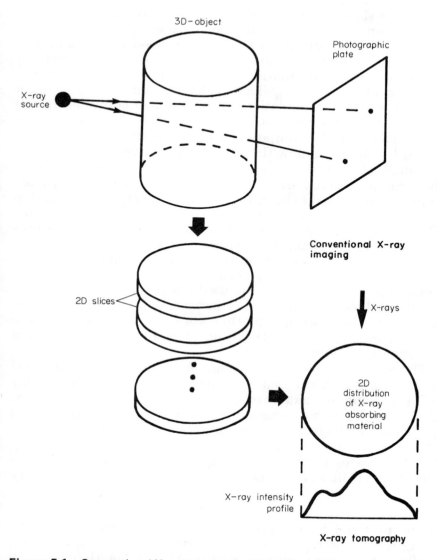

Figure 5.1   Conventional X-ray imaging (*top*) and X-ray tomography (*bottom*). By considering a three dimensional object to be composed of a stack of slices, we can investigate the distribution of material in a single slice by recording the corresponding X-ray intensity profile. This is known as X-ray tomography

terial in a slice. In other words, we only have one-dimensional information about a two-dimensional object just as in conventional X-ray radiography we only have two-dimensional information (i.e. an image) about a three-dimensional object. A further degree of information can be obtained by changing the direction of the X-rays. This is determined by the angle of rotation θ of the slice relative to the source or equivalently, the location of the source relative to the slice. Either way, further information on the composition of the material may be obtained by observing how the X-ray intensity profile varies with the angle of rotation. The basic question then arises of how the two-dimensional structure of a slice can be reconstructed from information on the X-ray intensity profiles as a function θ. One way is to use a computer-based arithmetic technique. This is where an initial estimate for the reconstruction is progressively updated until a sequence of simulated projections are obtained which are close to the experimental data. This is an iterative technique known as arithmetic reconstruction tomography (ART). It can be used effectively when relatively small databases are involved. However, ART is not an inverse solution to the problem. In other words, it is not an algorithm that reconstructs the distribution of material in a slice from the experimental data directly.

The addition of computer techniques to tomography has led to a method of X-ray imaging known a computer tomography (CT) or computer aided tomography (CAT) and the so-called CAT-scan. In X-ray images, computer tomography provides a quantitative image of the absorption coefficient for X-rays. To understand this, consider a single X-ray with initial intensity I_0. If it passes through a homogeneous material with an attenuation coefficient α over a length L, the resulting intensity is

$$I = I_0 \exp(-\alpha L)$$

If the material is inhomogeneous, we can consider the path along which the ray travels to consist of different attenuation coefficients α_i over elemental lengths $\Delta \ell_i$ (the length over which the attenuation coefficient is constant). The resulting intensity is then

$$I = I_0 \exp[-(\alpha_1 \Delta \ell_1 + \alpha_2 \Delta \ell_2 + ... + \alpha_N \Delta \ell_N)]$$

where

$$\sum_{i=1}^{N} \Delta \ell_i = L$$

As $\Delta\ell_i \to 0$, this result can be written as

$$I = I_0 \exp\left(-\int_L \alpha d\ell\right)$$

By computing the natural logarithm of I/I_0, we obtain the data

$$P = \int_0^L \alpha d\ell$$

where

$$P = -\ln(I/I_0)$$

The value of the intensity and therefore P depends upon the point where the ray passes through the object, which shall be denoted by z. It also depends on the orientation of the object relative to the ray. This is determined by the angle of rotation of the object about its centre θ. Hence, by adjusting the source of X-rays and the orientation of the attenuating object, a full sequence of projections can be obtained which are related to the two-dimensional attenuation coefficient $\alpha(x, y)$ by the equation

$$P(z, \theta) = \int_L \alpha(x, y) d\ell \qquad (5.1.1)$$

where $d\ell$ is an element of a line passing through the function $\alpha(x, y)$ and L depends on z and θ as shown in figure 5.2. The function P is a line integral through the two-dimensional X-ray absorption coefficient $\alpha(x, y)$. It is a projection of the function α that is characteristic of θ. The general name given to this type of imagery is therefore projection tomography. Here, the basic problem is to invert equation (5.1.1) to obtain $\alpha(x, y)$ when P is known for all values of z and θ. It is shown in the following section that equation (5.1.1) is just another way of writing the Radon transform of the function $\alpha(x, y)$ and how the inverse Radon transform can be used to reconstruct this function.

Although X-ray CT is one of the main applications of projection tomography, it can of course be applied to any source/detector system where:

1. The probe can be assumed to pass through the material like a ray.

2. A measurable property of the probe can be recorded that is associated with physical changes that take place along the path of the ray.

The term 'measurable property' includes the attenuation of X-rays or any other type of radiation that is attenuated by the object. However, there are properties of a field other than attenuation that may also be measured. For example, consider the case where a short pulse of radiation is emitted and the time taken for it to reach the detector recorded. If the material in which the pulse propagates is homogeneous, then the 'time-of-flight' for the pulse to traverse the distance between source and detector along a line L is given by the simple expression

$$t = \frac{L}{v}$$

where v is the velocity at which the pulse propagates through the material. Now, if the material is inhomogeneous along L, the time of flight becomes

$$t = \int_L \frac{dx}{v(x)}$$

If we record the time of flight for all lines through a slice of material with an inhomogeneous velocity profile $v(x,y)$, then, by analogy with equation (5.1.1), we can write

$$P(z, \theta) = \int_L \frac{d\ell}{v(x,y)}$$

In this case, a tomogram of the inhomogeneous velocity of the material can be found by inverting the above equation. This result is the basis for an imaging technique known as ultrasonic computer tomography (UCT). In this case, a short acoustic pulse is used as a probe. Alternatively, the decay in amplitude of the ultrasonic probe can be measured. This allows a tomogram of the acoustic attenuation to be obtained. Images of this kind may be interpreted as maps of the viscosity of the material since it is the viscous nature of a material that is responsible for attenuating acoustic radiation. By using electromagnetic probes, we can obtain information about the spatial distribution of the refractive index of a material using an appropriate

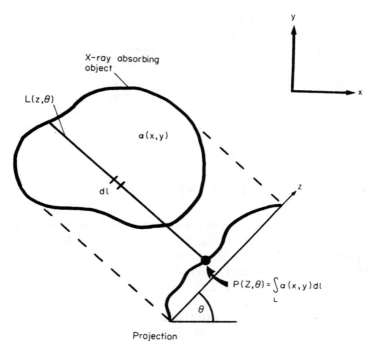

Figure 5.2 A projection is denoted by $P(z, \theta)$ where θ is the angle at which the projection is taken and z is the projection coordinate. This function is related to the variable X-ray absorption coefficient $\alpha(x, y)$ by the line integral shown. Projection tomography is based on measuring $P(z, \theta)$ for all values of z and θ and then inverting the line integral to recover $\alpha(x, y)$

time-of-flight experiment or the conductivity of a material by measuring the decay in amplitude of the electric or magnetic field.

In general, projection tomography involves an experiment where the projections $P(z, \theta)$ of a two-dimensional object $O(x, y)$ are recorded at different angles θ. A computer algorithm is then designed to invert the equation

$$P(z, \theta) = \int_L O(x, y)d\ell$$

159

numerically and reconstruct the object function O. The physical interpretation of the object function depends on the nature of the experiment, the type and frequency of the probe and the measurements that are made. The success of projection tomography as a useful quantitative imaging technique relies on how well the probe behaves like a ray. If the probe starts to diffract as a result of its interaction with the material, then projection tomography is inadequate and another method of imaging known as diffraction tomography must be used. This is discussed in Chapter 6.

5.2 THE RADON TRANSFORM

We have already seen in previous chapters, that a large proportion of the theory of imaging is closely related to the analytic properties of the delta function (e.g. the Fourier transform and the Green's function). Another important example is the Radon transform, named after Johannes Radon who first studied its properties in 1917. This transform has a variety of applications and is the mathematical basis for projection tomography. In this section, the Radon transform shall be derived entirely from the analytic properties of the two-dimensional delta function. Unless otherwise stated, all integrals lie between $-\infty$ and ∞.

Derivation of the Radon transform

Consider the two-dimensional delta function

$$\delta^2(\mathbf{r} - \mathbf{r}_0) = \delta(x - x_0)\delta(y - y_0)$$

We first define this function as

$$\delta^2(\mathbf{r} - \mathbf{r}_0) = \frac{1}{(2\pi)^2} \int \int \exp[-i\mathbf{k} \cdot (\mathbf{r} - \mathbf{r}_0)]d^2\mathbf{k}$$

Next, writing

$$\mathbf{k} = \hat{\mathbf{n}}k$$

where

$$\hat{\mathbf{n}} = \frac{\mathbf{k}}{k}$$

we note that

$$\int \delta(z - \hat{\mathbf{n}} \cdot \mathbf{r}) \exp(-ikz)dz = \exp(-ik\hat{\mathbf{n}} \cdot \mathbf{r})$$

where δ is the one-dimensional delta function. This result allows us to write the two-dimensional delta function, as

$$\delta^2(\mathbf{r} - \mathbf{r}_0) = \frac{1}{(2\pi)^2} \int \int \exp(ik\hat{\mathbf{n}} \cdot \mathbf{r}_0) \exp(-ik\hat{\mathbf{n}} \cdot \mathbf{r}) d^2\mathbf{k}$$

$$= \frac{1}{(2\pi)^2} \int \int d^2\mathbf{k} \exp(ik\hat{\mathbf{n}} \cdot \mathbf{r}_0) \int \delta(z - \hat{\mathbf{n}} \cdot \mathbf{r}) \exp(-ikz) dz$$

We now write this result in polar coordinates (k, θ) giving

$$\delta^2(\mathbf{r} - \mathbf{r}_0) = \frac{1}{(2\pi)^2} \int_0^{2\pi} d\theta \int_0^{\infty} dk\, k \int dz \exp[ik(\hat{\mathbf{n}} \cdot \mathbf{r}_0 - z)] \delta(z - \hat{\mathbf{n}} \cdot \mathbf{r})$$

$$= \frac{1}{(2\pi)^2} \int_0^{\pi} d\theta \int dk\, |\, k\,| \int dz \exp[ik(\hat{\mathbf{n}} \cdot \mathbf{r}_0 - z)] \delta(z - \hat{\mathbf{n}} \cdot \mathbf{r})$$

The next task involves a couple of simple analytical tricks. Using the definition of the sgn function, i.e.

$$\mathrm{sgn}(k) = \begin{cases} 1, & k \geq 0 \\ -1, & k < 0 \end{cases}$$

$|\, k\,|$ can be re-written as $k\,\mathrm{sgn}(k)$ so that

$$\delta^2(\mathbf{r} - \mathbf{r}_0) = \frac{1}{(2\pi)^2} \int_0^{\pi} d\theta \int dk\, k\, \mathrm{sgn}(k) \int dz \exp[ik(\hat{\mathbf{n}} \cdot \mathbf{r}_0 - z)] \delta(z - \hat{\mathbf{n}} \cdot \mathbf{r})$$

Re-writing the two-dimensional delta function in this form allows us to utilize the result

$$\int \left(\frac{\partial}{\partial z} \delta(z - \hat{\mathbf{n}} \cdot \mathbf{r}) \right) \exp(-ikz) dz = ik \int \delta(z - \hat{\mathbf{n}} \cdot \mathbf{r}) \exp(-ikz) dz$$

giving

$$\delta^2(\mathbf{r} - \mathbf{r}_0) = \frac{-i}{(2\pi)^2} \int_0^{\pi} d\theta \int dz \left(\frac{\partial}{\partial z} \delta(z - \hat{\mathbf{n}} \cdot \mathbf{r}) \right)$$

$$\times \int dk\, \mathrm{sgn}(k) \exp[ik(\hat{\mathbf{n}} \cdot \mathbf{r}_0 - z)]$$

Quantitative coherent imaging

We can progress further by using the definition of the sgn function in terms of the Fourier transform of $1/u$ (u being a dummy variable), i.e.

$$\int \frac{1}{u} \exp(-iku) du = -i\pi \, \text{sgn}(k)$$

On taking the inverse Fourier transform we obtain,

$$\frac{1}{u} = -\frac{i}{2} \int \text{sgn}(k) \exp(iku) dk$$

or, rearranging,

$$\int \text{sgn}(k) \exp(iku) dk = \frac{2i}{u}$$

The two-dimensional delta function can then be written as

$$\delta^2(\mathbf{r} - \mathbf{r}_0) = \frac{1}{2\pi^2} \int_0^\pi d\theta \int dz \frac{1}{\hat{\mathbf{n}} \cdot \mathbf{r}_0 - z} \frac{\partial}{\partial z} \delta(z - \hat{\mathbf{n}} \cdot \mathbf{r})$$

Observe, that all that has been done here, is to utilize various analytical results to write δ^2 in a different form. The reason for this, is that the definition of the forward and inverse Radon transforms is now very easy to derive as shall now be shown. Consider a continuous function O which shall be referred to as the object function. This function may be written as

$$O(\mathbf{r}_0) = \int O(\mathbf{r})\delta^2(\mathbf{r} - \mathbf{r}_0) d^2\mathbf{r}$$

Substituting our definition for δ^2 into the above equation leads to the expression

$$O(\mathbf{r}_0) = \int O(\mathbf{r}) \frac{1}{2\pi^2} \int_0^\pi d\theta \int dz \frac{1}{\hat{\mathbf{n}} \cdot \mathbf{r}_0 - z} \frac{\partial}{\partial z} \delta(z - \hat{\mathbf{n}} \cdot \mathbf{r}) d^2\mathbf{r}$$

or alternatively, interchanging the order of integration,

$$O(\mathbf{r}_0) = \frac{1}{2\pi^2} \int_0^\pi \int dz \frac{1}{\hat{\mathbf{n}} \cdot \mathbf{r}_0 - z} \frac{\partial}{\partial z} P(\hat{\mathbf{n}}, z) \tag{5.2.1}$$

where

$$P(\hat{\mathbf{n}}, z) = \int O(\mathbf{r})\delta(z - \hat{\mathbf{n}} \cdot \mathbf{r})d^2\mathbf{r}$$

The function P is defined as the Radon transform of O. If we write

$$P(\hat{\mathbf{n}}, z) = \hat{R}O(\mathbf{r}) = \int O(\mathbf{r})\delta(z - \hat{\mathbf{n}} \cdot \mathbf{r})d^2\mathbf{r} \qquad (5.2.2)$$

then $\hat{R}$ is known as the Radon operator. The object function can be recovered or reconstructed from P using equation (5.2.1). By writing

$$O(\mathbf{r}_0) = \hat{R}^{-1}P(\hat{\mathbf{n}}, z) = \frac{1}{2\pi^2} \int\limits_0^\pi d\theta \int dz \frac{1}{\hat{\mathbf{n}} \cdot \mathbf{r}_0 - z} \frac{\partial}{\partial z} P(\hat{\mathbf{n}}, z) \qquad (5.2.3)$$

we may define $\hat{R}^{-1}$ as the inverse Radon operator, $\hat{R}^{-1}P$ being the inverse Radon transform. The function P denotes the projection or line integral of O onto a line perpendicular to the direction of $\hat{\mathbf{n}}$. The unit vector $\hat{\mathbf{n}}$ defines the angle of rotation of the object function and so, we may write

$$P(\hat{\mathbf{n}}, z) \equiv P(\theta, z)$$

The variable z may be interpreted as defining the location of $\hat{\mathbf{n}}$ at which the rectilinear line integral through O is taken.

Useful operators

At this stage, it is useful to introduce two more operators, namely the Hilbert transform operator $\hat{H}$, defined by

$$\hat{H}f = \frac{1}{\pi} \int \frac{f(z)}{\hat{\mathbf{n}} \cdot \mathbf{r}_0 - z} dz$$

and the Back projection operator $\hat{B}$ given by

$$\hat{B}f = \frac{1}{2\pi} \int\limits_0^\pi f(\hat{\mathbf{n}}, \hat{\mathbf{n}} \cdot \mathbf{r}_0)d\theta$$

where f is a continuous function. From equation (5.2.3) the inverse Radon transform can then be written in terms of operators as

$$O(\mathbf{r}) = \hat{R}^{-1}P(\theta, z) = \hat{B}\hat{H}\partial_z P(\theta, z)$$

163

It is then clear that

$$\hat{R}^{-1} \equiv \hat{B}\hat{H}\partial_z$$

In other words, to compute the inverse Radon transform we need to differentiate, Hilbert transform and then back-project. This is known as filtered back-projection, the filtering being a result of implementing the operator $\hat{H}\partial_z$. The type of filter that is produced by this operation can be found by transforming $\hat{H}\partial_z P$ into Fourier space. For a fixed value of $\hat{n}$ this operation can be written as

$$\hat{H}\partial_z P = \frac{1}{\pi z} \otimes \frac{\partial P}{\partial z}$$

By taking the Fourier transform of this equation and using the convolution theorem we obtain

$$\hat{H}\frac{\partial P}{\partial z} \Longleftrightarrow -i\,\text{sgn}(k)ik\tilde{P}$$

Hence, we see that the filter produced by the operation $\hat{H}\partial_z$ is $\text{sgn}(k)k$ or $|k|$.

Physical pictures

Now that the main mathematical results have been presented, let us look at the physical significance of both a projection and back-projection. Writing $\hat{n} \cdot \mathbf{r}$ as $x\cos\theta + y\sin\theta$, the projection becomes (from equation (5.2.2))

$$P(\theta, z) = \int\int O(x,y)\delta(z - x\cos\theta - y\sin\theta)dxdy \qquad (5.2.4)$$

This function only exists when

$$z = x\cos\theta + y\sin\theta$$

the delta function being zero otherwise. We can think of a projection as being the family of line integrals through the object function when it is rotated by an angle θ. To illustrate this, consider the case when $\theta = 0$. The projection at this angle is given by

$$P(0, z) = \int\int O(x,y)\delta(z - x)dxdy = \int O(z,y)dy$$

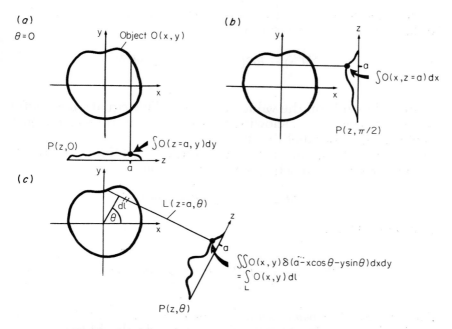

Figure 5.3 Projection of an object at different angles

In this case, it is easy to see that the projection $P(0, z)$ is obtained by integrating the object over y for all values of the projection coordinate z. This is shown in figure 5.3a. When $\theta = \pi/2$, the projection at this angle is

$$P(\pi/2, z) = \int\int O(x, y)\delta(z - y)dxdy = \int O(x, z)dx$$

and so, in this case, the projection is obtained by integrating along x as shown in figure 5.3b. It should now be clear that, for arbitrary values of θ, the line integral through O is along

165

a line L as shown in figure 5.3c. Another way of writing the Radon transform is therefore

$$P(\theta, z) = \hat{R}O(x, y) = \int_L O(x, y)d\ell$$

where L depends on the value of θ and z. This equation is useful as a conceptual guide, showing that the Radon transform is just a collection of parallel line integrals.

Let us now turn our attention to back-projection. The result of back-projecting a sequence of projections

$$P(\theta, z), \quad z = x\cos\theta + y\sin\theta$$

may be written as

$$B(x, y) = \frac{1}{2\pi} \int_0^\pi P(x\cos\theta + y\sin\theta, \theta)d\theta$$

The function $P(x\cos\theta+y\sin\theta, \theta)$ is the distribution of P along the family of lines L. In other words, for a fixed value of θ, $P(x\cos\theta+y\sin\theta, \theta)$ is constructed by assigning the value of the projection at z to all the points that lie along the line L. For example, referring to figure 5.3c, we take the value of the projection at $z = a$ and let all points along the line L have the same value. By repeating this process for all values of z, the function $P(x\cos\theta + y\sin\theta, \theta)$ is obtained for a given value of θ. The whole process is then repeated for all values of θ between 0 and π. This provides the function $P(x\cos\theta + y\sin\theta, \theta)$ for all vaules of θ. By summing all these results, the back-projection function is obtained. This is how the inverse Radon transform is obtained, except in this case, we back project the filtered projections (i.e. we back-project $\hat{H}\partial_z P(\theta, z)$ rather than just $P(\theta, z)$).

5.3 THE POINT SPREAD FUNCTION

The point spread function associated with the back-projection function can be found by reconstructing a point and observing how the reconstruction is spread about this point. Mathematically we can describe a point by a two-dimensional delta function. If we project a two-dimensional delta function, the result will be a sequence of one-dimensional delta functions at different angles. In terms of polar coordinates (r, θ_0) where $x = r \cos \theta_0$ and $y = r \cos \theta_0$, the back projection function becomes

$$B(r, \theta_0) = \frac{1}{2\pi} \int_0^{2\pi} \delta[r \cos(\theta_0 - \theta)] d\theta = \frac{1}{r}$$

The point spread function of the back projection function is therefore given by

$$P(x, y) = \frac{1}{\sqrt{(x^2 + y^2)}}$$

Hence, in general, the back projection function produced from an object $O(x, y)$ is given by

$$B(x, y) = P(x, y) \otimes \otimes O(x, y)$$

From this result, it is clear that we have another method of reconstructing the object function from its projections by inverting or deconvolving the above equation. From the convolution theorem, convolutions in real space are equivalent to multiplications if Fourier space. We can therefore write

$$\widetilde{B}(k_x, k_y) = \widetilde{P}(k_x, k_y) \widetilde{O}(k_x, k_y)$$

where

$$\widetilde{O} = \hat{F}_2 O$$

$$\widetilde{P} = \hat{F}_2 P$$

and

$$\widetilde{B} = \hat{F}_2 B$$

Re-arranging

$$\widetilde{O}(k_x, k_y) = \frac{\widetilde{B}(k_x, k_y)}{\widetilde{P}(k_x, k_y)}$$

The function $1/\widetilde{P}$ is known as the inverse filter and can fortunately be evaluated analytically since

$$\widetilde{P}(k_x, k_y) = \int \int \exp(-ik_x x) \exp(-ik_y y) \frac{1}{\sqrt{(x^2 + y^2)}} dx dy$$

$$= \frac{1}{\sqrt{(k_x^2 + k_y^2)}}$$

Hence the object function is given by

$$O(x,y) = \hat{F}_2^{-1}[\sqrt{(k_x^2 + k_y^2)}\tilde{B}(k_x, k_y)]$$

One may think of the back projection function as being a blurred image of the object because of the poor transmission of high spatial frequencies and the enhancement of low spatial frequencies. Any procedure that reverses this emphasis, helps to deblur the image. In other words, deconvolution amplifies the high spatial frequencies of the image which consequently enhances the resolution. Deconvolution is discussed in more detail in Part 3.

5.4 THE PROJECTION SLICE THEOREM

It is always useful to know how various operations in image or real space are related to Fourier space. The projection slice theorem gives the relationship between the Radon transform of an object and its two-dimensional Fourier transform. The theorem is as follows: The one-dimensional Fourier transform of a projection obtained at an angle θ, is the same as the radial slice taken through the two-dimensional Fourier domain of the object at the same angle. To show this, consider the two-dimensional Fourier transform of $O(x, y)$ given by

$$\tilde{O}(k\hat{\mathbf{n}}) = \hat{F}_2 O = \int O(\mathbf{r}) \exp(-ik\hat{\mathbf{n}} \cdot \mathbf{r}) d^2\mathbf{r}$$

We then use the result

$$\exp(-ik\hat{\mathbf{n}} \cdot \mathbf{r}) = \int \exp(-ikz)\delta(z - \hat{\mathbf{n}} \cdot \mathbf{r})dz$$

so that the Fourier transform may be written as

$$\tilde{O}(k\hat{\mathbf{n}}) = \int O(\mathbf{r}) \int \exp(-ikz)\delta(z - \hat{\mathbf{n}} \cdot \mathbf{r})dzd^2\mathbf{r}$$

Interchanging the order of integration, we then have

$$\tilde{O}(k\hat{\mathbf{n}}) = \int dz \exp(-ikz) \int O(\mathbf{r})\delta(z - \hat{\mathbf{n}} \cdot \mathbf{r})d^2\mathbf{r}$$

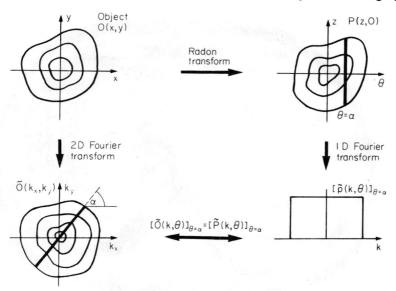

Figure 5.4 Illustration of the projection slice theorem

Hence, in terms of operators, we may write

$$\hat{F}_2 O(\mathbf{r}) = \hat{F}_1 \hat{R} O(\mathbf{r})$$

Observe that the two-dimensional Fourier transform of the object function is the same as the one-dimensional Fourier transform operating on the Radon transform of the object. Using polar coordinates, this result can be written as

$$\widetilde{O}(k, \theta) = \int \exp(-ikz) P(\theta, z) dz$$

where

$$\widetilde{O}(k, \theta) = \int_0^{2\pi} \int_0^\infty \exp[-ikr \cos(\phi - \theta)] O(r, \phi) r \, dr \, d\phi$$

The relationship between $\widetilde{O}$ at a fixed value of θ and $P(\theta, z)$ at the same angle is shown in figure 5.4. This figure can be taken as an illustration of the central slice theorem.

Quantitative coherent imaging

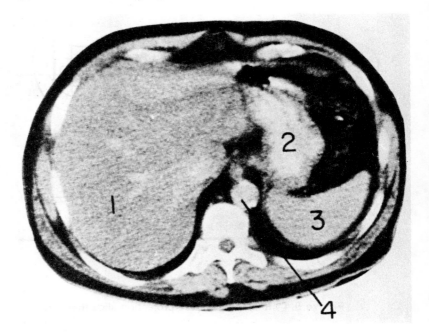

Figure 5.5 X-ray tomogram of a normal abdomen: 1, liver; 2, stomach, 3, spleen; 4, aorta

The projection slice theorem gives us yet another way by which the object function can be reconstructed from its parallel projections. That is, we take the Fourier transform of each projection and 'place it' along the appropriate radial slice. By repeating this process for all values of θ between 0 and π, Fourier inversion allows us to recover the object. In terms of the relevant operators this result may be expressed in the form

$$O(\mathbf{r}) = \hat{F}_2^{-1} \hat{F}_1 \hat{R} O(\mathbf{r})$$

The projection slice theorem is widely used to design FFT-based reconstruction algorithms for commercial X-ray CT. An example of the type of result obtainable using this method is given in figure 5.5 which shows an X-ray tomogram of a normal abdomen.

SUMMARY OF IMPORTANT RESULTS

Radon transform

$$P(z,\theta) = \hat{R}O(x,y) = \int \int O(x,y)\delta(z - x\cos\theta - y\sin\theta)dxdy$$

Inverse Radon transform

$$O(x,y) = \hat{R}^{-1}P(z,\theta) = \frac{1}{2\pi^2} \int \int \frac{1}{x\cos\theta + y\sin\theta - z} \frac{\partial}{\partial z} P(z,\theta)dzd\theta$$

Projection slice theorem

$$\hat{F}_2 O(x,y) = \hat{F}_1 \hat{R}O(x,y)$$

FURTHER READING

1. Herman G T, *Image Reconstruction for Projections*, Academic Press, 1980. A concise discussion of projection tomography and some of its applications.

2. Wells P N T, *Scientific Basis of Medical Imaging*, Churchill-Livingstone, 1982. This book provides a useful introduction to X-ray computer tomography in the second chapter.

3. Deans S R, *The Radon Transform and Some of Its Applications*, Wiley-Interscience, 1983. An excellent book which provides a comprehensive study and detailed account of the wide range of applications in which the Radon transform plays an essentail role. This book also contains one of the most comprehensive collections of references to scientific papers in the field. It also includes a translation of the original paper (written in German) by Johannes Radon.

4. Sanz J L C, Hinkle E B and Jain A K, *Radon and Projection Transform-Based Computer Vision (Algorithms, A Pipeline Architecture and Industrial Applications)*, Springer-Verlag (Series in Information Science), 1988. The application of the

Radon transform for the detection and recorgnition of lines and curves in grey level images is discussed.

5. Bates R H T and McDonnell M J, *Image Restoration and Reconstruction*, Clarendon Press, Oxford, 1986. Chapter 5 discusses reconstruction from projections.

6 Diffraction tomography

Diffraction tomography is an imaging method that attempts to reconstruct the internal structure of an inhomogeneous material by the way in which it diffracts radiation. This method of imaging is used when the wavelength of a probe λ is the same order of magnitude as the scatterer D, i.e. when

$$\lambda \sim D$$

In this case, the reconstruction methods used for projection tomography (which rely on the condition $\lambda \ll D$) are inadequate.

In practice, there is one very important difference between projection and diffraction tomography: whereas projection tomography is based on an exact reconstruction, diffraction tomography relies heavily on approximate solutions to the scattering problem. In other words, the inversion algorithm that enables us to recover the structure of an object from a sequence of projections is exact whereas in diffraction tomography, the inversion algorithm is based on an approximate solution for the diffracted field. The type of approximation that is used has already been discussed in Chapter 3. It is known as the Born approximation and provides a linear model for the diffracted field.

The problems discussed in this chapter are two-dimensional and like projection tomography are concerned with imaging a slice of material taken through a three-dimensional object. However, it should be stressed that the ideas and analytical techniques that are presented can easily be extended to three dimensions.

The principles of diffraction tomography are the same in both acoustic and electromagnetic imaging, but the theoretical details are different. In this chapter, attention is focused on the diffraction of an acoustic wavefield from a slice of material. The diffraction of a suitably polarized electromagnetic field from a conductive dielectric is briefly discussed at the end of this chapter.

6.1 DIFFRACTION TOMOGRAPHY USING CW FIELDS

Consider the ultrasonic imaging system illustrated in figure 6.1. A transducer emits a diverging wavefield at a fixed frequency which insonifies the scatterer completely. This field is transmitted through a homogeneous medium of uniform density ρ_0 and compressibility κ_0. The scatterer is assumed to be composed of variations in compressibility κ alone and confined to a region of space A. The inhomogeneous nature of this acoustic parameter causes diffraction to occur. The diffracted wavefield is detected by a second transducer which, like the acoustic source, is free to move around a circular frame which completely encloses the scatterer. As in projection tomography, the acoustic image obtained by this method is taken to be a cross section through a three-dimensional object. Our aim is to develop a scattering model for this system and obtain a suitable reconstruction algorithm.

Basic mathematical model

By considering the acoustic source to be a point source, the diverging incident wavefield can be described by the appropriate Green's function (in this case, the two-dimensional Green's function). The 2D wave equation for the Born scattered pressure field P_s at $\mathbf{r}$ due to the presence of a point acoustic source at $\mathbf{r}_i$ is then given by

$$(\nabla^2 + k^2)P_s(\mathbf{r}, \mathbf{r}_i, k) = -k^2\gamma_\kappa(\mathbf{r})g(\mathbf{r} \mid \mathbf{r}_i, k)$$

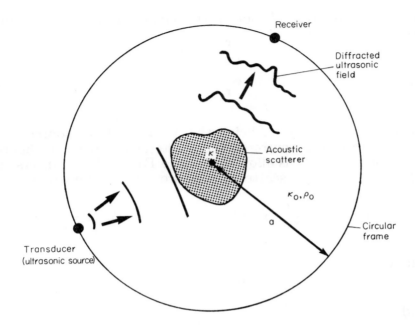

Figure 6.1 The type of experiment required to perform CW ultrasonic diffraction tomography. A transducer emits a wavefield oscillating at a fixed frequency through a homogeneous material with compressibility κ_0 and density ρ_0. The field is diffracted by an acoustic scatterer which in this case is composed of variations in the compressibility alone. By measuring the diffracted field as a function of the position of the source and receiver on the frame, the variations in the compressibility can be recovered

where

$$\gamma_\kappa = \frac{\kappa - \kappa_0}{\kappa_0}$$

Using the expression for the 2D Green's function, the solution to this equation at $\mathbf{r}_s$ is then

$$P_s(\mathbf{r}_s, \mathbf{r}_i, k) = \frac{ik}{8\pi} \int\limits_A \frac{\exp(ik \mid \mathbf{r} - \mathbf{r}_i \mid)}{\sqrt{\mid \mathbf{r} - \mathbf{r}_i \mid}} \frac{\exp(ik \mid \mathbf{r} - \mathbf{r}_s \mid)}{\sqrt{\mid \mathbf{r} - \mathbf{r}_s \mid}} \gamma_\kappa(\mathbf{r}) d^2\mathbf{r}$$

We shall develop a solution to this equation under the conditions

$$\frac{\mathbf{r}}{|\mathbf{r}_i|} << 1$$

and

$$\frac{\mathbf{r}}{|\mathbf{r}_s|} << 1$$

where $|\mathbf{r}_i| \simeq |\mathbf{r}_s| \simeq a$, a, being the distance of the source and receiver from the centre of the scatterer as shown in figure 6.1. These conditions allow us to use a Fourier-based inversion scheme because the scattered pressure field can be written as

$$P_s(\hat{\mathbf{n}}_i, \hat{\mathbf{n}}_s, k) = \frac{ik}{8\pi a} \exp(2ika) \int_A \exp[-ik(\hat{\mathbf{n}}_s - \hat{\mathbf{n}}_i) \cdot \mathbf{r}]\gamma_\kappa(\mathbf{r})d^2\mathbf{r}$$

where

$$\hat{\mathbf{n}}_i = -\frac{\mathbf{r}_i}{|\mathbf{r}_i|}$$

and

$$\hat{\mathbf{n}}_s = \frac{\mathbf{r}_s}{|\mathbf{r}_s|}$$

This equation is essentially a two-dimensional Fourier integral of the compressibility variations where $\hat{\mathbf{n}}_i$ and $\hat{\mathbf{n}}_s$ represent the direction of the incident and scattered fields respectively.

Geometry

If the scattered field is measured over a circular frame, then the appropriate co-ordinates to work with are polar co-ordinates. We therefore write

$$\hat{\mathbf{n}}_i = \hat{\mathbf{x}}\cos\phi_i + \hat{\mathbf{y}}\sin\phi_i$$

and

$$\hat{\mathbf{n}}_s = \hat{\mathbf{x}}\cos\phi_s + \hat{\mathbf{y}}\sin\phi_s$$

where ϕ_i and ϕ_s are the angles of incidence and scattering respectively. The scattered pressure field then becomes

$$P_s(k_x, k_y) = \frac{ik}{8\pi a} \exp(2ika) \int\int \exp(-ik_x x) \exp(-ik_y y)\gamma_\kappa(x, y)dxdy$$

$$(6.1.1)$$

where

$$k_x = k(\cos\phi_s - \cos\phi_i) \qquad (6.1.2)$$

and

$$k_y = k(\sin\phi_s - \sin\phi_i) \qquad (6.1.3)$$

Note, that k is constant and k_x and k_y are functions of ϕ_i and ϕ_s.

Measurments

Two basic parameters must be measured in an experiment of this kind: the amplitude of the scattered pressure field and its phase. In practice, the actual field that is measured in an imaging system of the type illustrated in figure 6.1 is not just the scattered field but the sum of the incident P_i and scattered fields, i.e. the total pressure field

$$P(k_x, k_y) = P_i(k_x, k_y) + P_s(k_x, k_y)$$

To recover γ_κ from P_s, we require information on the amplitude A and phase θ of P_i and P_s as a function of ϕ_i and ϕ_s. The amplitude and phase of the incident pressure field can be obtained by measuring the total pressure field in the absence of the scatterer. The incident pressure field as a function of these angles is then given by

$$P_i(\phi_i, \phi_s) = A_i(\phi_i, \phi_s)\exp[i\theta_i(\phi_i, \phi_s)]$$

Exactly the same procedure must then be repeated with the scatterer present, producing the total pressure field

$$P(\phi_i, \phi_s) = A(\phi_i, \phi_s)\exp[i\theta(\phi_i, \phi_s)]$$

The scattered pressure field is then given by

$$P_s(\phi_i, \phi_s) = P(\phi_i, \phi_s) - P_i(\phi_i, \phi_s) = A\cos\theta - A_i\cos\theta_i + i(A\sin\theta - A_i\sin\theta_i)$$

The behaviour of the incident pressure field is ultimately a function of the design of the acoustic imaging system and must be known *a priori* before the scatter is introduced. In other words the system must be calibrated before conducting an experiment. It is then a relatively simple procedure to compute the complex scattered field by measuring the amplitude of the total field and its shift in phase relative to the source. In practice this can be done using a quadrature filter.

Inversion

Having obtained the complex scattered pressure field, the compressibility fluctuations can be recovered by performing the appropriate Fourier inversion. Noting that γ_κ is a real function, we have from equation (6.1.1)

$$
\gamma_\kappa(x, y) = \text{Re}\left(\frac{2a}{\pi i k} \exp(-2ika) \right.
$$

$$
\left. \times \int \int \exp(ik_x x)\exp(ik_y y)P_s(k_x, k_y)dk_x dk_y \right) \tag{6.1.4}
$$

In this formula P_s is a function of k_x and k_y and not the experimental parameters ϕ_i and ϕ_s. Hence, to use this inversion, we need to know, how observations of the scattered field as a function of ϕ_i and ϕ_s are related to the spatial frequencies k_x and k_y. The relationship is provided by the parametric equations (6.1.2) and (6.1.3). Figure 6.2 shows the parametric curve in $k_x - k_y$ space produced by changing ϕ_s from 0 to 2π when ϕ_i is fixed according to these parametric equations. This curve is a circle with an origin at $[k_x = k\cos\phi_i, k_y = k\sin\phi_i]$. It is easy to show this analytically by decoupling equations (6.1.2) and (6.1.3) for ϕ_s which gives the equation for a circle,

$$
\frac{(k_x + k\cos\phi_i)^2}{k^2} + \frac{(k_y + k\sin\phi_i)^2}{k^2} = 1
$$

This relationship demonstrates that by changes the scattering angle, one is able to select the spatial frequencies of the scatterer which lie on a circle is Fourier space of radius k and origin $(k\cos\phi_i, k\sin\phi_i)$. By changing the value of ϕ_i (i.e. the position of the acoustic source), the origin of this circle is moved and a new set of spatial frequencies can be obtained by once again, measuring the scattered field at different scattering angles ϕ_s. By repeating this process for all values of ϕ_i between 0 and 2π, all the spatial frequencies of the scatterer can be measured up to and including $2k$. In other words, by recording the behaviour of the complex scattered field for all values of ϕ_i and ϕ_s between 0 and 2π, the complex spectrum of the scatterer can be obtained. This is illustrated in figure 6.3. Observe, that the

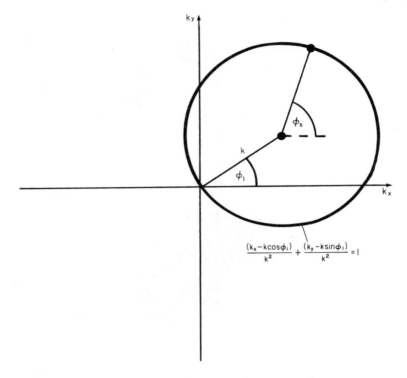

Figure 6.2 The geometric relationship between the spatial frequencies of the scatterer k_x and k_y and the incident and scattering angles (ϕ_i and ϕ_s respectively) is a circle of radius k (the wavenumber of the CW field used to insonify the scatterer) and origin ($k\cos\phi_i, k\sin\phi_i$)

maximum spatial frequency that can be obtained in this way is $2k$. To emphasize this, equation (6.1.4) should be written in a form where the double integral is bounded by the condition

$$\surd(k_x^2 + k_y^2) \leq 2k$$

Using vector notation, the inversion formula for the compressibility fluctuations can be written in the form

$$\gamma_\kappa = \mathrm{Re}\left(\frac{2a}{\pi i k} \exp(-2ika) \int\limits_{|\mathbf{k}|\leq 2k} \exp(i\mathbf{k}\cdot\mathbf{r})P_s(\mathbf{k})d^2\mathbf{k} \right)$$

179

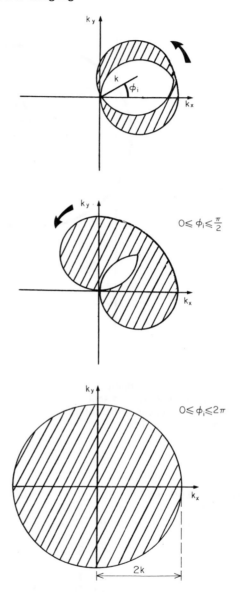

Figure 6.3 By changing the position of the acoustic source (determined by ϕ_i) and measuring the diffracted field as a function of ϕ_s, the spatial frequencies of the scatterer upto and including $2k$ can be determined. The scatterer can then be recovered by Fourier inversion

The available spatial resolution that can be obtained by this method is proportional to $1/2k$.

6.2
DIFFRACTION TOMOGRAPHY USING PULSED FIELDS

In the previous section, we examined how the compressibility fluctuations of an acoustic material can be recovered using a CW field and a scattering model that is based on the Helmholtz equation, the Born approximation and the far field approximation. Using exactly the same type of model, we shall now examine how the compressibility fluctuations can be reconstructed using a pulsed acoustic field.

Basic equations

To begin with, let us see how the basic equations change when a pulse is introduced. Using a pulse is equivalent to using a spectrum of different CW frequencies. If we denote the pulse by $p(\tau)$ where $\tau =$ time$\times$acoustic wave speed, then its characteristic spectrum can be written as

$$P(k) = \int_{-\infty}^{\infty} \exp(-ik\tau)p(\tau)d\tau$$

In this case, the scattered pressure field at $\mathbf{r}$ induced by a pulsed acoustic point source at $\mathbf{r}_i$ is determined by the wave equation

$$(\nabla^2 + k^2)P_s(\mathbf{r}, \mathbf{r}_i, k) = -k^2 P(k)\gamma_\kappa(\mathbf{r})g(\mathbf{r} \mid \mathbf{r}_i, k)$$

Following exactly the same procedure as before, the scattered pressure is given by

$$P_s(\hat{\mathbf{N}}, k) = \frac{ik}{8\pi a}P(k)\exp(2ika)\int_A \exp(-ik\hat{\mathbf{N}} \cdot \mathbf{r})\gamma_\kappa(\mathbf{r})d^2\mathbf{r}$$

where

$$\hat{\mathbf{N}} = \hat{\mathbf{n}}_s - \hat{\mathbf{n}}_i$$

The functions P_s describes the spectrum of the scattered pressure field. In practice, the spectrum of this field is not measured directly. What is actually measured is a time varying voltage (a signal with both positive and negative values) which is proportional to the time history of the scattered field. This is given by the inverse Fourier transform of P_s. Using the convolution theorem and remembering that ik in Fourier space yields a derivative in real space, we can write

$$p_s(\hat{\mathbf{N}}, \tau) = \frac{1}{8\pi a} \frac{\partial}{\partial \tau} \left(p(\tau) \otimes \delta(\tau + 2a) \otimes \int_A \gamma_\kappa \delta(\tau - \hat{\mathbf{N}} \cdot \mathbf{r}) d^2\mathbf{r} \right)$$

$$= \frac{1}{8\pi a} \frac{\partial}{\partial \tau} p(\tau + 2a) \otimes \int_A \gamma_\kappa(\mathbf{r}) \delta(\tau - \hat{\mathbf{N}} \cdot \mathbf{r}) d^2\mathbf{r} \qquad (6.2.1)$$

where

$$p_s(\hat{\mathbf{N}}, \tau) = \frac{1}{2\pi} \int_{-\infty}^{\infty} P_s(\hat{\mathbf{N}}, k) \exp(ik\tau) dk$$

This is a rather nice result because the integral over γ_κ in the above expression is just the Radon transform of γ_κ (cf. equation (5.2.2)). Hence, the techniques used to obtain the inverse Radon transform discussed in Chapter 5 can also be used here to reconstruct the compressibility fluctuations. The only additional problem that we have to contend with, is the convolution of the integral with $\partial_\tau p$.

Inversion

To extract the Radon transform of γ_κ we need to deconvolve p_s. This can be done by transforming back into Fourier space and constructing the appropriate inverse filter. We can then write

$$D(\hat{\mathbf{N}}, \tau) = \int_A \gamma_\kappa \delta(\tau - \hat{\mathbf{N}} \cdot \mathbf{r}) d^2\mathbf{r}$$

where D is the deconvolved data given by

$$D(\hat{\mathbf{N}}, \tau) = 8\pi a \hat{F}_1^{-1} \left(\frac{P_s(\hat{\mathbf{N}}, k)}{ikP(k)} \exp(-2ika) \right) \qquad (6.2.2)$$

Details of how to deconvolve in the presence of experimental noise and singular inverse filters such as this one, are given in Part 3.

Recalling the results of Chapter 5, the data D is completely equivalent to a projection with the exception that γ_κ is not an object function but a scattering function and D is not a projection but a deconvolved time trace. To reconstruct γ_κ from D we need to know the characteristic time traces for all values of $\hat{N}$. Because $\hat{N}$ is the difference between the scattered and incident unit vectors, there are a number of ways of choosing $\hat{N}$. We can choose to keep $\hat{n}_i$ fixed and vary $\hat{n}_s$ or vice versa. Alternatively, we may change both $\hat{n}_i$ and $\hat{n}_s$ keeping the angle between them fixed. This is equivalent to rotating the object by an angle ϕ while keeping the positions of the source and receiver fixed. Noting that

$$| \hat{N} |=| \hat{n}_s - \hat{n}_i |= \sqrt{[(\hat{n}_s - \hat{n}_i) \cdot (\hat{n}_s - \hat{n}_i)]}$$

$$= 2\sin\frac{\theta}{2}, \quad \theta = \cos^{-1}(\hat{n}_i \cdot \hat{n}_s)$$

where θ is the angle between the incident and scattered fields, we can write

$$\hat{N} \cdot \mathbf{r} = 2x \cos\phi \sin\frac{\theta}{2} + 2y \sin\phi \sin\frac{\theta}{2}$$

For a fixed value of θ, the deconvolved data can then be written as

$$D(\phi,\tau) = \int\int \gamma_\kappa(x,y)\delta\left(\tau - 2x\cos\phi\sin\frac{\theta}{2} - 2y\sin\phi\sin\frac{\theta}{2}\right) dx\,dy$$

This expression is identical to the formula for a projection (equation (5.2.4)) except for the coefficient $2\sin(\theta/2)$. In this case, using the expression for the inverse Radon transform, the compressibility fluctuations are given by

$$\gamma_\kappa(x,y) = \hat{R}^{-1}D$$

$$= \frac{1}{2\pi^2} \int\limits_0^\pi d\phi \int d\tau \frac{1}{2x\cos\phi\sin(\theta/2) + 2y\sin\phi\sin(\theta/2) - \tau} \frac{\partial}{\partial\tau}D(\phi,\tau)$$

6.3 THE DIFFRACTION SLICE THEOREM

It has been shown above that the deconvolved data generated by insonifying an acoustic scatterer with a pulse are related to the scattering function by the Radon transform. The spatial frequencies of the scattering function must therefore be related to the spectrum of these data in the same way that the spectrum of a projection is related to the spatial frequencies of the object function. In other words, the central slice theorem should apply. In this case, since we are dealing with a diffraction phenomenon, we refer to this theorem as the diffraction slice theorem. Its basic properties are the same as the projection slice theorem with one very important difference which arises from the presence of the additional parameter θ. Following the same procedure as in section 5.4 (for deriving the projection slice theorem) we write

$$\Gamma_\kappa(k\hat{\mathbf{N}}) = \int \gamma_\kappa(\mathbf{r}) \exp(-ik\hat{\mathbf{N}} \cdot \mathbf{r})d^2\mathbf{r}$$

$$= \int d^2\mathbf{r}\gamma_\kappa(\mathbf{r}) \int \exp(-ik\tau)\delta(\tau - \hat{\mathbf{N}} \cdot \mathbf{r})d\tau = \int D(\hat{\mathbf{N}}, \tau) \exp(-ik\tau)d\tau$$

In terms of the appropriate operators, this equation can be written as

$$\hat{F}_2\gamma_\kappa = \hat{F}_1\hat{R}\gamma_\kappa$$

As in the projection slice theorem, the Fourier transform of $\hat{R}\gamma_\kappa$ at a given angle is equal to a slice through the Fourier domain of γ_κ at the same angle. The length of the slice is determined by the maximum value of

$$\mid k\hat{\mathbf{N}} \mid = 2k\sin(\theta/2)$$

This is illustrated in figure 6.4. Using vector notation, the compressibility fluctuations can therefore be written in the form

$$\gamma_\kappa(\mathbf{r}) = \frac{1}{(2\pi)^2} \int\limits_{|\mathbf{k}|\leq 2k\sin\frac{\theta}{2}} \Gamma_\kappa(\mathbf{k}) \exp(i\mathbf{k} \cdot \mathbf{r})d^2\mathbf{k}$$

Observe that the bandwidth of the reconstruction and therefore its resolution do not depend on the wavenumber alone but also

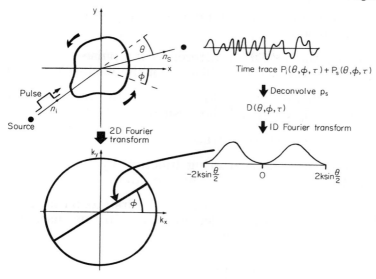

Figure 6.4 Illustration of the diffraction slice theorem

on the angle between the incident and scattered waves. Recall that the bandwidth of a CW reconstruction only depends on the magnitude of $2k$ whereas the value of the scattering angle plays a crucial role in defining the resolution of a reconstruction using pulsed fields. Note, that maximum resolution will be obtained when $\theta = 180^0$, i.e. when the back-scattered field is recorded. Also note that when θ is zero, only the DC component of the spectrum can be recovered, i.e.

$$\Gamma_\kappa(0,0) = \int\int \gamma_\kappa(x, y)dxdy$$

In addition to the scattering angle, the resolution also depends on the wavenumber k. With a pulsed system, the maximum value of k is determined by the band width of the pulse. Hence, the larger the band width of the pulse, the greater the resolution of the reconstruction. Since $\sqrt{k_x^2 + k_y^2} \leq 2k\sin(\theta/2)$, the maximum resolution available using an imaging system of this kind is obtained by measuring the back-scattered field. The resolution of the system is then determined by the bandwidth of the pulse alone. In this mode we may summarize the reconstruction as follows:

1. Insonify the acoustic scatterer with a pulse of acoustic radiation and record the time history of the back-scattered field.

2. Repeat this procedure for all angles by rotating the object or equivalently changing the position of the transducer.

3. Deconvolve each time trace.

4. Reconstruct the scattering function by taking the inverse Radon transform of the deconvolved data.

Another way of reconstructing γ_κ is first to back-project the time trace data with out deconvolving. In this case, the back-projection function is given by

$$B(x, y) = P(x, y) \otimes \otimes \gamma_\kappa(x, y)$$

where

$$P(x, y) = \frac{1}{8\pi ar} \otimes \frac{\partial}{\partial r} p(r + 2a), \quad r = \sqrt{x^2 + y^2}$$

We may then deconvolve the above equation by constructing the appropriate inverse filter. This is obtained by taking the Fourier transform of the point spread function which gives

$$\widetilde{P}(k_x, k_y) = \frac{1}{8\pi ak} ikP(k) \exp(2ika)$$

$$= \frac{i}{8\pi a} P(k) \exp(2ika)$$

where

$$k = \sqrt{k_x^2 + k_y^2}$$

The inverse filter is then given by $1/\widetilde{P}(k_x, k_y)$ and the scattering function can be reconstructed using the algorithm

$$\gamma_\kappa(x, y) = 8\pi a \hat{F}_2^{-1} \left(\exp(-2ika) \frac{\hat{F}_2 \widetilde{B}(k_x, k_y)}{iP(k)} \right)$$

6.4 QUANTITATIVE DIFFRACTION TOMOGRA-PHY

So far in this chapter, we have looked at two methods of recon-structing the compressibility fluctuations of an acoustic mate-rial using a CW or pulsed acoustic field. In both cases, only variations in one acoustic parameter is assumed to generate the scattered field. This model was chosen because it produced a relatively simple wave equation (the Helmholtz equation) which allowed us to study inverse solutions using the Born and far field approximations without the analysis becoming unduly complicated.

The two-parameter reconstruction problem

Now that the basic inversion method has been presented, let us go back and put some more physics in to the problem by considering a slightly more advance scattering model where variations in the density of the acoustic material also contribute to the scattered field. In this case, the wave equation is (see section 3.5)

$$(\nabla^2 + k^2)p = -k^2\gamma_\kappa p + \nabla \cdot (\gamma_\rho \nabla p)$$

where

$$\gamma_\rho = \frac{\rho - \rho_0}{\rho}$$

Once again, we use the Born and far field approximations to produce the integral equation

$$p_s(\hat{\mathbf{n}}_i, \hat{\mathbf{n}}_s, k) = \frac{ik}{8\pi a} \exp(2ika)\left(\int_A \exp[-ik(\hat{\mathbf{n}}_s - \hat{\mathbf{n}}_i) \cdot \mathbf{r}]\gamma_\kappa(\mathbf{r})d^2\mathbf{r} \right.$$

$$\left. -\frac{1}{k^2}\int_A \exp(-ik\hat{\mathbf{n}}_s \cdot \mathbf{r})\nabla \cdot [\gamma_\rho(\mathbf{r})\nabla \exp(ik\hat{\mathbf{n}}_i \cdot \mathbf{r})]d^2\mathbf{r} \right)$$

It is clear that the behaviour of the scattered field due to den-sity variations is compounded by one term which needs to be simplified. Our aim is to reduce this term to a form that is

187

compatible with the first, so that we may adopt the same type of inversion scheme. Integrating by parts we can write

$$\int_A \exp(-ik\hat{\mathbf{n}}_s \cdot \mathbf{r}) \nabla \cdot [\gamma_\rho \nabla \exp(ik\hat{\mathbf{n}}_i \cdot \mathbf{r})] d^2\mathbf{r}$$

$$= \int_A \nabla \cdot [\gamma_\rho \exp(-ik\hat{\mathbf{n}}_s \cdot \mathbf{r}) \nabla \exp(ik\hat{\mathbf{n}}_i \cdot \mathbf{r})] d^2\mathbf{r}$$

$$- \int_A \gamma_\rho \nabla \exp(-ik\hat{\mathbf{n}}_s \cdot \mathbf{r}) \cdot \nabla \exp(ik\hat{\mathbf{n}}_i \cdot \mathbf{r}) d^2\mathbf{r}$$

The second integral on the right hand side of the equation above can be evaluated and written in the form

$$\int_A \gamma_\rho \nabla \exp(-ik\hat{\mathbf{n}}_s \cdot \mathbf{r}) \cdot \nabla \exp(ik\hat{\mathbf{n}}_i \cdot \mathbf{r}) d^2\mathbf{r}$$

$$= -k^2 \int_A \hat{\mathbf{n}}_i \cdot \hat{\mathbf{n}}_s \gamma_\rho \exp[-ik(\hat{\mathbf{n}}_s - \hat{\mathbf{n}}_i) \cdot \mathbf{r}] d^2\mathbf{r}$$

We now need a physical reason for neglecting the integral over $\nabla \cdot [\bullet]$. To this end we can use Green's theorem in the plane to write

$$\int_A \nabla \cdot [\gamma_\rho \exp(-ik\hat{\mathbf{n}}_s \cdot \mathbf{r}) \nabla \exp(ik\hat{n}_i \cdot \mathbf{r})] d^2\mathbf{r}$$

$$= \oint_C \gamma_\rho \exp(-ik\hat{\mathbf{n}}_s \cdot \mathbf{r}^c) \nabla \exp(ik\hat{n}_i \cdot \mathbf{r}^c) \cdot \hat{\mathbf{n}} d\ell$$

where C is the contour enclosing A and $\mathbf{r}^c$ denotes the position vector on the contour C. We may now use one of two arguments: We can argue that the contribution to the scattered field due to scattering at just the boundary defined by C is negligible compared to the scattering produced by the interior of the scatterer itself. Alternatively we can introduce the boundary condition

$$\gamma_\rho(\mathbf{r}^c) = 0 \tag{6.4.1}$$

in which case the relevant integral vanishes completely. This condition implies that

$$\rho(\mathbf{r}^c) = \rho_0$$

In this form, it is clear that the density of the scatterer on the surface defining V must be the same as the homogeneous support. In this case, the expression for the scattered pressure field reduces to

$$p_s(\hat{\mathbf{n}}_i, \hat{\mathbf{n}}_s, k) = \frac{ik}{8\pi a} \exp(2ika) \int_A \exp[-ik(\hat{\mathbf{n}}_s - \hat{\mathbf{n}}_i) \cdot \mathbf{r}] f(\mathbf{r}, \theta) d^2\mathbf{r}$$

where

$$f(\mathbf{r}, \theta) = \gamma_\kappa(\mathbf{r}) + \gamma_\rho(\mathbf{r}) \cos\theta, \quad \cos\theta = \hat{\mathbf{n}}_i \cdot \hat{\mathbf{n}}_s$$

Hence, by using the additional boundary condition (6.4.1), the scattered field generated by variations in both the compressibility and density is reduced to the Fourier transform of a scattering function with one extra term, namely, $\gamma_\rho \cos\theta$. This result shows that the scattering of an acoustic field due to density fluctuations is a source of dipole radiation whereas variations in the compressibility represents a monopole source of scattering. This is illustrated in figure 6.5.

Our problem, is to find a way of reconstructing γ_κ and γ_ρ independently. This is known as a two-parameter reconstruction problem and its solution is based on exploiting the angular dependence of the density variations. To see how this works, suppose that we can recover the function $f(\mathbf{r}, \theta)$ at any θ of our choice. If we choose two different angles θ_1 and θ_2 where $\theta_1 \neq \theta_2$, then we can write two simultaneous equations of the form

$$f(\mathbf{r}, \theta_1) = \gamma_\kappa(\mathbf{r}) + \gamma_\rho(\mathbf{r}) \cos\theta_1$$

and

$$f(\mathbf{r}, \theta_2) = \gamma_\kappa(\mathbf{r}) + \gamma_\rho(\mathbf{r}) \cos\theta_2$$

Solving these equations, we then have

$$\gamma_\rho(\mathbf{r}) = \frac{f(\mathbf{r}, \theta_1) - f(\mathbf{r}, \theta_2)}{\cos\theta_1 - \cos\theta_2}$$

and

$$\gamma_\kappa(\mathbf{r}) = \frac{f(\mathbf{r}, \theta_1)\cos\theta_2 - f(\mathbf{r}, \theta_2)\cos\theta_1}{\cos\theta_2 - \cos\theta_1}$$

These solutions are quantitative reconstructions and this type of imagery is known as quantitative acoustic diffraction tomography. Let us examine how to obtain $f(\mathbf{r}, \theta)$. To do this, we introduce an experimental method which allows a two-

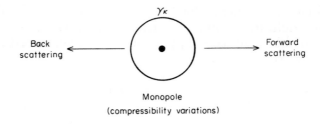

Monopole
(compressibility variations)

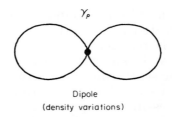

Dipole
(density variations)

Figure 6.5 The directivity patterns produced by scattering from variations in the compressibility (monopole) and density (dipole). The difference in directivity provides a method of recovering the density and compressibility independently. This is known as quantitative acoustic diffraction tomography

dimensional function to be reconstructed but at the same time, does not need the angle between the incident and scattered fields to be changed. In other words, we need a method of reconstructing the scattering function when the position of the receiver, relative to the source, is fixed. This rules out any reconstruction based on the use of a CW field because in this case, the scattered field must be measured at all scattering angles ϕ_s. Since θ is related to ϕ_i and ϕ_s by

$$\theta = \phi_s - \phi_i$$

this means that θ is a necessary experimental variable. The only experiment where θ can remain fixed has already been discussed in section 6.3, which examined a method of diffraction tomography using a pulsed field. Therefore, if we wish to conduct quantitative diffraction tomography based on a model where variations in the compressibility and density are responsible for the scattered field, we are forced to utilize a pulsed acoustic field. Following section 6.3, the scattered pressure field generated by a pulse $p(\tau)$ is given by

$$p_s(\hat{\mathbf{N}}, \tau) = \frac{1}{8\pi a} \frac{\partial}{\partial \tau} p(\tau + 2a) \otimes \int_A f(\mathbf{r}, \theta) \delta(\tau - \hat{\mathbf{N}} \cdot \mathbf{r}) d^2\mathbf{r}$$

Radon inversion then gives

$$f(\mathbf{r}, \theta) = \hat{R}^{-1} D(\phi, \tau, \theta)$$

where D is given by equation (6.3.2). By generating the data D at two different values of θ, γ_κ and γ_ρ can be recovered. Recall that for maximum resolution we need the value of θ to be as close to 180^0 as possible. It is therefore clear that one experiment should be based on measuring the back scattered field when $\theta = 180^0$ where the reconstruction is for the function

$$f(\mathbf{r}, \theta = 180^0) = \gamma_\kappa(\mathbf{r}) - \gamma_\rho(\mathbf{r})$$

This function is a measure of the acoustic impedance.

Quantitative acoustic diffraction tomography using CW fields

The solution to the two-parameter reconstruction problem given above assumes that the material is non-viscous. We shall now examine the type of inverse problem that occurs when a model is considered where, in addition to variations in the density and compressibility, scattering is also caused by variations in the bulk and shear viscosities. In this case, the appropriate wave equation (derived in section 3.5) is given by

$$(\nabla^2 + \xi^2)\Phi = -\xi^2 \nabla \cdot (\gamma_\rho \nabla \phi) + \frac{1}{1 + ik\ell} \nabla^2 (\gamma_\kappa \nabla^2 \phi)$$

$$- \frac{ik\ell}{1 + ik\ell} \left(\nabla^2 (\gamma_\alpha \nabla^2 \phi) + 2\nabla \cdot [\nabla \cdot (\gamma_\beta \nabla \nabla \phi)] \right)$$

where ϕ is the longitudinal velocity potential, $\Phi = \nabla^2 \phi$ is the acoustic dilatation, ℓ is the relaxation length and

$$\xi = \frac{k}{\sqrt{(1 + ik\ell)}}$$

191

Once again, using the Born and far field approximations, the scattered acoustic dilatation can be written in the form

$$\Phi_s(\hat{\mathbf{n}}_i, \hat{\mathbf{n}}_s, k) = \frac{i\xi}{8\pi a} \exp(2i\xi a)(I_1 + I_2 + I_3 + I_4)$$

where

$$I_1 = \int_A \exp(-i\xi\hat{\mathbf{n}}_s \cdot \mathbf{r})\nabla \cdot [\gamma_\rho \nabla \exp(i\xi\hat{\mathbf{n}}_i \cdot \mathbf{r})]d^2\mathbf{r}$$

$$I_2 = -\frac{1}{\xi^2(1 + ik\ell)} \int_A \exp(-i\xi\hat{\mathbf{n}}_s \cdot \mathbf{r})\nabla^2[\gamma_\kappa \nabla^2 \exp(i\xi\hat{\mathbf{n}}_i \cdot \mathbf{r})]d^2\mathbf{r}$$

$$I_3 = \frac{ik\ell}{\xi^2(1 + ik\ell)} \int_A \exp(-i\xi\hat{\mathbf{n}}_s \cdot \mathbf{r})\nabla^2[\gamma_\alpha \nabla^2 \exp(i\xi\hat{\mathbf{n}}_i \cdot \mathbf{r})]d^2\mathbf{r}$$

and

$$I_4 = \frac{2ik\ell}{\xi^2(1 + ik\ell)} \int_A \exp(-i\xi\hat{\mathbf{n}}_s \cdot \mathbf{r})\nabla \cdot \left(\nabla \cdot [\gamma_\beta \nabla\nabla \exp(i\xi\hat{\mathbf{n}}_i \cdot \mathbf{r})]\right)d^2\mathbf{r}$$

The above integrals can be simplified using the same method as before (i.e. the one used to solve the two-parameter problem). In each case, we integrate by parts and use Green's theorem in the plane to convert integrals over A to integral around C where C is the contour that completely encloses A. Using the boundary conditions

$$\gamma_f(\mathbf{r^c}) = 0$$

and

$$\hat{\mathbf{n}} \cdot \nabla\gamma_f(\mathbf{r^c}) = 0$$

where $f = \rho, \kappa, \alpha$ or β, the scattered dilatation becomes

$$\Phi_s(\hat{\mathbf{n}}_i, \hat{\mathbf{n}}_s, k) = -\frac{i\xi^3 \exp(2ika)}{8\pi a(1 + ik\ell)} \int_A \exp[-i\xi(\hat{\mathbf{n}}_s - \hat{\mathbf{n}}_i) \cdot \mathbf{r}]f(\mathbf{r}, \theta, k)d^2\mathbf{r} \quad (6.4.2)$$

where

$$f = \gamma_\kappa + \gamma_\rho \cos\theta + ik\ell(\gamma_\rho \cos\theta + \gamma_\alpha + 2\gamma_\beta \cos^2\theta) \quad (6.4.3)$$

Note, that the scattering function in this case depends on both the scattering angle θ and the wavenumber of the acoustic field.

Also, note that when the viscosity is zero so that $\ell = 0$, the scattering function reduces to

$$f = \gamma_\kappa + \gamma_\rho \cos\theta$$

The directional properties of scattering from variations in the bulk viscosity are the same as scattering from variations in the compressibility. However, scattering from fluctuations in the shear viscosity exhibits a $\cos^2\theta$ dependence on the scattering angle. When $k\ell$ is large, acoustic scattering is dominated by the scattering function

$$\gamma_\rho \cos\theta + \gamma_\alpha + 2\gamma_\beta \cos^2\theta$$

Let us now look at a quantitative reconstruction method using CW fields. Recall, that CW diffraction tomography requires the scattered field to be measured at all scattering angles. We therefore need a scattering function which is independent of θ. Thus, we consider a physical model where variations in the density and shear viscosity are negligible so that the scattering function becomes

$$f = \gamma_\kappa + ik\ell\gamma_\alpha$$

Fourier inversion of equation (6.4.2) then leads to the reconstruction

$$f(\mathbf{r}, k) = \frac{2ia(1 + ik\ell)}{\pi\xi^3} \exp(-2ika) \int\limits_{|\mathbf{k}| \leq 2|\xi|} \exp(i\mathbf{k} \cdot \mathbf{r})\Phi_s(\mathbf{k})d^2\mathbf{k}$$

By equating real and imaginary parts, we then obtain the quantitative reconstructions

$$\gamma_\kappa(\mathbf{r}) = \frac{2a}{\pi} \operatorname{Re}\left(\frac{i(1 + ik\ell)}{\xi^3} \exp(-2ika) \int\limits_{|\mathbf{k}| \leq 2|\xi|} \exp(i\mathbf{k} \cdot \mathbf{r})\Phi_s(\mathbf{k})d^2\mathbf{k}\right)$$

and

$$\gamma_\alpha(\mathbf{r}) = \frac{2a}{\pi k\ell} \operatorname{Im}\left(\frac{i(1 + ik\ell)}{\xi^3} \exp(-2ika) \int\limits_{|\mathbf{k}| \leq 2|\xi|} \exp(i\mathbf{k} \cdot \mathbf{r})\Phi_s(\mathbf{k})d^2\mathbf{k}\right)$$

Observe that the bandwidth of these reconstructions is determined by

$$2\mid\xi\mid=\frac{2k}{\sqrt{(1+k^2\ell^2)}}$$

Hence, in this case, the resolution is governed by the magnitude of both the wavenumber and the relaxation length. As the viscosity of the material increases, the resolution of the reconstructions decreases. This result has an obvious physical explanation: as the viscosity increases, both the incident and scattered field are absorbed by a greater amount and so there is less penetration of acoustic energy into and out of the scatterer. The measured scattered field therefore becomes weaker. When the viscosity is very large, there is practically no penetration of acoustic radiation into the scatterer and therefore no information on the internal structure of the scatterer can be obtained.

Quantitative diffraction tomography using EM fields

Before concluding this chapter, let us consider how the form of the electromagnetic scattering function compares with the acoustic scattering function using exactly the same type of model and approximations that have been presented in previous sections. Consider a model where a body composed of two-dimensional variations in the permittivity, permeability and conductivity is illuminated by an electromagnetic field (such as a millimetric microwave field) where the polarization of the electric vector is perpendicular to the two-dimensional plane. In this case, from equation (2.7.15), with

$$\widetilde{\mathbf{E}} = \hat{\mathbf{z}}\phi$$

we obtain

$$(\nabla^2 + k^2)\phi = -k^2\gamma_\epsilon\phi + ikz_0\sigma\phi + \nabla\cdot(\gamma_\mu\nabla\phi)$$

Using the same method as before it can then be shown that the Born scattered field is given by

$$\phi_s(\hat{\mathbf{n}}_s,\hat{\mathbf{n}}_i,k) = \frac{ikP}{8\pi a}\exp(2ika)\int_A \exp[-ik(\hat{\mathbf{n}}_s - \hat{\mathbf{n}}_i)\cdot\mathbf{r}]f(\mathbf{r},\theta,k)d^2\mathbf{r}$$

where

$$f = \gamma_\epsilon + \gamma_\mu \cos\theta - \frac{iz_0}{k}\sigma$$

Here, we see that γ_ϵ and γ_μ play an identical role to γ_κ and γ_ρ respectively.

SUMMARY OF IMPORTANT RESULTS

CW diffraction tomography

Data on diffraction pattern = Fourier transform of object.

Resolution $\propto$ wavelegth of CW field.

Pulsed diffraction tomography

Data on diffracted time trace = Radon transform of object.

Resolution $\propto$ Bandwidth of pulse $\times \sin$ (half the scattering angle).

Born scattering functions

Non-viscous acoustic medium

$$f(\mathbf{r}) = \gamma_\kappa(\mathbf{r}) + \gamma_\rho(\mathbf{r})\cos\theta$$

Non-conductive dielectric

$$f(\mathbf{r}) = \gamma_\epsilon(\mathbf{r}) + \gamma_\mu(\mathbf{r})\cos\theta$$

Viscous acoustic medium

$$f(\mathbf{r}, k) = \gamma_\kappa(\mathbf{r}) + \gamma_\rho(\mathbf{r})\cos\theta + ik\ell[(\gamma_\rho(\mathbf{r})\cos\theta + \gamma_\lambda(\mathbf{r}) + 2\gamma_\mu(\mathbf{r})\cos^2\theta)]$$

Conductive dielectric

$$f(\mathbf{r}, k) = \gamma_\epsilon(\mathbf{r}) + \gamma_\mu(\mathbf{r})\cos\theta - i\frac{z_0}{k}\sigma(\mathbf{r})$$

FURTHER READING

1. Morse P M and Ingard K U, *Theoretical acoustics*, McGraw-Hill, 1968. The scattering of acoustic waves is discussed in chapter 8 which includes mathematical details on acoustic scattering form an inhomogeneous material composed of variations in the density and compressibility using the Born approximation.

2. Devaney A J, *Diffraction Tomography*, Inverse Methods in Electromagnetic Imaging, Reidel, 1985. This is one of the best papers on the theoretical foundations of diffraction tomography.

3. Blackledge J M, Burge R E, Hopcraft K I and Wombell R J *Quantitative Diffraction Tomography I: Pulsed Acoustic Fields* and *II: Pulsed Elastic Waves*, Journal of Applied Physics D: Applied Physics, 1987, Volume 20, Pages 1-17. These papers discus the theory of quantitative diffraction tomography when a pulse of acoustic radiation insonifies a non-viscous material (Part I) and when an elastic wave is incident on a visco-elastic material (Part II).

7 Synthetic aperture imaging

Aperture synthesis is used in a wide range of applications including radar, sonar, diagnostic ultrasound and radio astronomy. The basic principle is really very simple. In one form or another, the resolution of an image is determined by the size of the aperture that is used for observation. To improve the resolution, the size of the aperture must be increased. In some cases, to achieve a given resolution, an aperture must be used which is impractical either to build of utilize effectively. However, if a smaller aperture (a real aperture) is used and its position changed while observations are being made, then in principle a much large aperture can be synthesized, the size of which depends on how far the smaller or real aperture has been moved. The improvement in resolution that can be obtained using this principle is quite spectacular. For example, simple radio interferometers can be successfully operated using array lengths of up to tens of kilometres. This allows maps to be constructed of radio emissions from the sky with resolutions of less than a minute of arc - better than the resolution of the human eye!

Although the principle of aperture synthesis is the same the details vary according to the application. This chapter focuses on aperture synthesis using radar. This is an electromagnetic coherent imaging technique which is used for remote sensing from space and both civilian and military reconnaissance.

7.1 SYNTHETIC APERTURE RADAR

Radar (**ra**dio **d**etection **a**nd **r**anging) has been used for many years to detect airborne objects using ground based antennas. Synthetic aperture radar (SAR) is a relatively recent development which is used to study the surface of the earth from both spaceborne and airborne platforms. The basic difference between spaceborne and airborne SAR is the 'look-down' angle of the microwave beam that is used. Spaceborne SAR uses look-down angles of $\sim 70^0$ whereas airborne systems use look-down angles $\sim 10^0$. Both systems attempt to classify the inhomogeneous nature of the earth's surface by repeatedly emitting a pulse of microwave radiation and recording the back-scattered field.

In this chapter, attention is focused on airborne SAR which is now used extensively for both civilian and military reconnaissance. To date, only one spaceborne SAR, called Seasat, has been operational. This satellite was launched in June 1978 but only functioned for a limited period of time (from July to October of the same year) owing to malfunction. It was designed to carry out studies of the ocean surface using a range of microwave sensors and was equipped with a 24 cm wavelength SAR. Another satellite system - the Earth Resources Satellite (ERS-1) - is due to be launched in the early 1990s. One of the payloads of the ERS-1 will be a 5cm wavelength SAR.

A conventional side-looking radar (a real aperture radar) operating at many tens of kilometres is only able to obtain lateral resolutions of about a kilometre. By synthesizing the aperture of the radar, one can obtain resolutions of a few metres. This enhancement of resolution by three orders of magnitude, together with the fact that radar can be used in cloud or fog, means that SAR is ideal for airborne reconnaissance. The quantity of data that must be recorded and processed in order to use SAR is typically a million independent pixels (discrete picture elements) every second. This immense amount of data has to be examined and positions of interest (targets) identified and extracted in real time.

Another important aspect of SAR reconnaissance is that in comparison with optical or infrared reconnaissance, radar can often pick out details on the ground which are either invisible or difficult to distinguish with the human eye. For example, it is possible to distinguish between different types of vegetation. In some cases, it is even possible to observe sub- surface structures in regions where the skin depth of the ground is small and the radar can penetrate further into the ground. Many ground-based objects are good reflectors of microwave radiation, particularly those objects that are composed from materials that are good conductors (i.e. metallic objects which have a relatively large radar cross-section). Objects of this kind can therefore be distinguished more easily using radar reconnaissance. This is why airborne SAR imaging is often used for the surveillance of military hardware.

SAR systems are usually classified in terms of the wavelength that is used. The two basic modes of operation are X-band, with a wavelength of 2.8 cm, and L-band, with a wavelength of 24 cm. In addition to different wavelengths, different polarizations can be used. One of the most commonly used types is vertical polarization. This is where an electric field is emitted which points in the vertical direction (relative to the orientation of the antenna). The back-scattered field that is produced with the same polarization is then measured. For this reason, the type of data that is produced is called vertical-vertical or VV polarization data. In addition to the vertically polarized return, scattering by the ground creates a new polarization which is at right angles to the incident electric vector and points along the horizontal axis. This is known as the depolarized return and the type of data that are produced by measuring it known as vertical-horizontal or VH polarization data. Alternatively, an incident electric field can be produced where the electric vector points along the horizontal axis. The data produced by measuring the like polarized field is known as the horizontal-horizontal or HH polarization data. The data produced by measuring the cross-polarized return in this case, is known as the horizontal-vertical or HV polarization data. Hence, in principle, there are four modes of operation that can be used. In practice VH and HV SAR images are not significantly different. However, the difference between VV, HH and VH or HV SAR images can be considerable.

An interesting example of a SAR image is given in figure 7.1. This is an airborne SAR image of a region of Northampton-shire in the UK using a 2.8 cm radar and VV polarization.

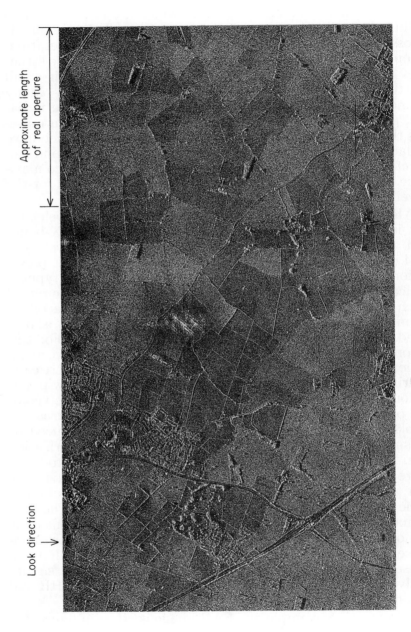

Look direction

Approximate length of real aperture

Figure 7.1 Synthetic aperture radar image of a region of Northamptonshire in the UK using 2.8 cm wavelength radar and vertical polarization

Figure 7.2 Optical image of the same region in figure 7.1

Optical image

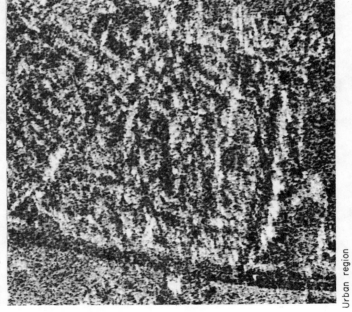

SAR image

Urban region

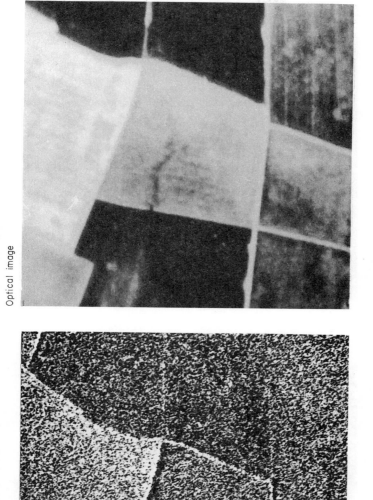

SAR image

Optical image

Naturally occurring terrain

Figure 7.3 SAR and optical images of a collection of fields and a small urban region

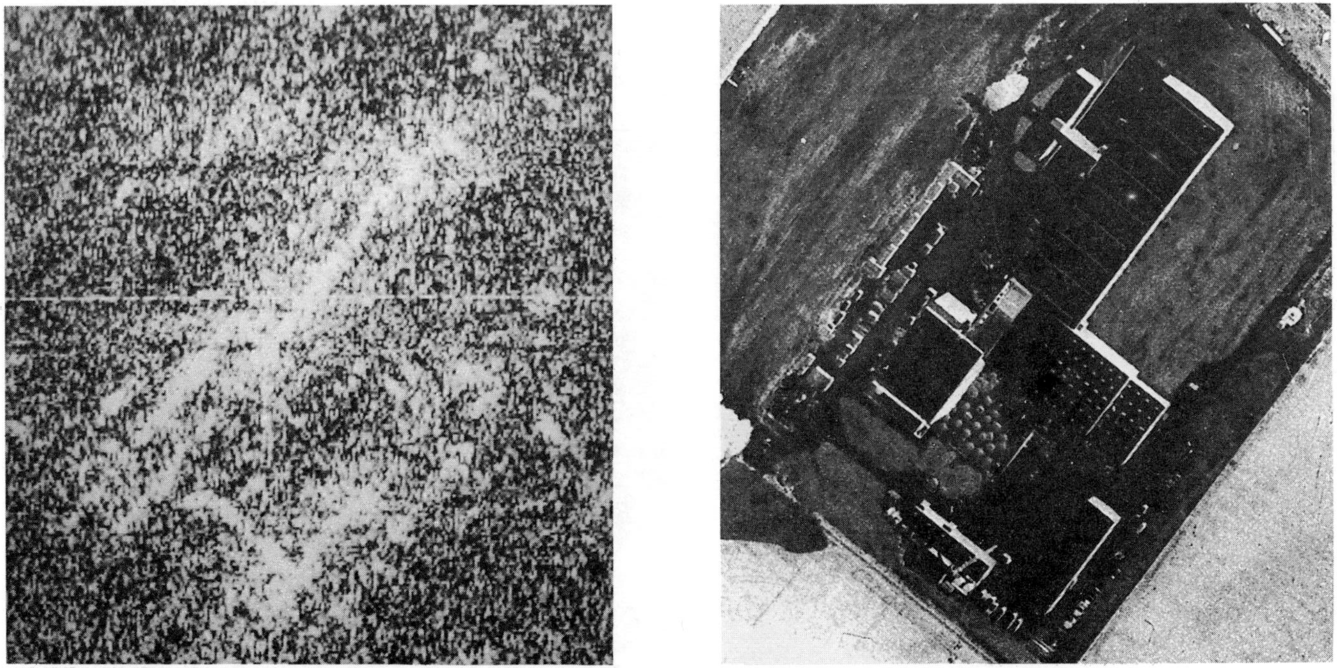

SAR image

Optical image

Figure 7.4 SAR and optical images of an object (a small factory) with a large radar cross-section

This type of image is known as a VVX SAR image (VV for vertical-vertical polarization and X for X-band). Each resolution cell in this image corresponds to a real length of about 1.5m. The range is approximately 50 km and the altitude is about 8 km. For comparison, an optical image (i.e. an overhead photograph) of the same area is given in figure 7.2.

There are a number of interesting features in this SAR image. A close inspection reveals that there are a variety of textures which change from one region of the image to the next. These textures are related to physical changes in the terrain such as the type of vegetation that is present. There is a particularly marked difference between rural and urban regions. An example of this (which has been taken from figure 7.1 and 7.2) is given in figure 7.3 which shows two SAR and matching optical images of a rural area consisting of a collection of fields and a small urban region. The latter SAR image consists of features which are geometrically related to the network of buildings. The large majority of buildings in this image are constructed from non-conductive materials (brick, concrete and wood etc.).

Much stronger reflections can be induced by structures that are made from conductive materials. An example of this is given in figure 7.4. which shows a SAR and optical image of a small factory. A large proportion of this object is constructed from metal panels which reflect a greater proportion of the incident microwaves than naturally occurring objects. Hence, this building has a relatively large radar cross-section which is why it stands out in figure 7.1 (i.e. the feature at approximately the centre of this figure).

7.2 PRINCIPLES OF SAR

Synthetic aperture radar is a pulse-echo system which utilizes the response of a scatterer as it passes through the beam, to synthesize the lateral resolution. This allows high resolution images of the type given in figure 7.1 to be obtained at a long range. The basic geometry of the system is given in figure 7.5. Here, and throughout the rest of this chapter, the range coordinate is denoted by x and the tracking coordinate along the flight path is denoted by y. The latter coordinate is referred to as the azimuth direction. The antenna emits a pulse of microwave radiation and the return signal or echo is recorded

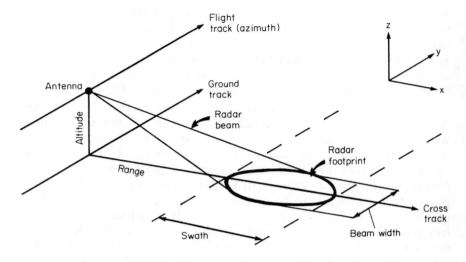

Figure 7.5 Basic geometry of synthetic aperture radar

at fixed time intervals along the flight path.

The radar pulse

SAR is a peak power limited system. In other words it operates at the maximum power available. The energy of the system is therefore given by

$$\text{Energy} = \text{Peak Power} \times \text{Time}$$

In order to transmit a microwave field with enough energy to establish a measurable return, the duration of the pulse must be made relatively long. If a simple on/off pulse is emitted, then the characteristic spectrum is a narrow band sinc function. The frequency content of this type of pulse is not usually broad enough to obtain adequate range resolution. For this reason, a frequency sweep or 'chirp' is applied over the duration of the pulse. Even with a frequency sweep applied to it, the pulse has a very narrow frequency band. In other words, the energy of the pulse is concentrated near to the carrier frequency. The

206

type of pulse that is actually used is given by (complex form)

$$p(\tau) = \exp(ik_0\tau)\exp(i\alpha\tau^2), \quad -T/2 \le \tau \le T/2$$

where

T - pulse length

τ - time $\times$ speed of light

α - quadratic chirp rate / (speed of light)^2

k_0 - carrier wave number (carrier frequency $= \frac{k_0}{2\pi} \times$ speed of light)

Note that in reality the pulse is of course not a complex but a real valued function of time. It is given by the real part of p, i.e. $\cos(k_0\tau + \alpha\tau^2)$. This type of pulse is just one of a number of different types of coded pulses that can in principle be used. It is used exstensively in radar systems because it has some very good properties for range resolution and can be implemented comparatively easily. The instantaneous phase of this pulse is $k_0\tau + \alpha\tau^2$. The rate of change of phase or frequency modulation is therefore $k_0 + 2\alpha\tau$ which is linear in τ. For this reason, the pulse is known as a linear frequency modulated (FM) chirp. In general, most SARs utilize values of k_0 and α where

$$k_0 \gg 1$$

and

$$\alpha \ll 1$$

For example, in the system used to produce the SAR image given in figure 7.1,

$$k_0 \simeq 224\mathrm{m}^{-1}$$

and the quadratic chirp rate was $2\pi \times 10^{13}\mathrm{sec}^{-2}$ giving

$$\alpha \simeq 7 \times 10^{-4}\mathrm{m}^{-2}$$

The range spectrum

The spectrum of the FM chirp is obtained by evaluating the integral

$$P(k) = \int\limits_{-T/2}^{T/2} \exp(ik_0\tau)\exp(-i\alpha\tau^2)\exp(-ik\tau)d\tau \qquad (7.2.1)$$

This is given by

$$P(k) = \sqrt{\frac{\pi}{2\alpha}} \left[K\left(\frac{\alpha T + u}{\sqrt{2\pi\alpha}}\right) + K\left(\frac{\alpha T - u}{\sqrt{2\pi\alpha}}\right) \right] \exp(-iu^2/4\alpha)$$

where $u = k + k_0$ and

$$K(x) = \int\limits_0^x \exp(i\pi x^2/2)dx = C(x) + iS(x)$$

with real and imaginary parts

$$C(x) = \int\limits_0^x \cos\frac{\pi}{2}x^2 dx$$

$$S(x) = \int\limits_0^x \sin\frac{\pi}{2}x^2 dx$$

The integrals above are known as Fresnel integrals. Figure 7.6 is a sketch of the real valued pulse $\cos(k_0\tau + \alpha\tau^2)$ and its characteristic amplitude spectrum. Observe that the bandwidth of the pulse is determined by the value of αT. With microwave systems, this is typically two to three orders of magnitude smaller than the carrier wavenumber k_0.

Range processing

Consider a single point scatterer which reflects a replica of the transmitted pulse. At the receiver, the return signal is coherently mixed down to base band (i.e. frequency demodulated). In practice, the field that is actually measured is of course not complex but a real valued signal. The imaginary part of this signal is obtained using a quadrature filter (see section 2.5 on the Hilbert transform). The complex or analytic signal that is obtained after demodulation is given by

$$\exp(i\alpha\tau^2), \quad -T/2 \le \tau \le T/2$$

At this stage, the range resolution is determined by the pulse length T. By applying a suitable process to the return signal, we can enhance the range resolution and hence obtain a more

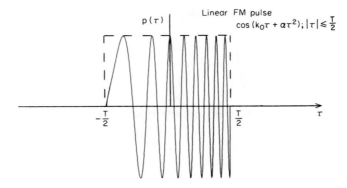

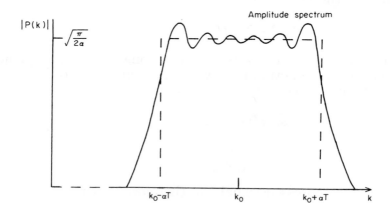

Figure 7.6 Sketch of the chirped linear frequency modulated pulse used in SAR and its characteristic amplitude spectrum

accurate record of the position in range of the point scatterer. This is achieved by correlating the signal with its complex reference function $\exp(-i\alpha\tau^2)$. In SAR and other pulse-echo systems which utilize a linear FM pulse, this process is known as range compression. The range compressed data $R(\tau)$ can be written

209

as (u being a dummy variable)

$$R(\tau) = \int\limits_{-T/2}^{T/2} \exp[-i\alpha(\tau + u)^2] \exp(i\alpha u^2) du$$

Expanding $(\tau + u)^2$, this equation becomes

$$R(\tau) = \exp(-i\alpha\tau^2) \int\limits_{-T/2}^{T/2} \exp(-2i\alpha u\tau) du$$

Evaluating the integral over u, we have

$$R(\tau) = T \exp(-i\alpha\tau^2) \operatorname{sinc}(\alpha T\tau)$$

The length of the pulse T is relatively long. As a consequence of this, the sinc function is very narrow compared to the exponential function. For this reason, we get

$$\cos(\alpha\tau^2) \operatorname{sinc}(\alpha T\tau) \simeq \operatorname{sinc}(\alpha T\tau)$$

and

$$\sin(\alpha\tau^2) \operatorname{sinc}(\alpha T\tau) \simeq 0$$

The range compressed signal can therefore be written as

$$R(\tau) \simeq T \operatorname{sinc}(\alpha T\tau), \quad T \gg 1$$

By defining the range resolution to be the distance between the first two zeros of the sinc function which occur when $\alpha T\tau = \pm\pi$, the range resolution is given by

Range resolution $= 2\pi/\alpha T$ metres

Observe that as the value of αT increases, the range resolution improves. For a 20 μs pulse, $T = 6$ km and with $\alpha = 7 \times 10^{-4}$ m^{-2}, the range resolution is approximately 1.5 metres.

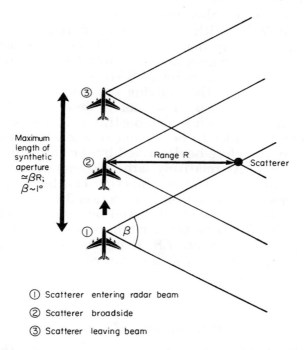

Maximum
length of
synthetic
aperture
$\simeq \beta R$;
$\beta \sim 1°$

Range R

Scatterer

③ entering radar beam
② broadside
① leaving beam

① Scatterer entering radar beam
② Scatterer broadside
③ Scatterer leaving beam

Figure 7.7 Plan view of SAR showing the maximum length of the synthetic aperture

Azimuth processing

As the radar travels along its flight path (repeatedly emitting a linear FM pulse and recording the back-scattered electric field that is generated by the ground), the radar beam illuminates an area of the ground which depends upon the grazing angle of the beam, its angle of divergence and the range at which the radar operates. The width of the beam in azimuth is given by $R \tan(\beta/2)$ where R is the range and β is the angle of divergence of the beam. For a SAR system, this value corresponds to the maximum length of the synthetic aperture as shown in figure 7.7. In practice $\beta \sim 1^0$ and so the width of the beam is approximately given by $R\beta/2$. This value determines the resolution in azimuth of the so called real aperture radar or RAR. At a range of of say 50 km with $\beta = 1^0$, this resolution is just under a kilometre which is very poor and of little practical use. Hence real aperture radar images are only useful when short ranges are involved. The whole point of SAR is to obtain high resolution at long ranges. By studying the response of the radar in azimuth as it passes by a scatterer, we can synthesize the resolution via the principle demonstrated in figure 7.8. We may consider the radar to be a point source. The field that is produced may therefore be described by the three-dimensional Green's function. At relatively large distances from the location of the source, the Green's function can be simplified using the Fresnel approximation (see section 3.1). This provides a description for the wavefield in the intermediate or Fresnel zone. The wave fronts in this zone have a curvature which is parabolic as shown in figure 7.8. Using the geometry shown in this figure, from Pythagoras' theorem, we have

$$(R + \delta R)^2 + y^2 = R^2$$

or

$$2R\delta R + (\delta R)^2 + y^2 = 0$$

If the angle of divergence of the beam is small, then δR is much less than 1. We can then ignore the nonlinear term $(\delta R)^2$ leaving the equation

$$2\delta R = -\frac{y^2}{R} \tag{7.2.2}$$

A simple plane wave travelling along the two-way path length $2(R + \delta R)$ can therefore be written as

$$\exp[(-2ik_0(R + \delta R)] = \exp(-2ik_0 R)\exp(-2ik_0\delta R)$$

where k_0 is the wavenumber. This wave has two phase factors. The first phase $2k_0 R$ is constant but the second phase $2k_0\delta R$ is, from equation (7.2.2) a function of y and given by $k_0 y^2/R$. Hence, as the radar moves past the scatterer a quadratic phase shift takes place. If we denote the width of the beam at R by L, then the complex azimuth response of the radar can be written as

$$\exp(ik_0 y^2/R), \quad -L/2 \leq y \leq L/2$$

where $-L/2$ is the point where the scatterer enters the beam and $L/2$ is the position where the scatterer leaves the beam. A

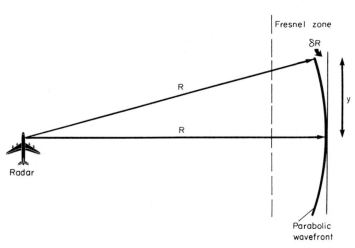

Figure 7.8 By the time the wavefield transmitted by the radar has reached a scatterer, the curvature of the wavefront is parabolic. Scattering occurs in the Fresnel zone. This gives a phase history which is proportional to the square of the distance moved in azimuth

plot of the azimuth response of a SAR is given in figure 7.9. In some cases, this response can be clearly observed with real data when the radar passes by a strong scatter with a large radar cross-section. An example of this is given in figure 7.10. If the beamwidth is small, then this effect is not significant. Also only if k_0 is sufficiently large will the effect be observed. In other words, the wavelength of the wavefield must be small compared with the range.

The analysis above demonstrates that the azimuth response of the radar is the same as the response in range to a linear FM pulse. Hence, by utilizing the principles of range compression, we can enhance the azimuth resolution. This is known as azimuth compression and, like range compression, is based on correlating the complex function $\exp(ik_0y^2/R)$ with its complex reference function $\exp(-ik_0y^2/R)$ over the beam width L. Hence,

213

$\cos(k_0 y^2/R)$

(a)

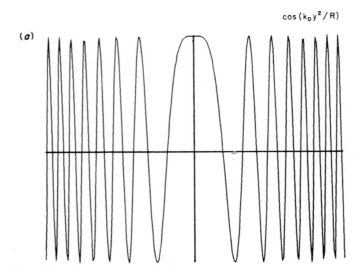

$\sin(k_0 y^2/R)$

(b)

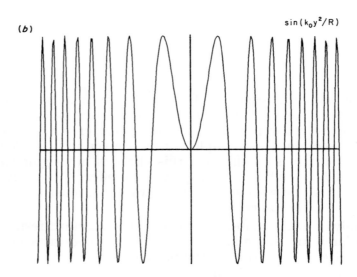

Figure 7.9 (a) Real and (b) imaginary components of the theoretical response in azimuth of the radar to a single point scatterer

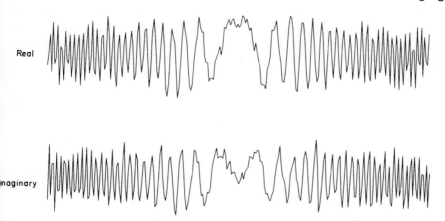

Figure 7.10 Example of the experimental response in azimuth of the radar to a single point scatterer

the azimuth compressed signal is given by

$$A(y) = \int_{-L/2}^{L/2} \exp[-ik_0(y+u)^2/R]\exp(ik_0 u^2/R)du$$

Expanding $(y+u)^2$ and evaluating the integral over u, we get

$$A(y) = L\exp(-ik_0 y^2/R)\operatorname{sinc}(k_0 Ly/R)$$

$$\simeq L\operatorname{sinc}(k_0 Ly/R), \quad L \gg 1$$

Observe, that azimuth compression is identical to range compression. In both cases, the correlation between the return signal and its reference may be computed in Fourier space using the correlation theorem and a FFT.

By defining the azimuth resolution to be the distance between the first zeros of the sinc function which occur when $k_0 Ly/R = \pm\pi$, the azimuth resolution is given by

$$\text{Azimuth resolution} = 2\pi R/k_0 L = 2\pi/\beta k_0 \text{ metres}$$

The microwave antenna (i.e. essentially the horn at the end of the microwave transmission line) acts like a rectangular aperture which diffracts an otherwise collimated beam of microwaves. The first zeros of the diffraction pattern determines the width of the radar beam (i.e. the first lobe). These zeros occur when

$$k_0 \frac{w}{2} \sin \frac{\beta}{2} = \pm\pi$$

where w is the width of the aperture of the radar (the real aperture). For small values of β,

$$\beta \simeq \frac{4\pi}{k_0 w}$$

and hence,

$$\text{Azimuth resolution} = \frac{w}{2}$$

The azimuth or synthetic resolution of the SAR is therefore independent of the wavelength!

By studying the response of the radar to a point scatterer in range and then in azimuth, we have established the form of the SAR point spread function. This is given by

$$P(x, y) = LT \operatorname{sinc}(\alpha T x) \operatorname{sinc}(\beta k_0 y)$$

A grey level display of the amplitude modulations of this function is given in figure 7.11. It is identical to the diffraction pattern produced by a rectangular aperture. The SAR data $D(x, y)$ generated by scattering from the ground is given by the convolution of the object function for the ground $O(x, y)$ with the appropriate point spread function, i.e.

$$D(x, y) = P(x, y) \otimes \otimes O(x, y) \qquad (7.2.3)$$

A SAR image is a grey level display of the amplitude modulations in the data, i.e.

$$I_{SAR}(x, y) = \mid D(x, y) \mid$$

The object function describes the imaged properties of the ground surface. The conventional model for this function is the point scattering model. This is where the object function is taken to be a distribution of point scatterers each of which

216

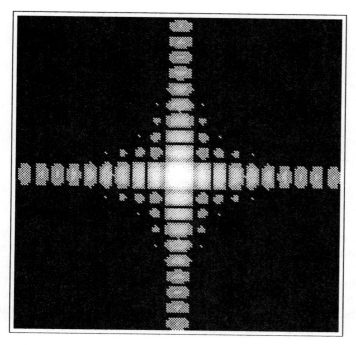

Figure 7.11   An example of the SAR point spread function $|\mathrm{sinc}(\alpha Tx)\,\mathrm{sinc}(\beta k_0 y)|$ for $\alpha T = \beta k_0$

reflects a replica of the transmitted pulse. In this case, the object function can be written in the form

$$O(x,y) = \sum_i \sum_j \delta(x - x_i)\delta(y - y_j)$$

Here nothing is said about the true physical nature of the ground surface such as its shape and material (dielectric) properties.

7.3 ELECTROMAGNETIC SCATTERING THEORY FOR SAR

By considering the response of the radar to a single point scatterer, the basic processing technique required to recover a SAR

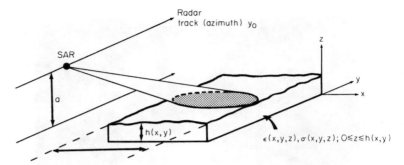

Figure 7.12 Physical model for airborne SAR

image can be established. However, this approach conveys no information about the possible physical interpretation of a SAR image. To do this, the relationship between the object function and the physical properties of the ground surface such as its dielectric properties and height fluctuations must be established. In this section, suitable expressions for the object functions associated with different polarizations are derived.

Physical model for SAR

Consider the model illustrated in figure 7.12. Here, x is the range coordinate, y is the azimuth coordinate and z is the vertical co-ordinate. The ground is composed of three-dimensional variations in the permittivity ϵ and conductivity σ and has height variations h. The relative permeability of the ground is one. Hence, the back-scattered field observed by the radar is produced by variations in $\epsilon(\mathbf{r})$ and $\sigma(\mathbf{r})$ over a region of space $\mathbf{r} = \hat{\mathbf{x}}x + \hat{\mathbf{y}}y + \hat{\mathbf{z}}z$, $0 \leq z \leq h(x,y), \hat{\mathbf{x}}x + \hat{\mathbf{y}}y \in A$ where A A is the total area of the ground illuminated by the radar beam (i.e. the radar footprint). For $z > h(x,y)$, ϵ and σ are equal to the permittivity and conductivity of the atmosphere. The permittivity of the atmosphere is taken to be the same as a vacuum and the conductivity of the atmosphere is assumed to be zero. Thus, if a denotes the altitude at which the radar operates, then for all values of z between h and a, $\epsilon = \epsilon_0$ and $\sigma = 0$

The field that is actually measured in SAR is the electric field and so we can work with equations for the electric field alone. From Maxwell's equations, we can write the basic wave equation for this field in the form (see chapter 3 section 5)

$$(\nabla^2 + k^2)\widetilde{\mathbf{E}} = -k^2\gamma\widetilde{\mathbf{E}} + ikz_0\sigma\widetilde{\mathbf{E}} - \nabla(\widetilde{\mathbf{E}} \cdot \nabla \ln \epsilon)$$

where

$$\gamma = \frac{\epsilon - \epsilon_0}{\epsilon_0}$$

k is the wavenumber and z_0 is the impedance of free space ($\simeq$ 376.6 ohms). Assuming that the scattered field only weakly perturbs the incident field, i.e.

$$\|\widetilde{\mathbf{E}}_s\| << \|\widetilde{\mathbf{E}}_i\|$$

and writing $\epsilon = \epsilon_r\epsilon_0$ where ϵ_r is the relative permittivity, we obtain

$$(\nabla^2 + k^2)\widetilde{\mathbf{E}}_s = -k^2\gamma\widetilde{\mathbf{E}}_i + ikz_0\sigma\widetilde{\mathbf{E}}_i - \nabla(\widetilde{\mathbf{E}}_i \cdot \nabla \ln \epsilon_r) \qquad (7.3.1)$$

where

$$\gamma = \epsilon_r - 1$$

Note, that the effects of using different polarizations are determined entirely by the term $\nabla(\widetilde{\mathbf{E}}_i \cdot \nabla \ln \epsilon_r)$. If this term is neglected, then the behaviour of the electric field is independent of its polarization (i.e. the wave equation remains the same when the direction of the electric field is changed). Our problem is to solve equation (7.3.1) for the scattered electric field $\mathbf{E}_s$ and write the solution in a form that is the same as equation (7.2.3) so that the object function can be defined in terms of the physical properties of the ground (ϵ_r, σ and h). To do this we need a suitable model for the incident field.

Green's function for airborne SAR

The field emitted by the radar is pulsed and diverges from what is in effect, a point source. We may therefore consider a model for the incident field of the form

$$\widetilde{\mathbf{E}}_i = \hat{n}Pg$$

where P is the spectrum of the pulse that the radar emits given by equation (7.2.1) and g is the three-dimensional Green's function given by

$$g(\mathbf{r} \mid \mathbf{r}_0, k) = \frac{\exp(ik \mid \mathbf{r} - \mathbf{r}_0 \mid)}{4\pi \mid \mathbf{r} - \mathbf{r}_0 \mid}$$

The geometry of an airborne SAR allows us to approximate the Green's function. Writing the path length $| \mathbf{r} - \mathbf{r}_0 |$ in Cartesian coordinates,

$$| \mathbf{r} - \mathbf{r}_0 | = (x - x_0) \left(1 + \frac{(y - y_0)^2}{(x - x_0)^2} + \frac{(z - z_0)^2}{(x - x_0)^2} \right)^{1/2}$$

and employing the conditions

$$\frac{(y - y_0)^2}{(x - x_0)^2} \ll 1$$

and

$$\frac{(z - z_0)^2}{(x - x_0)^2} \ll 1$$

a binomial expansion gives

$$| \mathbf{r} - \mathbf{r}_0 | \simeq x - x_0 + \frac{1}{2} \frac{(y - y_0)^2}{(x - x_0)} + \frac{1}{2} \frac{(z - z_0)^2}{(x - x_0)}$$

This result yields an expression for the Green's function in the Fresnel zone. In this case, we retain terms which are quadratic in both the azimuth and vertical directions. It is the inclusion of quadratic terms of this type which forms the theoretical basis for synthetic aperture imaging. Phyically, we are assuming that the wave front as a function of y and z has a curvature which is parabolic. The conditions required to do this place limits on the grazing angle θ and the angle of divergence of the radar beam β. In terms of θ and β, we may write these conditions in the form

$$\tan^2(\beta/2) \ll 1$$

and

$$\tan^2 \theta \ll 1$$

It is reasonable to restrict values of θ and β to being less than or equal to $10°$ when $\tan^2 \theta$ and $\tan^2(\beta/2)$ are two and three orders of magnitude less than 1 respectively. This upper limit for θ and β falls well within the values of these parameters that are used in airborne SAR systems where θ is typically $5° - 10°$ and $\beta \sim 1°$. The above expression for the path length can be simplified further by exploiting the fact that the range x_0 at which the radar operates is large compared to the width of ground that is illuminated by the beam (the swath width), i.e., we can introduce the condition

$$\frac{|x|}{x_0} << 1$$

This allows us to write

$$|\mathbf{r} - \mathbf{r}_0| = x - x_0 - \frac{(y - y_0)^2}{2x_0} - \frac{(z - z_0)^2}{2x_0}$$

The Green's function is then given by

$$g = \frac{1}{4\pi r_0} \exp[ik(x - x_0)] \exp[-ik(y - y_0)^2/2x_0] \exp[-ik(z - z_0)^2/2x_0]$$

The parameter r_0 remains fixed throughout the experiment and is known as the slant range (i.e. the distance between the radar and the scattering region).

Wave equations for SAR

The radar can emit a vertically polarized electric field of the form

$$\widetilde{\mathbf{E}}_i = (\hat{\mathbf{z}}\cos\theta + \hat{\mathbf{x}}\sin\theta)Pg \tag{7.3.2}$$

or a horizontally polarized electric field where $\mathbf{E}_i$ is given by

$$\widetilde{\mathbf{E}}_i = \hat{\mathbf{y}}Pg \tag{7.3.3}$$

Substituting equation (7.3.3) into equation (7.3.1) and taking the dot product of each term with $\hat{\mathbf{y}}$, the behaviour of the HH scattered field Φ_{HH} is determined by the wave equation

$$(\nabla^2 + k^2)\Phi_{HH} = -k^2\gamma Pg + ikz_0\sigma Pg$$

$$-\frac{\partial}{\partial y}\left(Pg\frac{\partial}{\partial y}\ln\epsilon_r\right), \quad \Phi_{HH} = \hat{\mathbf{y}}\cdot\widetilde{\mathbf{E}}_s \tag{7.3.4}$$

The cross polarized scattered field in this case is obtained by taking the dot product of each term with $\hat{\mathbf{z}}\cos\theta + \hat{\mathbf{x}}\sin\theta$ giving

$$(\nabla^2 + k^2)\Phi_{HV} = -\left(\cos\theta\frac{\partial}{\partial z} + \sin\theta\frac{\partial}{\partial x}\right)\left(Pg\frac{\partial}{\partial y}\ln\epsilon_r\right),$$

$$\simeq g \frac{\partial^2}{\partial y^2} \ln \epsilon_r$$

provided

$$L_y << \frac{x_0}{k_0 \mid y - y_0 \mid}$$

where L_y is the characteristic scale length over which variations in $\ln \epsilon_r$ occur. For an X-band radar operating at a range of 50 km with a beamwidth of 1 km,

$$L_y << 22\text{cm}$$

which is physically reasonable. This result allows us to reduce equation (7.3.4) and write it in the form.

$$(\nabla^2 + k^2)\Phi_{HH} \simeq -k^2\gamma Pg + ikz_0\sigma Pg - Pg\frac{\partial^2}{\partial y^2} \ln \epsilon_r \qquad (7.3.8)$$

Similarly, equations (7.3.5)-(7.3.7) become

$$(\nabla^2 + k^2)\Phi_{HV} \simeq -\cos\theta Pg\frac{\partial^2}{\partial z\partial y} \ln \epsilon_r - \sin\theta Pg\frac{\partial^2}{\partial x\partial y} \ln \epsilon_r \qquad (7.3.9)$$

$$(\nabla^2 + k^2)\Phi_{VV} \simeq -k^2\gamma Pg + ikz_0\sigma Pg - \cos^2\theta Pg\frac{\partial^2}{\partial z^2} \ln \epsilon_r$$

$$-2\cos\theta\sin\theta Pg\frac{\partial^2}{\partial z\partial x} \ln \epsilon_r - \sin^2\theta Pg\frac{\partial^2}{\partial x^2} \ln \epsilon_r \qquad (7.3.10)$$

$$(\nabla^2 + k^2)\Phi_{VH} \simeq -\cos\theta Pg\frac{\partial^2}{\partial y\partial z} \ln \epsilon_r - \sin\theta Pg\frac{\partial^2}{\partial y\partial x} \ln \epsilon_r \qquad (7.3.11)$$

Determination of the back-scattered fields

Now that an appropriate set of wave equations has been derived, we can concentrate on developing a solution for the back-scattered field that is observed by the radar. To start with, we shall develop a solution for the HH field. For the time being, let us consider the reduced wave equation

$$(\nabla^2 + k^2)\Phi = -k^2 Pg\gamma + ikz_0 Pg\sigma \qquad (7.3.13)$$

After demonstrating the basic analytical method we shall return to equations (7.3.8)-(7.3.11). Remember, we are aiming at a solution for the processed SAR data which gives a mathematical expression for the object function in terms of ϵ_r, σ and h.

The Green's function solution to equation (7.3.13) for the the back-scattered field is

$$\Phi = P \int (k^2\gamma - ikz_0\sigma)g^2 d^3\mathbf{r} \qquad (7.3.14)$$

The radar measures the back-scattered field at a fixed range x_0 and altitude z_0 over a finite distance in azimuth. Denoting the fixed range and altitude by R and a respectively, the kernel of equation (7.4.14) becomes

$$g^2 = \frac{1}{16\pi^2 r_0^2} \exp[2ik(x-R)] \exp[-ik(y-y_0)^2/R] \exp[-ik(z-a)^2/R]$$

Writing

$$X = x - R$$

$$Y = y - y_0$$

and

$$Z = z - a$$

the back-scattered field as a function of y_0 and k is given by

$$\Phi(y_0, k) = \frac{P}{16\pi^2 r_0^2} \int \int \int \exp[ik(2X - Y^2/R - Z^2/R)](k^2\gamma - ikz_0\sigma)dxdydz$$

Because the band width of the pulse is so small compared to the carrier frequency we can write $k^2\gamma$ and $ikz_0\sigma$ as $k_0^2\gamma$ and $ik_0z_0\sigma$ respectively. By taking the inverse Fourier transform of the integral equation above, the back-scattered field can be written in terms of its measured time history $\phi(y_0, \tau)$ at different points in azimuth y_0. Using the convolution theorem we then obtain

$$\phi(y_0, \tau) = \frac{1}{16\pi^2 r_0^2} \int \int \int p(\tau + 2X - Y^2/R - Z^2/R)(k_0^2\gamma - ik_0z_0\sigma)dxdydz$$

where

$$\phi(y_0, \tau) = \frac{1}{2\pi} \int_{-\infty}^{\infty} \Phi(y_0, k) \exp(ik\tau)dk$$

223

Noting that $k_0 \gg 1$ and $\alpha \ll 1$, by comparing the magnitude of terms which make up the kernel p we obtain

$$p(\tau + 2X + 2Z - Y^2/R) \simeq p(\tau + 2X) \exp(-ik_0Y^2/R) \exp(-ik_0Z^2/R)$$

This simplification is a consequence of the result

$$k_0 - \alpha(Y^2 + Z^2)/R \simeq k_0$$

and allows the scattered field to be written as

$$\phi(y_0, \tau) = \int \int p(\tau + 2X) \exp(-ik_0Y^2/R) f(x, y) dx dy$$

where f is the scattering function given by

$$f(x, y) = \frac{1}{16\pi^2 r_0^2} \int_0^h (k_0^2 \gamma - ik_0 z_0 \sigma) \exp[-ik_0(z-a)^2/R] dz$$

We now have an integral equation where our processing variables τ and y_0 have been separated into two different functions. This is why SAR data can be processed in range and azimuth separately. A futher simplification can now be made to f by noting that

$$\frac{z}{a} \ll 1, \quad 0 \le z \le h$$

for an airborne SAR so that

$$(z - a)^2 = z^2 - 2za + a^2 \simeq -2za + a^2$$

Hence, since $a/R = \tan\theta$ where θ is the grazing angle, the scattering function can be written as

$$f(x, y) = \frac{1}{16\pi^2 r_0^2} \exp(-ik_0 a \tan\theta) \int_0^h (k_0^2 \gamma - ik_0 z_0 \sigma) \exp(2ik_0 z \tan\theta) dz$$

We now introduce a couple of tricks which are designed entirely to write the scattered field in a more convenient form. First of all we use the properties of the delta function to write

$$\int \int p(\tau + 2X) \exp(-ik_0 Y^2/R) f(x, y) dx dy$$

$$= \int d\tau' p(\tau') \int \int \delta(\tau' - \tau - 2X) \exp(-ik_0 Y^2/R) f(x,y) dx dy$$

$$= \int d\tau' p(\tau') \int f[\tau'/2 - \tau/2 + R, y] \exp(-ik_0 Y^2/R) dy$$

Next, we let $x = 2R - \tau$ and $x' = \tau' + x$. Then, $\tau' = x' - x$, $\tau'/2 - \tau/2 + R = x'/2$ and $d\tau' = dx'$ and the scattered field can be written in the form

$$\phi(y_0, x) = \int dx' p(x' - x) \int f(x', y) \exp[-ik_0(y - y_0)^2/R] dy$$

To be consistent with the notation now being used for the range variable we write y as y' and y_0 as y. The scattered field can then be written as

$$\phi(x, y) = \int \int \exp[ik_0(x' - x)] \exp[i\alpha(x' - x)^2] \exp[-ik_0(y' - y)^2/R]$$

$$\times f(x', y') dx' dy'$$

At the receiver, the scattered field, modelled by the above equation, is coherently mixed down to baseband. This is equivalent to multiplying it by $\exp(ik_0 x)$ and provides the data

$$d(x, y) = \exp(ik_0 x) \phi(x, y)$$

$$= \int \int \exp[i\alpha(x' - x)^2] \exp[-ik_0(y' - y)^2/R] \exp(ik_0 x') f(x', y') dx' dy'$$

This is a convolution equation and so we may write,

$$d(x, y) = \exp(i\alpha x^2) \exp(-ik_0 y^2/R) \otimes \otimes O(x, y)$$

where O is the object function given by

$$O(x, y) = \exp(ik_0 x) f(x, y)$$

We can now apply the processing method which was explained in section 7.2. Correlating this data with the functions $\exp(-i\alpha x^2)$ and $\exp(ik_0 y^2/R)$ over the pulse length T and beam width L respectively, we obtain

$$D(x, y) = \beta RT \, \mathrm{sinc}(\alpha Tx) \, \mathrm{sinc}(\beta k_0 y) \otimes \otimes O(x, y) \tag{7.3.15}$$

where

$$D(x,y) = d(x,y) \odot \odot \exp(-i\alpha x^2)\exp(ik_0 y^2/R)$$

and $\beta(= L/R)$ is the angle of divergence of the beam. The SAR image in then given by

$$I_{SAR}(x,y) =\mid D(x,y)\mid = \beta RT \mid \operatorname{sinc}(\alpha Tx)\operatorname{sinc}(\beta k_0 y) \otimes \otimes O(x,y)\mid$$

Observe, that this equation for D is the same as equation 7.2.3. However, in this case, the object function is defined in terms of a scattering function for the ground f.

By taking the two-dimensional Fourier transform of $D(x,y)$, equation (7.3.15) can then be written in $k_x - k_y$ space as

$$\widetilde{D}(k_x, k_y) = \frac{\pi^2 R}{\alpha k_0} F(k_x - k_0, k_y), \quad -\alpha T \le k_x \le \alpha T,$$

$$-\beta k_0 \le k_y \le \beta k_y \tag{7.3.16}$$

where

$$\widetilde{D}(k_x, k_y) = \int\limits_{-\infty}^{\infty} \int\limits_{-\infty}^{\infty} D(x,y)\exp(-ik_x x)\exp(-ik_y y)dxdy$$

and

$$F(k_x - k_0, k_y) = \int\limits_{-\infty}^{\infty} \int\limits_{-\infty}^{\infty} \exp(ik_0 x)f(x,y)\exp(-ik_x x)\exp(-ik_y y)dxdy$$

From equation (7.3.16), it is clear that range compression provides a sample of the spectrum F of width $2\alpha T$ located at k_0. Unlike the range spectrum, the azimuth spectrum is not the result of a spectral shift from GHz to MHz. The azimuth spectrum therefore gives base band information on the nature of the scattering function f band limited by $2\beta k_0$. The spectral content of f that is acquired, is therefore a rectangle of area $4\alpha\beta k_0 T$ centred on $(-k_0, 0)$ in $k_x - k_y$ space. This is shown in figure 7.13 which illustrates that the spectral information (in contrast to resolution) on the ground depends on the wavelength of the microwaves. The wavelength determines the characteristic scale length over which scattering takes place. This leads to a marked difference between SAR images obtained at different

226

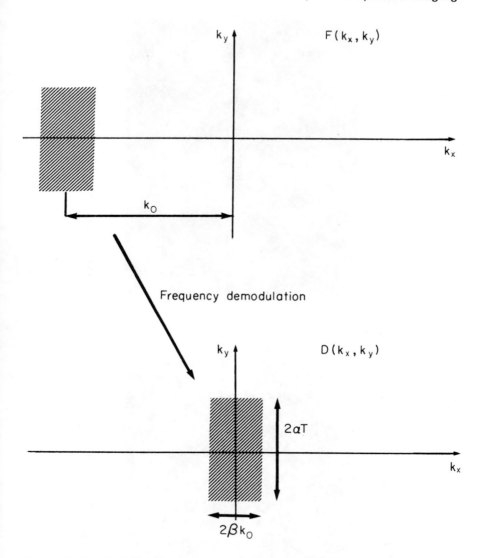

Figure 7.13 The shaded region represents the band of spatial frequencies on the scattering function for the ground that is obtained with SAR

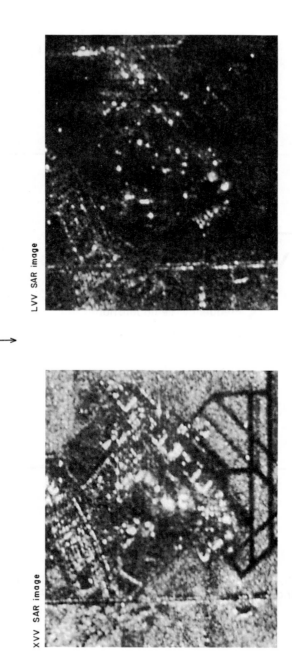

Look direction →

XVV SAR image

LVV SAR image

Figure 7.14 Comparison of two SAR images of the same region using different wavelengths (*left*, λ = 2·8 cm; *right*, λ = 24 cm)

wavelengths. An example of this is shown in figure 7.14 which compares an XVV and LVV SAR image of the same region.

Let us now return to equations (7.3.8)-(7.3.11). Recall that we worked with the reduced wave equation (7.4.13) in order to demonstrate the basic analytic method. Now that this has been done, we are in a position to go back and repeat the calculation for equations (7.3.8)-(7.3.11). From equation (7.3.8), the back-scattered HH field is

$$\Phi_{HH} = P \int \int \int \left(k^2 \gamma - i k z_0 \sigma + \frac{\partial^2}{\partial y^2} \ln \epsilon_r \right) g^2 \, dx \, dy \, dz$$

This equation is identical in form to equation (7.3.13). The processed SAR data can therefore be written without further proof as

$$D_{HH}(x, y) = TR\beta \operatorname{sinc}(\alpha Tx) \operatorname{sinc}(\beta k_0 y) \otimes \otimes O_{HH}(x, y)$$

where the HH object function is given by

$$O_{HH} = \frac{1}{16\pi^2 r_0^2} \exp(-i k_0 a \tan \theta) \exp(i k_0 x) \int_0^h \left(k_0^2 \gamma - i k_0 z_0 \sigma \right.$$

$$\left. + \frac{\partial^2}{\partial y^2} \ln \epsilon_r \right) \exp(2 i k_0 z \tan \theta) dz \tag{7.3.17}$$

A similar type of model can be generated for different polarization data. To begin with, we can evaluate the cross polarized scattered field. From equation (7.3.9), the back-scattered HV field is given by

$$\Phi_{HV} = P \int \int \int \left(\cos\theta \frac{\partial^2}{\partial z \partial y} \ln \epsilon_r + \sin\theta \frac{\partial^2}{\partial x \partial y} \ln \epsilon_r \right) g^2 \, dx \, dy \, dz$$

Once again, the form of this equation is identical to equation (7.3.13). Hence, the processed HV SAR data is

$$D_{HV}(x, y) = TR\beta \operatorname{sinc}(\alpha Tx) \operatorname{sinc}(\beta k_0 y) \otimes \otimes O_{HV}(x, y)$$

where the HV object function is given by

$$O_{HV} = \frac{1}{16\pi^2 r_0^2} \exp(-i k_0 a \tan \theta) \exp(i k_0 x) \int_0^h \left(\cos\theta \frac{\partial^2}{\partial z \partial y} \ln \epsilon_r \right.$$

229

$$+\sin\theta\frac{\partial^2}{\partial x\partial y}\ln\epsilon_r\Bigg)\exp(2ik_0z\tan\theta)dz \qquad (7.3.18)$$

From equation (7.3.10) it is easy to show that D_{VV} is given by

$$D_{VV}(x,y) = TR\beta\,\mathrm{sinc}(\alpha Tx)\,\mathrm{sinc}(\beta k_0y)\otimes\otimes O_{VV}(x,y)$$

where

$$O_{VV} = \frac{1}{16\pi^2r_0^2}\exp(-ik_0a\tan\theta)\exp(ik_0x)\int_0^h\Bigg(k_0^2\gamma - ik_0z_0\sigma$$

$$+2\cos\theta\sin\theta\frac{\partial^2}{\partial z\partial x}\ln\epsilon_r$$

$$+\sin^2\theta\frac{\partial^2}{\partial x^2}\ln\epsilon_r + \cos^2\theta\frac{\partial^2}{\partial z^2}\ln\epsilon_r\Bigg)\exp(2ik_0z\tan\theta)dz \qquad (7.3.19)$$

Finally, from equation (7.3.11), we get

$$D_{VH}(x,y) = TR\beta\,\mathrm{sinc}(\alpha Tx)\,\mathrm{sinc}(\beta k_0y)\otimes\otimes O_{VH}(x,y)$$

where

$$O_{VH} = \frac{1}{16\pi^2r_0^2}\exp(-ik_0z\tan\theta)\exp(ik_0x)\int_0^h\Bigg(\cos\theta\frac{\partial^2}{\partial y\partial z}\ln\epsilon_r$$

$$+\sin\theta\frac{\partial^2}{\partial y\partial x}\ln\epsilon_r\Bigg)\exp(i2ik_0z\tan\theta)dz \qquad (7.3.20)$$

7.4 POLARIZATION EFFECTS

SAR images are highly sensitive to the polarization of the field that is emitted or received. In principle, this result can be used to classify regions of an image when it is known *a priori,* how certain types of terrain effect different polarized radiation. One of the most dramatic effects occurs when microwaves are scattered by the sea surface at low grazing incidence.

An example of this is shown in figure 7.15. This figure shows two real aperture radar or RAR images of the sea surface using

Time (s)

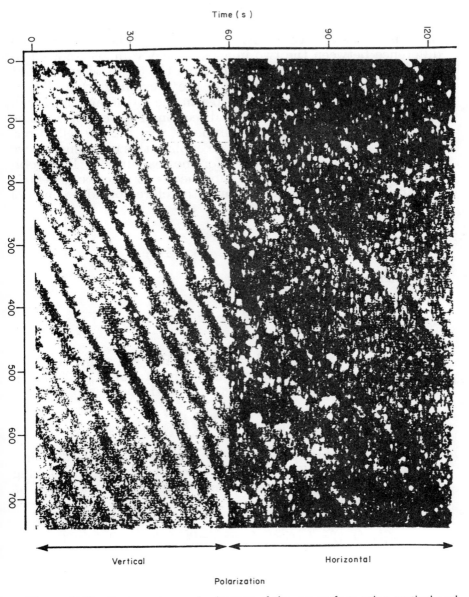

Vertical Horizontal

Polarization

Figure 7.15 Real aperture radar images of the sea surface using vertical and horizontal polarization

X-band HH and VV polarization. In this example, a pulse is emitted in a fixed time interval and the VV return measured over a set period of time (approximately 60 seconds). The radar is then switched to HH mode. Clearly, there is a marked difference between the two images. The VV image shows features which are due to reflections from the crests of waves that are aligned along the direction of the prevailing wind. These features are almost completely lost in the HH image, although it is just possible to observe the direction of wave motion. The HH image is dominated by a number of very intense reflections which are known as sea spikes. To explain this phenomenon we need to setup a suitable model for the sea surface. To a good approximation, the sea is a homogeneous conductive dielectric of varying height $h(x, y)$. We may therefore consider a model where

$$\epsilon_r(x, y, z) = \epsilon_{ro}, \quad z \le h(x, y)$$

$$\sigma(x, y, z) = \sigma_0, \quad z \le h(x, y)$$

and where

$$\left[\frac{\partial \epsilon_r}{\partial x}\right]_{z<h} = \left[\frac{\partial \epsilon_r}{\partial y}\right]_{z<h} = \left[\frac{\partial \epsilon_r}{\partial z}\right]_{z<h} = 0$$

Typical values for ϵ_{ro} and σ_0 are 81 and 4.3 siemens/metre respectively. In this case, for an X-band radar $(k_0 \simeq 224m^{-1})$, $k_0^2 \gamma_0 \simeq 4 \times 10^6 m^{-2}$ and $k_0 z_0 \sigma_0 \simeq 3.6 \times 10^5$ so that

$$k_0^2 \gamma_0 - i k_0 z_0 \sigma_0 \simeq k_0^2 \gamma_0$$

A simple mathematical model for the VV and HH RAR images given in figure 7.15 can be obtained by letting the grazing angle θ approaches zero. All terms involving $\sin \theta$ can then be neglected giving

$$I_{RAR}^{ij}(x, y) = T \mid \text{sinc}(\alpha Tx) \exp(-ik_0 y^2 / R) \otimes \otimes O_{ij}(x, y) \mid$$

where

$$O_{VV} = \frac{1}{16\pi^2 R^2} \exp(ik_0 x) \int_0^h \left(k_0^2 \gamma_0 + \frac{\partial^2}{\partial z^2} \ln \epsilon_r\right) dz, \quad \gamma_0 = \epsilon_{ro} - 1$$

and

$$O_{HH} = \frac{1}{16\pi^2 R^2} \exp(ik_0 x) \int_0^h \left(k_0^2 \gamma_0 + \frac{\partial^2}{\partial y^2} \ln \epsilon_r \right) dz$$

The VV object function is easy to evaluate, giving

$$O_{VV} = \frac{1}{16\pi^2 R^2} \exp(ik_0 x) \left(k_0^2 \gamma_0 h + \frac{1}{\epsilon_{ro}} \left[\frac{\partial \epsilon_r}{\partial z} \right]_{z=h} \right)$$

The HH object function can be evaluated by using Leibniz' formula for the integral of a derivative, i.e.

$$\int_{a(x)}^{b(x)} \frac{\partial}{\partial x} f(x,y) dy = \frac{\partial}{\partial x} \int_{a(x)}^{b(x)} f(x,y) dy$$

$$+ \left[f(x,y) \right]_{y=a(x)} \frac{da}{dx} - \left[f(x,y) \right]_{y=b(x)} \frac{db}{dx}$$

We then obtain

$$O_{HH} = \frac{1}{16\pi^2 R^2} \exp(ik_0 x) \left(k_0^2 \gamma_0 h - \frac{1}{\epsilon_{ro}} \left[\frac{\partial \epsilon_r}{\partial y} \right]_{z=h} \frac{\partial h}{\partial y} \right)$$

Noting that

$$\int_0^h \frac{\partial}{\partial z} \left(\frac{\partial \ln \epsilon_r}{\partial y} \right) dz = \frac{1}{\epsilon_{ro}} \left[\frac{\partial \epsilon_r}{\partial y} \right]_{z=h}$$

and (using Leibniz' formula again)

$$\int_0^h \frac{\partial}{\partial y} \left(\frac{\partial \ln \epsilon_r}{\partial z} \right) dz = -\frac{1}{\epsilon_{ro}} \left[\frac{\partial \epsilon_r}{\partial z} \right]_{z=h} \frac{\partial h}{\partial y}$$

we have

$$\left[\frac{\partial \epsilon_r}{\partial y} \right]_{z=h} = - \left[\frac{\partial \epsilon_r}{\partial z} \right]_{z=h} \frac{\partial h}{\partial y}$$

since

$$\int_0^h \frac{\partial}{\partial z} \left(\frac{\partial}{\partial y} \ln \epsilon_r \right) dz = \int_0^h \frac{\partial}{\partial y} \left(\frac{\partial}{\partial z} \ln \epsilon_r \right) dz$$

A relatively simple expression for the VV and HH RAR images can then be obtained by letting

$$\frac{1}{\epsilon_{ro}} \left[\frac{\partial \epsilon_r}{\partial z} \right]_{z=h} = k_0 \gamma_0 \simeq 1.8 \times 10^4 \mathrm{m}^{-1}$$

Here, it is assumed that the gradient in the vertical direction due to a change in the permittivity across the interface between the sea and air is equal to $k_0 \gamma_0 \epsilon_{ro} \simeq 1.3 \times 10^6 \mathrm{m}^{-1}$ over the imaged scene. This allows us to write the VV and HH RAR images as

$$I_{RAR}^{VV}(x, y) = A \mid \mathrm{sinc}(\alpha T x) \exp(-ik_0 y^2/R) \otimes \otimes \exp(ik_0 x) [1 + k_0 h(x, y)] \mid$$

and

$$I_{RAR}^{HH}(x, y) = A \mid \mathrm{sinc}(\alpha T x) \exp(-ik_0 y^2/R) \otimes \otimes \exp(ik_0 x) \left[k_0 h(x, y) \right.$$

$$\left. + \left(\frac{\partial}{\partial y} h(x, y) \right)^2 \right]$$

where A is given by

$$A = \frac{\gamma_0 k_0 T}{16 \pi^2 R^2} \simeq \frac{114 T}{R^2}$$

In this form, it is clear that the VV RAR image is a map of the height variations h of the sea surface whereas the HH RAR image is a map of both h and $(\partial_y h)^2$. Compared to h, the non-linear term $(\partial_y h)^2$ is very sensitive to the sea state. From this result we deduce that sea spikes are caused by rapid variations in the height of the sea surface as a function of the azimuth direction. In other words, the HH RAR image is dominated by features which map the location of points where

$$\mid \frac{\partial h}{\partial y} \mid >> k_0 h$$

A simple illustration of this is given in figure 7.16 which shows images of $\mid 1 + s_{i,j} \mid$ and $\mid s_{i,j} + (s_{i,j} - s_{i,j-1})^2 \mid$, $s_{i,1} = s_{i,2}$ where $s_{i,j}$ is a randomly generated surface. Features appear which resemble sea spikes at locations where the difference between the jth and $(j-1)^{th}$ elements of $s_{i,j}$ is relatively large and the nonlinear term $(s_{i,j} - s_{i,j-1})^2$ dominates.

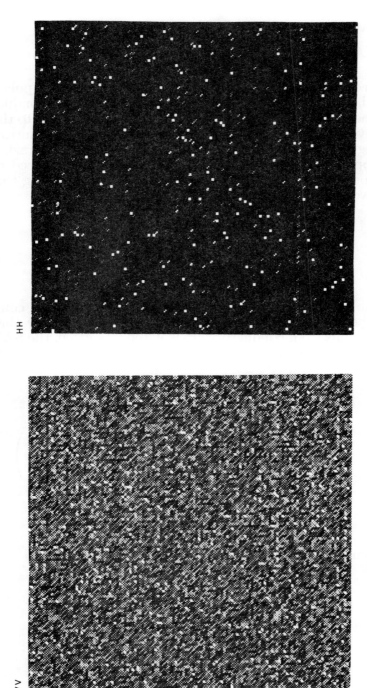

Figure 7.16 Simulation of sea spikes using a rough surface model for the sea

7.5 QUANTITATIVE IMAGING WITH SAR

The object functions for a SAR image show that the VV polarization data are related to both the permittivity and conductivity whereas the VH cross polarization data are related to the permittivity alone. This result provides a method of quantitative imaging using SAR. Consider a model where the grazing angle approaches zero and where the ground is composed of conductors embedded in a homogeneous dielectric. Using this model, we can employ the following conditions

$$\epsilon_r(x, y, z) = \epsilon_{ro}, \quad 0 \leq z \leq h(x, y)$$

and

$$\left[\frac{\partial \epsilon_r}{\partial x}\right]_{z<h} = \left[\frac{\partial \epsilon_r}{\partial y}\right]_{z<h} = \left[\frac{\partial \epsilon_r}{\partial z}\right]_{z<h} = 0$$

The problem is then reduced to that of processing and combining the VV and VH polarization data in such a way that the reflections from conductors are isolated. As $\theta \to 0$, the SAR data for ij polarization is given by

$$D_{ij}(x, y) = P(x, y) \otimes \otimes O_{ij}(x, y)$$

where

$$O_{VV} = \frac{1}{16\pi^2 R^2} \exp(ik_0 x) \left(k_0^2 \gamma_0 h + \frac{1}{\epsilon_{ro}} \left[\frac{\partial \epsilon_r}{\partial z}\right]_{z=h} - ik_0 z_0 \int_0^h \sigma dz\right)$$

and

$$O_{VH} = \frac{1}{16\pi^2 R^2} \exp(ik_0 x) \frac{1}{\epsilon_{ro}} \left[\frac{\partial \epsilon_r}{\partial z}\right]_{z=h} \frac{\partial h}{\partial y}$$

If we then consider the case when

$$\frac{1}{\epsilon_{ro}} \left[\frac{\partial \epsilon_{ro}}{\partial z}\right]_{z=h} = k_0 \gamma_0$$

the object functions reduced to

$$O_{VV} = \frac{k_0 \gamma_0}{16\pi^2 R^2} \exp(ik_0 x) \left(1 + k_0 h - \frac{iz_0}{\gamma_0} \int_0^h \sigma dz\right)$$

and

$$O_{VH}(x,y) = \frac{k_0\gamma_0}{16\pi^2 R^2} \exp(ik_0 x)\frac{\partial h}{\partial y}$$

The VV and HH processed SAR data are then given

$$D_{VV} = \frac{k_0\gamma_0}{16\pi^2 R^2} P \otimes \otimes \exp(ik_0 x)\left(1 + k_0 h - \frac{iz_0}{\gamma_0}\int_0^h \sigma dz\right)$$

and

$$D_{VH} = \frac{\gamma_0}{16\pi^2 R^2} P \otimes \otimes \exp(ik_0 x)\frac{\partial}{\partial y}(1 + k_0 h)$$

The last equation can be integrated directly giving

$$\frac{k_0\gamma_0}{16\pi^2 R^2} P \otimes \otimes \exp(ik_0 x)(1 + k_0 h) = k_0 \int^y D_{VH}dy$$

and hence, the VV polarization data can be written as

$$D_{VV} = k_0 \int^y D_{VH}dy - \frac{ik_0 z_0}{16\pi^2 R^2} P \otimes \otimes \exp(ik_0 x)\int_0^h \sigma dz$$

By defining the SAR image of the conductivity variations as

$$I^\sigma_{SAR}(x,y) = \frac{k_0\gamma_0}{16\pi^2 R^2} \mid P(x,y) \otimes \otimes \exp(ik_0 x)\int_0^{h(x,y)} \sigma(x,y,z)dz \mid$$

we then obtain

$$I^\sigma_{SAR}(x,y) = \mid D_{VV}(x,y) - k_0 \int^y D_{VH}(x,y)dy \mid$$

According to the formula above, a quantitative SAR image of the conductivity of the ground may be obtained by a relatively simple procedure. All that is required is a suitable method of integrating the cross polarization data D_{VH}.

7.6 SYNTHETIC APERTURE SONAR

Sonar is divided into two clasees: passive sonar and active sonar. Passive sonar is used for detecting objects in the sea by analysing the sound that they make using short time Fourier analysis. The time signature is divided into equal segments and the amplitude spectrum of each segment is computed. An image is then generated of the amplitude modulations as a function of frequency and time. This reveals any dominant frequency components in the signal and hence a possible acoustic source. If the source moves, then a Doppler shift occurs which can be observed in the image. This effect can be used to detect moving acoustic sources such as submarines.

Active sonar uses acoustic waves to detect and locate objects or image regions of the seabed. The principles of active sonar are very similar to radar. They include sideways looking sonars which are used to produce surveys of the seabed and sub-bottom profiling where high resolution information regarding the sub-bottom of the sea bed is obtained to a depth of about ten metres. Compared to radar, the environment (i.e. the sea) in which a sonar must operate is much noisier due to the wide range of physical effects that can occur. For example, turbulence in the sea (caused by temperature gradients) generates random density fluctuations which may refract or even diffract the sonar beam. Another important difference between radar and sonar is that the absorption and dispersion of acoustic waves in the sea are much greater than the absorption and dispersion of microwaves in the atmosphere. The absorption of acoustic radiation is proportional to the square of the frequency. Hence, unlike radar the resolution of a sonar image (i.e. its high frequency content) is limited by the range at which it operates.

Sideways looking sonars are usually real aperture systems. They may utilize either amplitude coded or frequency coded pulses but more commonly resort to frequency modulated chirps with carrier frequencies of the order of 10 kHz. In such cases, the principle is identical to a real aperture radar. The range resolution is given by $2\pi/\alpha T$ metres where α is the quadratic chirp rate/(speed of sound in sea water)^2 and T is the length of the pulse. Also, as in real aperture radar, the lateral resolution is determined by the width of the beam.

The principle of aperture synthesis may also be applied to

sonar. One of the major problems with this is due to the relatively low velocity of sound in water ($\sim 10^3 \mathrm{ms}^{-1}$ compared with $3 \times 10^8 \mathrm{ms}^{-1}$ for microwaves in air). This means that the pulse repetition frequency for synthetic aperture sonar or SAS is much lower than in SAR. In order to adequately sample the synthetic aperture, the position of the transducer must not change along the track by a distance greater than its length (the real aperture). This condition means that either the survey speed is very low or the real aperture is relatively large. For a maximum effective range R, the period between successive transmissions is of the order of $2R/c$ where c is the sound velocity in sea water. If the survey speed is v, then the transducer will have moved between consecutive transmissions by a distance

$$d = \frac{2vR}{c}$$

For a survey speed of $3\mathrm{ms}^{-1}$, a sonar operating at a range of say 10 km requires a real aperture length of 60 metres if aperture synthesis is to be utilized effectively. Clearly to generate a 60 metre real aperture, a single transducer must be replaced by a linear array of transducer. Practical problems then arise of how the overall length of the real aperture can be kept rigid to avoid ambiguities caused by the non-ideal behaviour of the systems platform. Nevertheless, in principle, SAS can be used to acquire detailed high resolution surveys. We can consider the same type of model for a SAS as the one presented for SAR. This is illustrated in figure 7.17.

Assuming that the sea is a lossless homogeneous medium with density ρ_0 and compressibility κ_0 and the seabed has height variations $h(x,y)$ and compressibility variations $\kappa(x,y,z)$, then it can be shown that the SAS image is given by

$$I_{SAS}(x,y) = \mid \beta T R \operatorname{sinc}(\alpha T x) \operatorname{sinc}(\beta k_0 y) \otimes \otimes O(x,y) \mid$$

where

$$O(x,y) = \frac{k_0^2}{16\pi^2 r_0^2} \exp(-ik_0 a \tan\theta) \exp(ik_0 x)$$

$$\times \int_0^{h(x,y)} \gamma_\kappa(x,y,z) \exp(2ik_0 z \tan\theta) dz,$$

$$\gamma_\kappa = \frac{\kappa - \kappa_0}{\kappa_0}$$

Quantitative coherent imaging

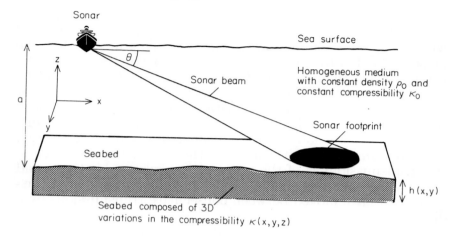

Figure 7.17 Geometry and physical model for synthetic aperture sonar

The parameters in the above equations are

β - angle of divergence of the sonar beam

T - length of the sonar pulse

R - range

α - quadratic chirp rate/(velocity of sound)^2

k_0 - carrier wavenumber of pulse

r_0 - slant range of sonar beam

θ - grazing angle of sonar

h - height variations of the seabed

κ - compressibility of seabed

κ_0 - compressibility of the sea

ρ_0 - density of the sea

This result has been obtained by solving the wave equation

$$(\nabla^2 + k^2)p = -k^2\gamma_\kappa Pg$$

for the pressure field p using the analysis provided in section 7.3. The model used to derive this result, assumes that the sea and the seabed are density matched. It also assumes that acoustic absorption by the sea is negligible.

SUMMARY OF IMPORTANT RESULTS

SAR point spread function

$$P(x,y) = \beta RT \operatorname{sinc}(\alpha T x) \operatorname{sinc}(\beta k_0 y)$$

Resolution

Range resolution $= 2\pi/\alpha T$ metres

Azimuth resolution $=$ Half the length of the real aperture

SAR image

For ij polarization,

$$I_{SAR}^{ij}(x,y) = |\, P(x,y) \otimes \otimes O_{ij}(x,y) \,|$$

where O_{ij} is given by equations (7.3.17)-(7.3.20).

FURTHER READING

1.   Rihaczek A W, *Principles of High Resolution Radar*, McGraw-Hill, 1969. An introduction to both real and synthetic aperture radar systems.

2. Harger R O, *Synthetic Aperture Radar Systems*, Academic Press, 1970. A good text on the engineering of SAR.

3. Kovaly J J, *Synthetic Aperture Radar*, Artech, 1976. A useful text which is a collection of original papers on a large range of important aspects of synthetic aperture radar imaging.

4. Mitchell R L, *Radar Signal Simulation*; MARK Resources, 1985. This book discusses the simulation of radar signals that occur at various point in a radar system and also provides a good introduction to radar signal processing.

5. Ulaby F T, Moore R K and Fung A K, *Microwave Remote Sensing (Active and Passive)*, Addison-Wesley, 1981 (Volume 1), 1982 (Volume 2) and 1986 (Volume 3). These volumes are a series of advanced level texts which cover a wide range of topics on both the theory of microwave scattering and remote sensing with microwaves. Synthetic Aperture Radar is discussed in volume 2 (chapter 9).

6. Barber B C, *Theory of Digital Imaging from Orbital Synthetic Aperture Radar*, International Journal of Remote Sensing, 1985, Volume 6, Number 7, Pages 1009-1057. This paper is one of the most informative and readable scientific papers available on the basic digital processing used in SAR imagery.

Data Processing

PART THREE
Data Processing

8 Deconvolution I: Linear restoration

A large number of inverse problems are in one form or another, essentially deconvolution. We have already seen a number examples of this in previous chapters where, after solving for the Born scattered field, we obtain an expression of the form

$$s(x) = p(x) \otimes f(x)$$

where s is the recorded signal, p is some instrument function and f is the object function which we want to reconstruct. In previous chapters we have presented simple solutions to this problem without discussing the variety of computational problems that can arise in practice due to the effect additive noise n, when the signal is given by

$$s(x) = p(x) \otimes f(x) + n(x)$$

This chapter, together with chapters 9 and 10, are designed to serve the reader with a survey of the variety of techniques that have been developed to cope with this type of problem. In this chapter, linear restoration methods shall be discussed.

8.1 THE LEAST SQUARES METHOD AND THE ORTHOGONALITY PRINCIPLE

The least squares method and the orthogonality principle are used extensively in signal processing and will be used repeatedly in this and the chapters to follow. Hence, we shall start by providing details on some basic analytical results.

The least squares principle

Suppose, we have a real function $f(x)$ which we want to approximate by a function $\hat{f}(x)$. We construct $\hat{f}$ in such a way that its functional behaviour can be controlled be adjusting the value of a parameter a. We can then adjust the value of a to find get the best estimte $\hat{f}$ of f. So what is the best value of a to choose? To solve this problem, we construct the mean square error

$$e = \int [f(x) - \hat{f}(x,a)]^2 dx$$

This error is a function of a. The value of a which produces the best approximation $\hat{f}$ of f is therefore the one where $e(a)$ is a minimum. Hence, a must be chosen so that

$$\frac{\partial e}{\partial a} = 0$$

Substituting the expression for e into the above equation and differentiating we obtain

$$\int [f(x) - \hat{f}(x,a)] \frac{\partial}{\partial a} \hat{f}(x,a) dx = 0$$

Solving this equation for $\hat{f}$ provides the minimum mean square estimate for f. This method is known generally as the least squares principle.

Linear polynomial models

To use the least squares principle, some sought of model for the estimate $\hat{f}$ must be introduced. Suppose we expanded $\hat{f}$ in terms of a linear combination of (known) basis functions $y_n(x)$, i.e.

$$\hat{f}(x) = \sum_n a_n y_n(x)$$

where

$$\sum_n \equiv \sum_{n=-N/2}^{N/2}$$

For simplicity let us first assume that f is real (complex signals shall be dealt with later on). Since, the basis functions are known, to compute $\hat{f}$ the coefficients a_n must be found. Using the least squares principle, we require a_n such that the mean square error

$$e = \int \left(f(x) - \sum_n a_n y_n(x) \right)^2 dx$$

is a minimum. This occurs when

$$\frac{\partial e}{\partial a_m} = 0$$

Differentiating,

$$\frac{\partial}{\partial a_m} \int \left(f(x) - \sum_n a_n y_n(x) \right)^2 dx$$

$$= 2 \int \left(f(x) - \sum_n a_n y_n(x) \right) \frac{\partial}{\partial a_m} \left(f(x) - \sum_n a_n y_n(x) \right) dx$$

We then have

$$\frac{\partial}{\partial a_m} \left(f(x) - \sum_n a_n y_n(x) \right) = -\frac{\partial}{\partial a_m} \sum_n a_n y_n(x)$$

$$= -\frac{\partial}{\partial a_m} (... + a_1 y_1(x) + a_2 y_2(x) + ... + a_n y_n(x) + ...)$$

$$= -y_1(x), \quad m = 1$$

$$= -y_2(x), \quad m = 2$$

.

.

.

$$= -y_m(x), \quad m = n$$

Hence, we get

$$\frac{\partial e}{\partial a_m} = -2 \int \left(f(x) - \sum_n a_n y_n(x) \right) y_m(x) dx = 0$$

The coefficients a_n which minimize the mean square error for a linear polynomial model are therefore obtained by solving the equation

$$\int f(x) y_m(x) = \sum_n a_n \int y_n(x) y_m(x) dx$$

for a_n.

The orthogonality principle

The result derived above demonstrates that the coefficients a_n are such that the error $f - \hat{f}$ is orthogonal to the signals y_m. We write this result in the form

$$\langle f - \hat{f}, y_m \rangle \equiv \int [f(x) - \hat{f}(x)] y_m(x) dx = 0$$

This is known as the orthogonality principle.

Complex signals, norms and Hilbert spaces

Let us now consider the case where f is a complex signal. In this case, $\hat{f}$ must be a complex estimate of this signal. We also assume that both y_n and a_n are complex. The mean square error is then given by

$$e = \int | f(x) - \sum_n a_n y_n(x) |^2 \, dx$$

The operation

$$\left(\int | f(x) | \, dx \right)^{1/2}$$

defines the norm of the function f which is denoted by the sign $\| \bullet \|$. Hence, using this notation, we can write the mean square error in the form

$$e = \| f(x) - \hat{f}(x) \|^2$$

which saves having to write integral signs all the time. This notation shall be used in later work.

The error function above defines a Hilbert space which is a vector space. It is a function of the complex coefficients a_n and is a minimum when

$$\frac{\partial e}{\partial a_m} = 0$$

To evaluate this result requires differentiation with respect to a complex variable. Since we shall be considering complex signals later, the opportunity is taken here to provide the details of this result. Substituting the expression for e into the equation above and differentiating, we get

$$\frac{\partial}{\partial a_m} \int |f - \sum_n a_n y_n|^2 \, dx = \int \Big[\Big(f - \sum_n a_n y_n\Big) \frac{\partial}{\partial a_m} \Big(f - \sum_n a_n y_n\Big)^*$$

$$+ \Big(f - \sum_n a_n y_n\Big)^* \frac{\partial}{\partial a_m} \Big(f - \sum_n a_n y_n\Big) \Big] dx = 0$$

We then use the results

$$\frac{\partial}{\partial a_m} \Big(f - \sum_n a_n y_n\Big) = -y_m$$

and

$$\frac{\partial}{\partial a_m} \Big(f - \sum_n a_n y_n\Big)^* = -y_m^* \frac{\partial a_m^*}{\partial a_m} = 0$$

The last result is obtained by using the formula

$$2\frac{\partial}{\partial z} = \frac{\partial}{\partial x} - i\frac{\partial}{\partial y}, \quad z = x + iy$$

from which it follows that

$$\frac{\partial z^*}{\partial z} = \frac{1}{2}\Big(\frac{\partial}{\partial x} - i\frac{\partial}{\partial y}\Big)(x - iy) = 0$$

From these results we find that e is a minimum when

$$\int \Big(f - \sum_n a_n y_n\Big)^* y_m \, dx = 0$$

or alternatively, taking the complex conjugate of this equation,

$$\int \Big(f - \sum_n a_n y_n\Big) y_m^* \, dx = 0$$

249

Hence, we obtain a more general definition of the orthogonality principle for complex signals (of which real signals are just a special case) which is that the optimum coefficients a_n which minimize the mean square error $\|f - \hat{f}\|^2$ are such the the error $f - \hat{f}$ is orthogonal to the signals y_m^* or

$$\langle f - \hat{f}, y_m^* \rangle = 0$$

Linear convolution models

So far we have demonstrated the least squares principle for approximating a function using a model for the estimate $\hat{f}$ of the form

$$\hat{f}(x) = \sum_n a_n y_n(x)$$

Another model which has a number of useful applications is the linear convolution model

$$\hat{f}(x) = y(x) \otimes a(x)$$

In this case, the least squares principle can again be used to find the function a. The simplest way to show how this can be done is to demonstrate the technique for digital signals and then use a limiting arguement for contiuous functions.

Digital signals

If f_i is a real digital signal consisting of a set of numbers $f_1, f_2, f_3, \dots$ etc., then we may use a linear convolution model for the discrete estimate $\hat{f}_i$ given by

$$\hat{f}_i = \sum_j y_{i-j} a_j$$

In this case, using the least squares principle, we find a_i by minimizing the mean square error

$$e = \sum_i (f_i - \hat{f}_i)^2$$

This error is a minimum when

$$\frac{\partial}{\partial a_k} \sum_i \left(f_i - \sum_j y_{i-j} a_j \right)^2 = 0$$

Differentiating, we get

$$-2\sum_i \left(f_i - \sum_j y_{i-j}a_j \right) \frac{\partial}{\partial a_k} \sum_j y_{i-j}a_j$$

$$= -2\sum_i \left(f_i - \sum_j y_{i-j}a_j \right) y_{i-k} = 0$$

and rearranging, we have

$$\sum_i f_i y_{i-k} = \sum_i \left(\sum_j y_{i-j}a_j \right) y_{i-k}$$

The left hand side of this equation is just the discrete correlation of f_i with y_i and the right hand side is a correlation of y_i with

$$\sum_j y_{i-j}a_j$$

which is itself just a discrete convolution of y_i with a_i. Hence, using the appropriate symbols we can write this equation as

$$f_i \odot y_i = (y_i \otimes a_i) \odot y_i$$

Real analogue signals

With real analogue signals, the optimum function a which minimizes the mean square error

$$e = \int [f(x) - \hat{f}(x)]^2 dx$$

where

$$\hat{f}(x) = a(x) \otimes y(x)$$

is obtained by solving the equation

$$[f(x) - a(x) \otimes y(x)] \odot y(x) = 0$$

This result is based on extending the result derived above for digital signals to infinte sums and using a limiting arguement to integrals.

Complex digital signals

If the data are a complex discrete function f_i where f_i corresponds to a set of complex numbers $f_1, f_2, f_3, ...$, then we use the mean square error defined by

$$e = \sum_i | f_i - \hat{f}_i |^2$$

and a linear convolution model of the form

$$\hat{f}_i = \sum_j y_{i-j} a_j$$

In this case, the error is a minimum when

$$\frac{\partial e}{\partial a_k} = \sum_i \left(f_i - \sum_j y_{i-j} a_i \right)^* y_{i-k} = 0$$

or

$$f_i \odot y_i^* = (y_i \otimes a_i) \odot y_i^*$$

Complex analogue signals

If $\hat{f}(x)$ is a complex estimate given by

$$\hat{f}(x) = a(x) \otimes y(x)$$

then the function $a(x)$ which minimizes the error

$$e = \| f(x) - \hat{f}(x) \|^2$$

is given by solving the equation

$$[f(x) - a(x) \otimes y(x)] \odot y^*(x) = 0$$

This result is just another version of the orthogonality principle.

Notation

Notice that in the work presented above, the signs $\otimes$ and $\odot$ have been used to denote convolution and correlation respectively for both continuous and discrete data. With discrete signals $\otimes$ and $\odot$ denote convolution and correlation sums respectively. This is indicated by the presence of subscripts on the appropriate functions. If subscripts are not present, then the functions in question are continuous and $\otimes$ and $\odot$ are taken to denote convolution and correlation integrals respectively.

Two dimensions

In two dimensions, the least squares method may also be used to approximate a function using the same methods that have been presented above. For example, suppose we wish to approximate the complex 2D function $f(x, y)$ using an estimate of the form

$$\hat{f}(x, y) = \sum_n \sum_m a_{nm} \phi_{nm}(x, y)$$

In this case, the mean square error is given by

$$e = \int \int \mid f(x, y) - \hat{f}(x, y) \mid^2 dx dy$$

Using the orthogonality principle, this error is a minimum when

$$\int \int \left[f(x, y) - \sum_n \sum_m a_{nm} \phi_{nm}(x, y) \right] \phi_{pq}^*(x, y) dx dy = 0$$

This is just a two dimensional version of the orthogonality principle.

Another important linear model that is used for designing two dimensional digital filters is

$$\hat{f}_{ij} = \sum_n \sum_m y_{i-n, j-m} a_{nm}$$

In this case, for complex data, the mean square error

$$e = \sum_i \sum_j \mid f_{ij} - \hat{f}_{ij} \mid^2$$

is a minimum when

$$\sum_i \sum_j \left(f_{ij} - \sum_n \sum_m y_{i-n, j-m} a_{nm} \right) y_{i-p, j-q}^* = 0$$

Using the appropriate symbols we can write this equation in the form

$$f_{ij} \odot \odot y_{ij}^* = (y_{ij} \otimes \otimes a_{ij}) \odot \odot y_{ij}^*$$

Similarly, for continuous functions, when

$$\hat{f}(x,y) = y(x,y) \otimes \otimes a(x,y)$$

the error

$$e = \int \int \mid f(x,y) - \hat{f}(x,y) \mid^2 dxdy$$

is a minimum when

$$[f(x,y) - a(x,y) \otimes \otimes y(x,y)] \odot \odot y^*(x,y) = 0$$

8.2 THE INVERSE FILTER

The inverse filter is a straightforward approach to deconvolving the equation

$$s(x) = p(x) \otimes f(x) + n(x)$$

In the absence of any useful information about the noise n, we may ignore it under the assumption that its total contribution to the signal s is small. We then set about inverting the reduced equation

$$s(x) = p(x) \otimes f(x)$$

The basic approach to solving this problem is to process the data s in Fourier space. Using the convolution theorem, we have

$$S(k) = P(k)F(k)$$

Reordering and taking the inverse Fourier transform, we get

$$f(x) = \hat{F}_1^{-1} \left(\frac{S(k)}{P(k)} \right)$$

$$= \hat{F}_1^{-1} \left(\frac{P^*(k)S(k)}{\mid P(k) \mid^2} \right)$$

The function $1/P$ is known as the inverse filter.

Criterion for the inverse filter

The criterion for the inverse filter is that the mean square of the noise is a minimum. In other words, f is chosen in such a way that the mean square error

$$e = \|n(x)\|^2 = \|s(x) - p(x) \otimes f(x)\|^2$$

is a minimum. Using the orthogonality principle, this error is a minimum when

$$[s(x) - p(x) \otimes f(x)] \odot p^*(x) = 0$$

Using the correlation and convolution theorems, in Fourier space, this equation becomes

$$[S(k) - P(k)F(k)]P^*(k) = 0$$

Hence, solving for F, we obtain the same result as before, namely,

$$F(k) = \frac{P^*(k)}{|P(k)|^2} S(k)$$

The inverse filter is therefore given by

$$\text{inverse filter} = \frac{P^*}{|P|^2}$$

Computational problems

In principle, the inverse filter provides an exact solution to the problem when $n(x)$ is close to zero. However, in practice this solution is fraught with difficulties. First, the inverse filter is invariably a singular function due to zeros occurring in $|P|$. Equally bad is the fact that even if the inverse filter is not singular, it is usually ill conditioned. This is where the magnitude of P goes to zero so quickly as k increases that $1/|P|^2$ rapidly aquires extremely large values. The effect of this is to amplify the noisy high frequency components of S. This can lead to a reconstruction for f which is dominated by the noise in s. The inverse filter can therefore only be used when:

1. The inverse filter is nonsingular.

2. The signal to noise ratio of the data is very small.

Unfortunately, such conditions are rare.

The computational problems associated with the inverse filter can be avoided by implementing a variety of different filters whose individual properties and characteristics are suited to certain types of experimental data.

8.3 THE WEINER FILTER

The Weiner filter is a minimum mean square filter. It is one of the most commonly used filters and is named after the American mathematician Norbert Weiner, who was among the first to discuss its properties. The problem is as follows: Given the data

$$s(x) = p(x) \otimes f(x) + n(x)$$

find an estimate for f denoted by $\hat{f}$ of the form

$$\hat{f}(x) = q(x) \otimes s(x)$$

Clearly, the problem is to find q or equivalently its Fourier transform Q. The Weiner filter is based on utilizing the least squares principle to find q. Thus, q is found is such a way that the error

$$e = \|f(x) - \hat{f}(x)\|^2$$

is a minimum. Using the orthogonality principle, this error is a minimum when

$$[f(x) - q(x) \otimes s(x)] \odot s^*(x) = 0$$

Hence, using the correlation and convolution theorems, in Fourier space we can write

$$F(k)S^*(k) = Q(k)S(k)S^*(k)$$

or

$$Q(k) = \frac{S^*(k)}{|S(k)|^2} F(k)$$

Since

$$S(k) = P(k)F(k) + N(k)$$

Q can be written in terms of P, F and N giving,

$$Q(k) = \frac{P^*(k) \mid F(k) \mid^2 + N^*(k)F(k)}{\mid P(k) \mid^2 \mid F(k) \mid^2 + \mid N(k) \mid^2 + D(k)}$$

where

$$D(k) = P(k)F(k)N^*(k) + N(k)P^*(k)F^*(k)$$

Special case: Signal independent noise

The Weiner filter can be simplified if we assume that the correlation of the noise with the object function f is zero and vice versa or

$$n^*(x) \odot f(x) = 0$$

and

$$f^*(x) \odot n(x) = 0$$

In situations where this is true (which fortunately includes many practical situations), the noise is referred to as signal independent noise. From these results it follows that (using the correlation theorem)

$$N^*(k)F(k) = 0$$

and

$$F^*(k)N(k) = 0$$

In this case, $D = 0$ and the Weiner filter Q reduces to

$$\text{Weiner filter} = \frac{P^*(k)}{\mid P(k) \mid^2 + \mid N(k) \mid^2 / \mid F(k) \mid^2}$$

The estimate $\hat{f}$ obtained by applying this filter is given by

$$\hat{f}(x) = \hat{F}_1^{-1}[Q(k)S(k)]$$

To implement the Weiner filter, the power spectra of the noise $\mid N(k) \mid^2$ and the object $\mid F(k) \mid^2$ need to be known *a priori*. This filter has the following properties:

1. As the noise tends to zero so that $\mid N \mid^2 \to 0$, it reduces to the inverse filter. Hence with minimal noise, the Weiner filter behaves like the inverse filter.

2. As the power of the object goes to zero (i.e. as $|F|^2 \to 0$), the Weiner filter has zero gain. This solves problems associated with zeros in $|P|$ and means that the Weiner filter is well conditioned.

Problems and practical implementation

The main problem with the Weiner filter is that in practice, accurate estimates of $|N|^2$ and $|F|^2$ are usually not available. We are therefore forced to make use of any known statistical properties of the data provided. For this reason, an approximate form for the Weiner filter is usually constructed which is given by

$$\text{Weiner filter} = \frac{P^*}{|P|^2 + \Gamma}$$

where Γ is a suitable constant. We shall see in the following chapter, that this approximation provides a *maximum a posteriori* (MAP) estimate for the object. The value of Γ ideally reflects some form of prior knowledge about the signal to noise ratio (SNR) of the data, i.e.

$$\Gamma = \frac{1}{(SNR)^2}$$

In practice, it is not uncommon for one to apply the Weiner filter over a range of different values of Γ and then choose the reconstruction (i.e. the version of $\hat{f}$ for a given value of Γ) which optimizes the interpretation of the data. This depends as much on the users own preference and individual requirements as it does on the performance of the Weiner filter.

8.4 THE POWER SPECTRUM EQUALIZATION FILTER

As the name implies, the power spectrum equalization (PSE) filter is based on finding an estimate $\hat{f}$ whose power spectrum is equal to the power spectrum of the desired function f. In other words $\hat{f}$ is obtained by employing the criterion

$$|F(k)|^2 = |\hat{F}(k)|^2$$

together with the linear convolution model

$$\hat{f}(x) = q(x) \otimes s(x)$$

N.B. Be careful not to confuse the complex spectrum of the estimate $\hat{F}$ with the Fourier transform operator $\hat{F}_1$ or the inverse Fourier transform operator $\hat{F}_1^{-1}$.

Like the Weiner filter, the PSE filter also assumes that the noise is signal independent. Since

$$\hat{F} = QS = Q(PF + N)$$

and given that $N^*F = 0$ and $F^*N = 0$, we have

$$| \hat{F} |^2 = \hat{F}\hat{F}^* = | Q |^2 \, (| P |^2 | F |^2 + | N |^2)$$

The criterion above can therefore be written as

$$| F |^2 = | Q |^2 \, (| P |^2 | F |^2 + | N |^2)$$

Solving for $| Q |$, $\hat{f}$ is then given by

$$\hat{f}(x) = \hat{F}_1^{-1}(| Q | S)$$

where $| Q |$ is the PSE filter given by

$$\text{PSE filter} \;=\; \left(\frac{1}{| P |^2 + | N |^2 / | F |^2} \right)^{1/2}$$

Like the Weiner filter, in the absence of accurate estimates for $| N |^2$ and $| F |^2$, we approximate the PSE filter by

$$\text{PSE filter} \;\simeq\; \left(\frac{1}{| P |^2 + \Gamma} \right)^{1/2}$$

where

$$\Gamma = \frac{1}{(\text{SNR})^2}$$

Note, that the criterion used to derive this filter can be written in the form

$$\int (| F(k) |^2 - | \hat{F}(k) |^2) dk = 0$$

or using Parseval's theorem

$$\int (| f(x) |^2 - | \hat{f}(x) |^2) dx = 0$$

cf. Criterion for the Weiner filter, i.e.

$$\text{minimize} \quad \int \mid f(x) - \hat{f}(x) \mid^2 dx$$

8.5 THE MATCHED FILTER

Matched filtering is based on correlating the signal s with the complex conjugate of the instrument function p. The estimate $\hat{f}$ of f can therefore be written as

$$\hat{f}(x) = p^*(x) \odot s(x)$$

Assuming that $n(x) = 0$, so that

$$s(x) = p(x) \otimes f(x)$$

we have

$$\hat{f}(x) = p^* \odot p(x) \otimes f(x)$$

which in Fourier space is

$$\hat{F}(k) = \mid P(k) \mid^2 F(k)$$

Observe, that the amplitude spectrum of $\hat{F}$ is given by $\mid P \mid^2 \mid F \mid$ and that the phase information is determined by F alone (i.e. the phase spectrum of $\hat{F}$ is given by $\arg(F)$).

Criterion for the matched filter

The criterion for the matched filter is as follows. Given that

$$s = p \otimes f + n$$

the match filter provides an estimate for f of the form

$$\hat{f} = q \otimes s$$

where q is chosen in such a way that the ratio

$$R = \frac{\mid \int QP dk \mid^2}{\int \mid N \mid^2 \mid Q \mid^2 dk}$$

is a maximum. The matched filter Q is found by first writing

$$QP = \mid N \mid Q \times \frac{P}{\mid N \mid}$$

and then using the Schwarz inequality

$$\left|\int QP dk\right|^2 = \left|\int |N| Q \frac{P}{|N|} dk\right|^2 \leq \int |N|^2 |Q|^2 \, dk \int \frac{|P|^2}{|N|^2} dk$$

From this result and the definition of R given above we get

$$R \leq \int \frac{|P|^2}{|N|^2} dk$$

Now, recall that the criterion for the matched filter is that R is a maximum. If this is the case, then

$$R = \int \frac{|P|^2}{|N|^2} dk$$

or

$$\left|\int |N| Q \frac{P}{|N|} dk\right|^2 = \int |N|^2 |Q|^2 \, dk \int \frac{|P|^2}{|N|^2} dk$$

This is true, if and only if

$$|N| Q = \frac{P^*}{|N|}$$

because we then have

$$\left|\int \frac{|P|^2}{|N|^2} dk\right|^2 = \int \frac{|P|^2}{|N|^2} dk \int \frac{|P|^2}{|N|^2} dk$$

Thus, R is a maximum when

$$Q = \frac{P^*}{|N|^2}$$

White noise

If the noise n is white, then its power spectrum is a constant, i.e.

$$|N(k)|^2 = N_0^2$$

In this case

$$Q = \frac{P^*}{N_0^2}$$

and

$$\hat{F} = \frac{P^*}{N_0^2} S$$

Hence, for white noise, the match filter provides an estimate which may be written in the form

$$\hat{f} = \frac{1}{N_0^2} p^* \odot s$$

Deconvolution of chirped pulses

The matched filter is frequently used in systems that utilize linear frequency modulated (FM) pulses. Pulses of this type are known as chirped pulses. Examples where this particular type of pulse is used include radar, active sonar and some forms of seismic prospecting called Vibroseis. The application of this technique to coherent radar imaging has already been covered in Chapter 7.

The linear FM pulse is given by

$$p(x) = \exp(i\alpha x^2), \quad |x| \le X$$

where α is a constant and X is the length of the pulse. The phase of this pulse is αx^2 and the instantaneous frequency is given by

$$\frac{d}{dx}(\alpha x^2) = 2\alpha x$$

which varies linearly with x. Hence, the frequency modulations are linear which is why the pulse is referred to as a linear FM pulse. In this case, the signal that is received is given by (neglecting additive noise)

$$s(x) = \exp(i\alpha x^2) \otimes f(x), \quad |x| \le X$$

After matched filtering, we get

$$\hat{f}(x) = \exp(-i\alpha x^2) \odot \exp(i\alpha x^2) \otimes f(x)$$

Now,

$$\exp(-i\alpha x^2) \odot \exp(i\alpha x^2) = \int\limits_{-X/2}^{X/2} \exp[-i\alpha(y+x)^2] \exp(i\alpha y^2) dy$$

$$= \exp(-i\alpha x^2) \int\limits_{-X/2}^{X/2} \exp(2i\alpha yx)dy$$

Evaluating the integral over y, we have

$$\exp(-i\alpha x^2) \odot \exp(i\alpha x^2) = X \exp(-i\alpha x^2) \operatorname{sinc}(\alpha X x)$$

and hence

$$\hat{f}(x) = X \exp(-i\alpha x^2) \operatorname{sinc}(\alpha X x) \otimes f(x)$$

In some systems the length of the linear FM pulse is relatively long. For example, some radars utilize pulses where $X \sim 3000$ m. In this case,

$$\cos(\alpha x^2) \operatorname{sinc}(\alpha X x) \simeq \operatorname{sinc}(\alpha X x)$$

and

$$\sin(\alpha x^2) \operatorname{sinc}(\alpha X x) \simeq 0$$

and so

$$\hat{f}(x) \simeq X \operatorname{sinc}(\alpha X x) \otimes f(x)$$

In Fourier space, this last equation can be written as

$$\hat{F}(k) = \frac{\pi}{\alpha} F(k), \quad | \, k \, | \leq X$$

$$= 0, \quad \text{otherwize}$$

The estimate $\hat{f}$ is therefore a band limited estimate of f whose bandwidth is determined by the product of the chirping parameter α with the length of the pulse X.

8.6 CONSTRAINED DECONVOLUTION

Constrained deconvolution provides a filter which gives the user additional control over the deconvolution process. This method is based on minimizing a linear operation on the object f of the form $g \otimes f$ subject to some other constraint. Using the least squares approach, we find an estimate for f by minimizing $\|g \otimes f\|^2$ subject to the constraint

$$\|s - p \otimes f\|^2 = \|n\|^2$$

Using this result, we can write

$$\|g \otimes f\|^2 = \|g \otimes f\|^2 + \lambda(\|s - p \otimes f\|^2 - \|n\|^2)$$

because quantity inside the brackets on the right hand side is zero. The constant λ is called the Lagrange multiplier. Using the orthogonality principle, $\|g \otimes f\|^2$ is a minimum when

$$(g \otimes f) \odot g^* - \lambda(s - p \otimes f) \odot p^* = 0$$

In Fourier space, this equation becomes

$$|G|^2 F - \lambda(SP^* - |P|^2 F) = 0$$

Solving for F, we get

$$F = \frac{SP^*}{|P|^2 + \gamma |G|^2}$$

where γ is the reciprocal of the Lagrange multiplier ($= 1/\lambda$). Hence, the constrained least squares filter is given by

$$\text{Constrained least squares filter} = \frac{P^*}{|P|^2 + \gamma |G|^2}$$

The important point about this filter is that it allows the user to change G to suite a particular application. This filter can be thought of as a generalization of the other filters. For example, if $\gamma = 0$ then the inverse filter is obtained, if $\gamma = 1$ and $|G|^2 = |N|^2 / |F|^2$ then the Weiner is obtained, and if $\gamma = 1$ and $|G|^2 = |N|^2 - |P|^2$ then the matched filter is obtained.

Discussion

Table 8.1 lists the filters discussed in this chapter. Although the discussion has been restricted to one dimension-functions, these filters can also be derived using an equivalent two-dimensional analysis. Also, in both cases, they can be used to process digital data. The list of filters given in Table 8.1 can therefore be used to deconvolve both digital signals and digital images. In each case, the filter Q provides a solution to the inversion of the following equations for f

$$s = p \otimes f + n \qquad \qquad 1D$$

Table 8.1 The filters Q used to deconvolve a signal or an image with additive noise using linear restoration. (The symbols are defined below.)

Name of filter	Formula	Condition
Inverse filter	$Q = P*/|P|^2$	Minimize $\|n\|^2$
Weiner filter	$Q = \dfrac{P*}{|P|^2 + |F|^2/|N|^2}$	Minimize $\|f - q \otimes s\|^2$
		$N*F = 0; F*N = 0$
PSE filter	$Q = \left(\dfrac{1}{|P|^2 + |F|^2/|N|^2}\right)^{\frac{1}{2}}$	$|F|^2 = |QS|^2$
		$N*F = 0; F*N = 0$
Matched filter	$Q = P*/|N|^2$	Maximize $\left(\dfrac{\|\int QP\,dk\|^2}{\int|N|^2|Q|^2\,dk}\right)$
Constrained deconvolution	$Q = \dfrac{P*}{|P|^2 + \gamma|G|^2}$	Minimize $\|g \otimes f\|^2$

P Fourier transform of the point spread function p
f object function
F Fourier transform of f
s signal (1D) or image (2D)
S Fourier transform of s
n noise
N Fourier transform of n
γ $1/2\lambda$ where λ is the Lagrange multiplier

or

$$s = p \otimes \otimes f + n \qquad\qquad 2D$$

The solution for f is given by

$$f = \mathrm{IFT}(QS)$$

where IFT stands for the 1D or 2D inverse Fourier transform and S is the Fourier transfrom (complex spectrum) of the signal s.

8.7 A LINEAR DECONVOLUTION PROGRAM: 2D WEINER FILTER

As an introduction to linear deconvolution programming, an example of a routine for computing the 2D Weiner filter is presented below. This program employs the subroutine FFT2D given in section 2.11 and requires the user to specify the point spread function and the signal to noise ratio of the image.

(a)

(b)

(*c*)

Figure 8.1   Weiner-filtered optical image of the planet Saturn using a Gaussian point spread function: (*a*) original image; (*b*) Weiner-filtered (SNR = 4); (*c*) Weiner-filtered (SNR = 8)

```
      SUBROUTINE WEINER(S,P,F,N,SNR)
C
C FUNCTION: THIS SUBROUTINE DECONVOLVES AN IMAGE
C           USING THE WEINER FILTER.
C
      REAL S(64,64),P(64,64),F(64,64)
      REAL SS(64,64),PP(64,64),FF(64,64)
C
C S - IMAGE
C P - POINT SPREAD FUNCTION
C F - OUTPUT (DECONVOLVED IMAGE)
C SNR - SIGNAL TO NOISE RATIO.
C
C COMPUTE THE SQUARE OF 1/SNR.
C
```

267

```
      GAMMA=1./(SNR*SNR)
C
C INITIALIZE IMAGINARY ARRAYS.
C
      DO J=1,N
      DO I=1,N
      SS(I,J)=0.
      PP(I,J)=0.
      FF(I,J)=0.
      ENDDO
      ENDDO
C
C COMPUTE THE FOURIER TRANSFORMS OF THE
C IMAGE S AND THE POINT SPREAD FUNCTION P.
C
      CALL FFT2D(S,SS,N,-1)
      CALL FFT2D(P,PP,N,-1)
C
C COMPUTE THE WEINER FILTER AND MULTIPLY
C WITH THE COMPLEX SPECTRUM OF THE IMAGE.
C
      DO J=1,N
      DO I=1,N
      DENOM=P(I,J)*P(I,J)+PP(I,J)*PP(I,J)+GAMMA
      F(I,J)=(P(I,J)*S(I,J)+PP(I,J)*SS(I,J))/DENOM
      FF(I,J)=(P(I,J)*SS(I,J)-PP(I,J)*S(I,J))/DENOM
      ENDDO
      ENDDO
C
C COMPUTE THE INVERSE FOURIER TRANSFORM.
C
      CALL FFT2D(F,FF,N,1)
C
      RETURN
      END
```

An example of Weiner filtering using the subroutine above is given in figure 8.1. This shows a blurred optical (incoherent) image of the planet Saturn before and after it has been Weiner filtered using a Gausian point spread function (variance = 10 pixels) and SNR=4 and 8.

SUMMARY OF IMPORTANT RESULTS

Least squares principle

If $\hat{f}$ is an estimate of f, then the least squares estimate is obtained by finding $\hat{f}$ such that

$$e = \|f(x) - \hat{f}(x)\|^2$$

is a minimum.

Orthogonality principle

1. Linear polynomial model: If

$$\hat{f}(x) = \sum_n a_n y_n(x)$$

then the coefficients a_n which minimize the mean square error e defined above are found be solving the equation

$$\langle f - \hat{f}, y_m^* \rangle = 0$$

The error $f - \hat{f}$ is orthogonal to the signals y_m^*.

2. Linear convolution model: If

$$\hat{f}(x) = a(x) \otimes y(x)$$

then the function a which minimizes the mean square error e defined above is obtained by solving the equation

$$(f - \hat{f}) \odot y^* = 0$$

Linear deconvolution

1. Weiner filter: If

$$s(x) = p(x) \otimes f(x) + n(x)$$

the object function f is found by minimizing the mean square error

$$e = \|f(x) - \hat{f}(x)\|^2$$

where
$$\hat{f}(x) = q(x) \otimes s(x)$$
The solution to this problem (i.e. the solution for Q) is called the Weiner filter. For signal independent noise, the Weiner filter is given by
$$Q(k) = \frac{P^*(k)}{|P(k)|^2 + |N(k)|^2 / |F(k)|^2}$$

2. Matched filter: If
$$s(x) = p(x) \otimes f(x) + n(x)$$
then the matched filtered estimate of f is given by
$$\hat{f}(x) = p^*(x) \odot s(x)$$
This filter is used extensively in cases when p is a linear FM or chirped pulse of the form
$$p(x) = \exp(i\alpha x^2)$$

FURTHER READING

1. Papoulis A, *Signal Analysis*, McGraw-Hill, 1977. This is a mathematically intensive book but it covers a wide range of relavent topics including the least squares principle and the orthogonality principle. It also provides a detailed discussion on the Weiner filter and matched filter.

2. Rosenfeld A and Kak A C, *Digital Picture Processing*, Computer Science and Applied Mathematics, Academic Press, 1980. This book includes a readable derivation of the 2D Weiner filter.

3. Bates R H T and McDonnell M J, *Image Restoration and Reconstruction*, Clarendon Press, Oxford, 1986. Deconvolution is discussed in chapter 3. Some good examples of Weiner filtering are provided at the end of this chapter.

4. Robinon E A and Silvia M T, *Digital Signal Processing and Time Series Analysis*, Holden-Day, 1978. As well as being a useful introduction to digital signal processing, this book contains chapters on seismic deconvolution (chapter 10) and speech deconvolution.

9 Deconvolution II: Nonlinear restoration

The processes discussed in the last chapter did not take into account the statistical nature of the noise or the signal. To do this, another type of theory must be used which is nonlinear. Just as the least squares principle is the basis for linear restoration, the basis of nonlinear restoration is a result in probability theory called Bayes rule.

9.1 BAYES RULE AND BAYESIAN ESTIMATION

The probability of an event

Suppose we toss a coin, observe whether we get heads or tails and then repeat this process a number of times. As the number of trials increases, we expect that the number of times heads or tails occurs is half that of the number of trials. In other words, the probability of getting heads is $1/2$ and the probability of getting tails is also $1/2$. Similarly, if a dice with six faces is thrown repeatedly, then the probability of it landing on any one particular face is $1/6$. In general, if an experiment is repeated N times and an event A occurs n times, then the probability of this event $P(A)$ is defined as

$$P(A) = \lim_{N \to \infty} \left(\frac{n}{N} \right)$$

The probability is the relative frequency of an event as the number of trials tends to infinity. In practice, only a finite number of trials can be conducted and we therefore define the probability of an event A as

$$P(A) = \frac{n}{N}$$

In the analysis that follows, N is taken to approach infinity.

The joint probability

Suppose we have two coins which we label $C1$ and $C2$. We toss both coins simultaneously N times and record the number of times $C1$ is heads, the number of times $C2$ is heads and the number of times $C1$ and $C2$ are heads together. What is the probability that $C1$ and $C2$ are heads together ? Clearly, if m is the number of times out of N trials that heads occurs simultaneously, then the probability of such an event must be given by

$$P(C1 \ \text{heads} \ \text{and} \ C2 \ \text{heads}) = \frac{m}{N}$$

This is known as the joint probability of $C1$ being heads when $C2$ is heads. In general, if two events A and B are possible and m is the number of times both events occur simultaneously, then the joint probability is given by

$$P(A \ \text{and} \ B) = \frac{m}{N}$$

The conditional probability

Suppose we setup an experiment in which two events A and B can occur. We conduct N trials and record the number of times A occurs (which is n) and the number of times A and B occur simultaneously (which is m). In this case, the joint probability may written as

$$P(A \ \text{and} \ B) = \frac{m}{N} = \frac{m}{n} \times \frac{n}{N}$$

Now, the quotient n/N is the probability $P(A)$ that event A occurs. The quotient m/n is the probability that events A and B occur simultaneously given that event A has already occurred.

The latter probability is known as the conditional probability and is written as

$$P(B \mid A) = \frac{m}{n}$$

where the symbol $B \mid A$ means 'B given A'. Hence, the joint probability can be written as

$$P(A \text{ and } B) = P(A)P(B \mid A)$$

Suppose that we do a similar type of experiment but this time we record the number of times p that event B occurs and the number of times q that event A occurs simultaneously with event B. In this case, the joint probability of events B and A occurring together is given by

$$P(B \text{ and } A) = \frac{q}{N} = \frac{q}{p} \times \frac{p}{N}$$

The quotient p/N is the probability $P(B)$ that event B occurs and the quotient q/p is the probability of getting events B and A occurring simultaneously given that event B has already occurred. The latter probability is just the probability of getting A 'given' B, i.e.

$$P(A \mid B) = \frac{q}{p}$$

Hence, we have

$$P(B \text{ and } A) = P(B)P(A \mid B)$$

Bayes rule

The probability of getting A and B occurring simultaneously is exactly the same as getting B and A together, i.e.

$$P(A \text{ and } B) = P(B \text{ and } A)$$

Hence, by using the definition of these joint probabilities in terms of the conditional probabilities we arrive at the following formula

$$P(A)P(B \mid A) = P(B)P(A \mid B)$$

or alternatively

$$P(B \mid A) = \frac{P(B)P(A \mid B)}{P(A)}$$

This result is known as Bayes rule. It relates the conditional probability of B given A to that of A given B.

Bayesian estimation

In signal analysis Bayes rule is written in the form

$$P(f \mid s) = \frac{P(f)P(s \mid f)}{P(s)}$$

where f is the object that we want to recover from the signal

$$s(x) = p(x) \otimes f(x) + n(x)$$

This result is the basis for a class of nonlinear restoration methods which are known collectively as Bayes estimators.

In simple terms, Bayesian estimation attempts to recover f in such a way that the probability of getting f given s is a maximum. In practice this is done by assuming that $P(f)$ and $P(s \mid f)$ obey certain statistical distributions which are consistent with the experiment in which s is measured. In other words, models are chosen for $P(f)$ and $P(s \mid f)$ and then f is computed at the point where $P(f \mid s)$ reaches its maximum value. This occurs when

$$\frac{\partial}{\partial f} P(f \mid s) = 0$$

The functions P are known as the probability density functions or pdfs. The pdf $P(f \mid s)$ is called the *a posteriori* pdf. Since the logarithm of a function varies monatonically with that function, the *a posteriori* pdf is also a maximum when

$$\frac{\partial}{\partial f} \ln P(f \mid s) = 0$$

Now, using Bayes rule, we can write this equation as

$$\frac{\partial}{\partial f} \ln P(s \mid f) + \frac{\partial}{\partial f} \ln P(f) = 0 \tag{9.1.1}$$

Because the solution to this equation for f maximizes the *a posteriori* pdf, this method is known as the maximum *a posteriori* or MAP method. To illustrate the principles of Baysian estimation, we shall now present some simple examples of how this technique can be applied to data analysis.

Example 1: Suppose that we measure a single sample s (one real number) in an experiment where it is known *a priori* that

$$s = f + n$$

where n is noise (a random number). Suppose that it is also known *a priori* that the noise is determined by a Gaussian distribution of the form

$$P(n) = \frac{1}{\sqrt{2\pi\sigma_n^2}} \exp(-n^2/2\sigma_n^2)$$

where σ_n^2 is the standard deviation of the noise. Now, the probability of measuring s given f (i.e. the conditional probability $P(s \mid f)$) is determined by the noise since

$$n = s - f$$

We can therefore write

$$P(s \mid f) = \frac{1}{\sqrt{2\pi\sigma_n^2}} \exp[-(s - f)^2/2\sigma_n^2]$$

To find the MAP estimate, the pdf for f must also be known. Suppose that f also has a zero-mean Gaussian distribution of the form

$$P(f) = \frac{1}{\sqrt{2\pi\sigma_f^2}} \exp(-f^2/2\sigma_f^2)$$

Then,

$$\frac{\partial}{\partial f} \ln P(s \mid f) + \frac{\partial}{\partial f} \ln P(f) = \frac{(s - f)}{\sigma_n^2} - \frac{f}{\sigma_f^2} = 0$$

Solving this equation for f gives

$$f = \frac{s\Gamma^2}{1 + \Gamma^2}$$

where Γ is the signal to noise ratio

$$\Gamma = \frac{\sigma_f}{\sigma_n}$$

Notice, that as $\sigma_n \to 0$, $f \to s$ which must be true since $s = f + n$ and n has a zero-mean Gaussian distribution. Also, note that the solution we acquire for f is entirely dependent on the prior information we have on the pfd for f. A different pdf produces an entirely different solution. For example, suppose it is known

275

or we have good reason to assume that f obeys a Rayleigh distribution of the form

$$P(f) = \frac{f}{\sigma_f^2} \exp(-f^2/2\sigma_f^2), \quad f \geq 0$$

$$0, \quad f < 0$$

In this case,

$$\frac{\partial}{\partial f} \ln P(f) = \frac{1}{f} - \frac{f}{\sigma_f^2}$$

and equation (9.1.1) becomes (still assuming that the noise obeys the same zero-mean Gaussian distribution)

$$\frac{(s-f)}{\sigma_n^2} + \frac{1}{f} - \frac{f}{\sigma_f^2} = 0$$

This equation is quadratic in f. Solving this equation, we get

$$f = \frac{s\Gamma^2}{2(1+\Gamma^2)} \left(1 \pm \sqrt{1 + \frac{4\sigma_n^2}{s^2\Gamma^2}\left(1 + \frac{1}{\Gamma^2}\right)} \right)$$

The solution for f which maximizes the value of $P(f \mid s)$, can then be written in the form

$$f = \frac{s}{2a}\left(1 + \sqrt{1 + \frac{4a\sigma_n^2}{s^2}}\right)$$

where

$$a = 1 + \frac{1}{\Gamma^2}$$

This is a nonlinear estimate for f. If

$$\frac{2\sigma_n\sqrt{a}}{s} \ll 1$$

then

$$f \simeq \frac{s}{a}$$

In this case, f is linearly related to s. In fact, this linearized estimate is identical to the MAP estimate obtained earlier where it was assumed that f had a Gaussian distribution.

From equation (9.1.1) and the example given above, it should now be clear that Bayesian estimation (i.e. the MAP method) is only as good as the prior information on the statistical behaviour of f - the object for which we seek a solution. However, when $P(f)$ is broadly distributed compared with $P(s \mid f)$, the peak value of the *a posteriori* pdf will lie close to the peak value of $P(f)$. In particular, if $P(f)$ is roughly constant, then $\partial \ln P(f)/\partial f$ is close to zero and therefore

$$\frac{\partial}{\partial f} \ln P(f \mid s) \simeq \frac{\partial}{\partial f} \ln P(s \mid f)$$

In this case, the *a posteriori* pdf is a maximum when

$$\frac{\partial}{\partial f} \ln P(s \mid f) = 0$$

The estimate for f that is obtained by solving this equation for f is called the maximum likelihood or ML estimate. To obtain this estimate, only prior knowledge on the statistical fluctuations of the conditional probability is required. If, as in the previous example, we assume that the noise is a zero-mean Gaussian distribution, then the ML estimate is given by

$$f = s$$

Note that this is the same as the MAP estimate when the standard deviation of the noise is zero.

The basic and rather important difference between the MAP and ML estimates is that the ML estimate ignores prior information about the statistical fluctuations of the object f. It only requires a model for the statistical fluctuations of the noise. For this reason, the ML estimate is usually easier to compute. It is also the estimate to use in cases where there is a complete lack of knowledge about the statistical behaviour of the object.

Example 2: To further illustrate the difference between the MAP and ML estimate and to show their use in signal analysis, consider the case where we measure N samples of a real signal s in the presence of additive noise n which is the result of transmitting a known signal f modified by a random amplitude factor a. The samples of the signal are given by

$$s_i = a f_i + n_i; \quad i = 1, 2, ..., N$$

277

The problem is to find an estimate for a. To solve problems of this type using Bayes estimation, we must introduce multidimensional probability theory. In this case, the pdf is a function of not just one number s but a set of numbers $s_1, s_2, ..., s_N$. It is therefore is vector space. To emphasize this, we use the vector notation

$$P(\mathbf{s}) \equiv P(s_1, s_2, s_3, ..., s_N)$$

The **ML estimate** is given by solving the equation

$$\frac{\partial}{\partial a} \ln P(\mathbf{s} \mid a) = 0$$

for a where

$$P(\mathbf{s} \mid a) \equiv P(s_1, s_2, ..., s_N \mid a)$$

Let us again assume that the noise is described by a zero-mean Gaussian distribution of the form

$$P(\mathbf{n}) \equiv P(n_1, n_2, ..., n_N) = \frac{1}{\sqrt{2\pi\sigma_n^2}} \exp\left(-\frac{1}{2\sigma_n^2} \sum_{i=1}^{N} n_i^2\right)$$

The conditional probability is then given by

$$P(\mathbf{s} \mid a) = \frac{1}{\sqrt{2\pi\sigma_n^2}} \exp\left(-\frac{1}{2\sigma_n^2} \sum_{i=1}^{N} (s_i - af_i)^2\right)$$

and

$$\frac{\partial}{\partial a} \ln P(\mathbf{s} \mid a) = \frac{1}{\sigma_n^2} \sum_{i=1}^{N} (s_i - af_i)f_i = 0$$

Solving this last equation for a we obtain the ML estimate

$$a = \frac{\displaystyle\sum_{i=1}^{N} s_i f_i}{\displaystyle\sum_{i=1}^{N} f_i^2}$$

The **MAP estimate** is obtained by solving the equation

$$\frac{\partial}{\partial a} \ln P(\mathbf{s} \mid a) + \frac{\partial}{\partial a} \ln P(a) = 0$$

for a. Using the same distribution for the conditional pdf, let us assume that a has a zero-mean Gaussian distribution of the form

$$P(a) = \frac{1}{\sqrt{2\pi\sigma_a^2}} \exp(-a^2/2\sigma_a^2)$$

where σ_a^2 is the standard deviation of a. In this case,

$$\frac{\partial}{\partial a} \ln P(a) = -\frac{a}{\sigma_a^2}$$

and hence, the MAP estimate is obtained by solving the equation

$$\frac{\partial}{\partial a} \ln P(\mathbf{s} \mid a) + \frac{\partial}{\partial a} \ln P(a)$$

$$= \frac{1}{\sigma_n^2} \sum_{i=1}^{N} (s_i - af_i)f_i - \frac{a}{\sigma_a^2} = 0$$

for a. The solution to this equation is given by

$$a = \frac{\frac{\sigma_a^2}{\sigma_n^2} \sum_{i=1}^{N} s_i f_i}{1 + \frac{\sigma_a^2}{\sigma_n^2} \sum_{i=1}^{N} f_i^2}$$

Note, that if $\sigma_a \gg \sigma_n$, then,

$$a \simeq \frac{\sum_{i=1}^{N} s_i f_i}{\sum_{i=1}^{N} f_i^2}$$

which is the same as the ML estimate.

9.2 MAXIMUM LIKELIHOOD FILTER

In the last section, the principles of Bayesian estimation were presented. We shall now use these principles to design deconvolution algorithms. The problem is as follows: Given the complex digital signal

$$s_i = \sum_j p_{i-j} f_j + n_i$$

find an estimate for f_i when p_i is known together with the statistics for n_i. In this section, the ML estimate is derived.

The ML estimate for f_i is determined by solving the equation

$$\frac{\partial}{\partial f_k} \ln P(s_1, s_2, .., s_N \mid f_1, f_2, ..., f_N) = 0$$

As before, the algebraic form of the estimate depends upon the model that is chosen for the pdf. Let us assume that the noise has a zero-mean Gaussian distribution. In this case, the conditional pdf is given by

$$P(\mathbf{s} \mid \mathbf{f}) = \frac{1}{\sqrt{2\pi\sigma_n^2}} \exp\left(-\frac{1}{2\sigma_n^2} \sum_i \mid s_i - \sum_j p_{i-j}f_j \mid^2\right)$$

where σ_n^2 is the standard deviation of the noise. Substituting this result into the previous equation and differentiating, we get

$$\frac{1}{\sigma_n^2} \sum_i \left(s_i - \sum_j p_{i-j}f_j\right) p_{i-k}^* = 0$$

or

$$\sum_i s_i p_{i-k}^* = \sum_i \left(\sum_j p_{i-j}f_j\right) p_{i-k}^*$$

Using the appropriate symbols, we may write this equation in the form

$$s_n \odot p_n^* = (p_n \otimes f_n) \odot p_n^*$$

where $\odot$ and $\otimes$ denote the correlation and convolution sums respectively. The ML estimate is obtained by solving the equation above for f_n. This can be done by transforming it into Fourier space. Using the correlation and convolution theorems, in Fourier space this equation becomes

$$S_m P_m^* = (P_m F_m)P_m^*$$

and thus

$$f_n = \hat{F}_1^{-1} F_m = \hat{F}_1^{-1}\left(\frac{S_m P_m^*}{\mid P_m \mid^2}\right)$$

where $\hat{F}_1^{-1}$ is taken to denote the inverse DFT. Hence for Gaussian statistics, the ML filter is given by

$$\text{ML filter} \quad = \frac{P_m^*}{\mid P_m \mid^2}$$

which is identical to the inverse filter.

9.3 MAXIMUM *A POSTERIORI* FILTER

This filter is obtained by finding f_i such that

$$\frac{\partial}{\partial f_k} \ln P(s_1, s_2, ..., s_n \mid f_1, f_2, ..., f_n) + \frac{\partial}{\partial f_k} \ln P(f_1, f_2, ..., f_n) = 0$$

Consider the following models for the pdfs

1. Gaussian statistics for the noise

$$P(\mathbf{s} \mid \mathbf{f}) = \frac{1}{\sqrt{2\pi\sigma_n^2}} \exp\left(\frac{1}{2\sigma_n^2} \sum_i \mid s_i - \sum_j p_{i-j} f_j \mid^2\right)$$

2. Zero-mean Gaussian distribution for the object

$$P(\mathbf{f}) = \frac{1}{\sqrt{2\pi\sigma_f^2}} \exp\left(-\frac{1}{2\sigma_f^2} \sum_i \mid f_i \mid^2\right)$$

By substituting these expressions for $P(\mathbf{s} \mid \mathbf{f})$ and $P(\mathbf{f})$ into the equation above, we obtain

$$\frac{1}{\sigma_n^2} \sum_i \left(s_i - \sum_j p_{i-j} f_j\right) p_{i-k}^* - \frac{1}{\sigma_f^2} f_k = 0$$

Rearranging, we may write this result in the form

$$s_n \odot p_n^* = \frac{\sigma_n^2}{\sigma_f^2} f_n + (p_n \otimes f_n) \odot p_n^*$$

In Fourier space, this equation becomes

$$S_m P_m^* = \frac{1}{\Gamma^2} F_m + \mid P_m \mid^2 F_m$$

The MAP filter for Gaussian statistics is therefore given by

$$\text{MAP} \quad \text{filter} = \frac{P_m^*}{\mid P_m \mid^2 + 1/\Gamma^2}$$

where

$$\Gamma = \frac{\sigma_f}{\sigma_n} - \text{the signal to noise ratio}$$

Note, that this filter is the same as the Weiner filter under the assumption that the power spectra of the noise and object are constant. Also, note that

$$\lim_{\sigma_n \to 0} (\text{MAP} \quad \text{filter}) = \text{ML} \quad \text{filter}$$

9.4 THE MAXIMUM ENTROPY FILTER

The entropy of a system describes its disorder. In other words, it is a measure of the lack of information about the exact state of a system. In signal analysis, the entropy of a signal is a measure of its fluctuation. A highly fluctuating signal with large changes in its phase and amplitude modulations over small time steps has a large entropy whereas a smoothly varying signal has a relatively low entropy. Maximum entropy analysis is useful in cases where it is known *a priori* that the object which one is attempting to reconstruct by deconvolving the signal, is a rapidly fluctuating function. In the absence of accurate knowledge about the exact entropy of the object (which is usually the case in practice), we aim at a reconstruction whose entropy is a maximum. Similarly, if the object is known to be a smoothly vary function with a low entropy then we aim at a reconstruction for the object with minimum entropy (i.e. we apply a minimum entropy analysis).

The general definition for the entropy of a system E is

$$E = \sum_i P_i \ln P_i$$

where P_i is the probability that the system is in a state i. Maximum entropy deconvolution is based on modelling the object f as a pdf using Maxwell-Boltzmann statistics. A reconstruction for f is found such that

$$E = \sum_i f_i \ln f_i$$

is a maximum. Because of the nature of the logarithmic function this type of solution must be restricted to cases where f_i is real and positive.

The signal s_i is given by

$$s_i = \sum_j p_{i-j} f_j + n_i$$

We can therefore write the entropy as

$$E = \sum_i f_i \ln f_i + \lambda \left(\sum_i | s_i - \sum_j p_{i-j} f_j |^2 - \sum_i | n_i |^2 \right)$$

where λ is the Lagrange multiplier. This entropy is a maximum when

$$\frac{\partial E}{\partial f_k} = 0$$

Differentiating, we obtain

$$1 + \ln f_n - \lambda(s_n \odot p_n^* - p_n \otimes f_n \odot p_n^*) = 0$$

or rearranging

$$f_n = \exp[-1 + \lambda(s_n \odot p_n^* - p_n \otimes f_n \odot p_n^*)]$$

This equation is transcendental in f_n and as such, requires that f_n is evaluated iteratively, i.e.

$$f_n^{k+1} = \exp[-1 + \lambda(s_n \odot p_n^* - p_n \otimes f_n^k \odot p_n^*)]$$

The rate of convergence of this solution is determined by the value of the Lagrange multiplier. The efficiency and overall success of maximum entropy deconvolution therefore depends on the value of the Lagrange multiplier chosen by the user. In general, the iterative nature of this nonlinear solution is undesirable because it is time consuming and may require many iterations before convergence is achieved. For this reason a linear approximation is useful. This is obtained by retaining just the first two terms (i.e. the linear terms) in the Taylor series expansion of the exponential function which gives the following equation

$$f_n = \lambda(s_n \odot p_n^* - p_n \otimes f_n \odot p_n^*)$$

283

Table 9.1 List of filters Q used to deconvolve a signal or image with additive noise using nonlinear restoration methods. (The symbols are defined below)

Name of filter	Formula	Condition
Maximum likelihood	$Q = P^*/|P|^2$	Gaussian noise
Maximum *a posteriori*	$Q = \dfrac{P^*}{|P|^2 + \sigma_n^2/\sigma_f^2}$	Gaussian noise and object
Maximum entropy	$Q = \dfrac{P^*}{|P|^2 + 1/\lambda}$	Linear approximation

P Fourier transform of the point spread function
σ_f Variance of the object
σ_n Variance of the noise
λ Lagrange multiplier

In Fourier space, this equation is

$$F_m = \lambda S_m P_m^* - \lambda \mid P_m \mid^2 F_m$$

Solving for F_m, we get

$$F_m = \frac{S_m P_m^*}{\mid P_m \mid^2 + 1/\lambda}$$

The linearized maximum entropy filter is therefore given by

$$\text{Maximum entropy filter} = \frac{P_m^*}{\mid P_m \mid^2 + 1/\lambda}$$

Notice, that the algebraic form of this function is very similar to the MAP filter in the sense that $1/\mid P_m \mid^2$ is regularized by a user defined constant. This filter together with a list of the other filters which have been discussed so far in this chapter are given in Table 9.1.

9.5 HOMOMORPHIC FILTER

The homomorphic filter employs the properties of the logarithm to write the equation

$$S(k) = P(k)F(k)$$

in the form

$$\ln S(k) = \ln P(k) + \ln F(k)$$

In this case, the object function f can be recovered using the formula

$$f = \hat{F}_1^{-1}[\exp(\ln S - \ln P)] \tag{9.5.1}$$

This type of operation is known as homomorphic filtering. In practice, deconvolution by homomorphic processing replaces the problems associated with computing the inverse filter $1/P$ with computing the logarithm of a complex function (i.e. computing the functions $\ln S$ and $\ln P$).

By writing the complex sepctra S and P in terms of their amplitude and phase spectra, we get

$$S = A_S \exp(i\theta_S)$$

and

$$P = A_P \exp(i\theta_P)$$

where A_S and A_P are the amplitude spectra of S and P respectively and θ_S and θ_P are the phase spectra of S and P respectively. These parameters are defined by the equations

$$A_S = \sqrt{S_r^2 + S_i^2}; \quad S_r = \text{Re}[S], \quad S_i = \text{Im}[S]$$

$$A_P = \sqrt{P_r^2 + P_i^2}; \quad P_r = \text{Re}[P], \quad P_i = \text{Im}[P]$$

$$\theta_S = \tan^{-1}\left(\frac{S_i}{S_r}\right), \quad -\frac{\pi}{2} \leq \theta_S \leq \frac{\pi}{2}$$

$$\theta_P = \tan^{-1}\left(\frac{P_i}{P_r}\right), \quad -\frac{\pi}{2} \leq \theta_P \leq \frac{\pi}{2}$$

Using these results, equation (9.5.1) can be written in the form

$$f = \hat{F}_1^{-1}[\exp(\ln A_S - \ln A_P)\cos(\theta_S - \theta_P) + i\exp(\ln A_S - \ln A_P)\sin(\theta_S - \theta_P)]$$

9.6 BLIND DECONVOLUTION

All the methods of deconvolution that have been discussed so far (both in this chapter and chapter 8) assume that the instrument function or point spread function is known *a priori*. In some cases however, this function may either by difficult to obtain experimentally or simply not available. In such cases, it must be estimated from the data alone. This is known as blind deconvolution.

Blind deconvolution can be implamented relatively easily if it is known *a priori* that the spectrum of the object is 'white' (i.e. the average value of each Fouirer component is roughly the same over the entire frequency spectrum). In this case, any large scale variations which change the shape of the data spectrum will be due to the frequency distribution of the instrument function. By smoothing the data spectrum, an estimate of the instrument function can be established. This estimate may then be used to deconvolve the data by employing an appropriate filter.

SUMMARY OF IMPORTANT RESULTS

Bayes rule (for signal analysis)

$$P(f \mid s) = \frac{P(s \mid f)P(f)}{P(s)}$$

where P is the probability distribution function and

$$s(x) = p(x) \otimes f(x) + n(x)$$

Maximum likelihood deconvolution: Find f such that

$$\frac{\partial}{\partial f} \ln P(s \mid f) = 0$$

Maximum *a posteriori* deconvolution: Find f such that

$$\frac{\partial}{\partial f} \ln P(s \mid f) + \frac{\partial}{\partial f} \ln P(f) = 0$$

N.B. The MAP estimate is only as good as the prior information on the statistical behaviour of the object f (i.e. the statistical model for $P(f)$).

Maximum entropy deconvolution: Find f such that

$$E = \int f(x) \ln f(x) dx$$

is a maximum. N.B. Maximum entropy analysis may only be considered in cases when f is real and nonnegative.

FURTHER READING

1. Schwartz M and Shaw L, *Signal Processing*, McGraw-Hill, 1975. The estimation of signals in noise using Bayesian estimators is discussed in Chapter 6.

2. Andrews H C and Hunt B R, *Digital Image Reconstruction*, Prentice-Hall, 1977. The principles and applications of both linear and nonlinear reconstruction methods are presented.

10 Deconvolution III: Super resolution

The effect of deconvolving a signal or image is to recover the information it contains by compensating for the blur caused by the instrument function. The resolution of the information obtained by this process is determined by the bandwidth of the data which in turn, is controlled by the finite frequency response of the instrument function. Super resolution is a process which attempts to overcome the limited resolving power of an instrument by designing algorithms which extrapolate the complex spectrum of the information from a finite sample of data. This is known as spectral extrapolation.

10.1 BANDLIMITED FUNCTIONS AND SPECTRAL EXTRAPOLATION

A bandlimited function is a function whose spectral bandwidth is finite. Most real signals are bandlimited functions. The bandwidth determinesthe resolution of a signal. This leads one to consider the problem of how the bandwidth and hence the resolution of the signal, can be increased synthetically. In other words, how can we extrapolate the spectrum of a bandlimited function from an incomplete sample. Solutions to this type of problem are important in signal analysis when a resolution is required that is not a characteristic of the signal provided and is difficult or even impossible to achieve experimentally. The type of resolution obtained by extrapolating the spectrum of a bandlimited function is referred to as super resolution.

The basic problem is an inverse problem. In its simplest form, it is concerned with the inversion of the integral equation

$$s(x) = \int_{-\infty}^{\infty} f(y) \frac{\sin[K(x-y)]}{\pi(x-y)} dy$$

for f where K determines the bandwidth of the signal s and hence the resolution of f. The equation above is a convolution, over the interval $[-\infty, \infty]$. Hence, we may view our problem (i.e. the super resolution problem) in terms of deconvolving s to recover the object f in the special case when the intrument function is a sinc function.

In practice, signals have a finite duration and so

$$f(x) = 0, \quad |x| > X$$

In this case, we can restrict the convolution integral to the interval $[-X, X]$ and model the signal as

$$s(x) = \int_{-X}^{X} f(y) \frac{\sin[K(x-y)]}{\pi(x-y)} dy \tag{10.1.1}$$

In this form, the problem has been studied thoroughly. It is well known that the object can be expressed in the following form

$$f(x) = \sum_{n=0}^{\infty} \lambda_n^{-1} \left[\int_{-X}^{X} s(y)\phi_n(y)dy \right] \phi_n(x)$$

where the eigenfunctions ϕ_n are the prolate spheroidal wave functions given by the solution to the equation

$$\int_{-X}^{X} \phi_n(y) \frac{\sin[K(x-y)]}{\pi(x-y)} dy = \lambda_n \phi_n(x)$$

and λ_n are the associated eigenvalues. Like other theoretical inverse solutions, this solution is extremely sensitive to errors in measuring s (i.e. experimental noise). It is therefore difficult to achieve a stable solution using this method with real signals. Hence, in practice, this solution is of little value.

Using the convolution theorem, we can write equation (10.1.1) in Fourier space as

$$S(k) = H(k)F(k), \quad |k| \le \infty$$

where

$$H(k) = \begin{cases} 1, & |k| \le K \\ 0, & |k| > K \end{cases}$$

or alternatively

$$S(k) = \begin{cases} F(k), & |k| \le K \\ 0, & \text{otherwise} \end{cases}$$

Here, S and F are the Fourier transforms of s and f respectively. In this form, our problem is to recover $F(k)$ for all values of k from $S(k)$. Because f has finite support, its spectrum is analytic and can therefore, in principle, be analytically continued beyond $[-K, K]$ to provide higher resolution. This can be done by computing the Taylor series for F, i.e.

$$F(k) = \sum_{n=-\infty}^{\infty} F^{(n)}(0) \frac{k^n}{n!}$$

The derivatives $F^{(n)}$ of F at $k = 0$ can be determined from the finite segment $F(k), |k| \le K$ which is equal to S. Hence, we can write

$$F(k) = \sum_{n=-\infty}^{\infty} S^{(n)}(0) \frac{k^n}{n!}$$

This method of extrapolation is known as analytic continuation. Once again, although of theoretical interest, in practice this method is fraught with problems. First, it not possible to evaluate $S^{(n)}(0)$ accurately when the signal is noisy. Secondly, the truncation of the Taylor series (which is necessary in practice) yields large errors for large k, and since knowledge of $F(k)$ is required for all values of k, errors of this kind are unacceptable. Thus, in practice, analytic continuation fails even in the presence of small amounts of noise.

There are two important features of equation (10.1.1), and therefore its inversion, which in practice are entirely unsuitable. First, it is assumed that the signal s can be measured without any experimental error; secondly, it is assumed that all the functions are continuous. In practice, we are usually provided with a digital signal which is a discrete set of real or complex numbers. From this digital signal, we can generate discrete Fourier data (via the discrete Fourier transform). These data is related to s via the transform

$$S_n \equiv S(k_n) = \int_{-X}^{X} s(x)\exp(-ik_n x)dx, \quad |k_n| \le K \qquad (10.1.2)$$

where

$$s(x) = f(x) + n(x)$$

They are a set of N numbers and define the bandlimited signal

$$s_{BL}(x) = \sum_{n=-N/2}^{N/2} S_n \exp(ik_n x)$$

This signal may be complex, real and of alternating or fixed polarity depending on the type of experiment that is conducted. In each case, the problem is to reconstruct the object f from N spectral samples in the presence of additive noise n.

The first thing that the reader should understand and always bear in mind is that there no exact, unique or even correct solution to the type of problem that has been presented above. In other words, it is simply not possible to derive a solution as such for f from S_n, only an estimate for it. There are two reasons for this. First, the exact value of the noise n at x is not known, only (at best) the probability of n having a particular value at x. Secondly, even in the absence of noise, this type of problem is ill posed. A problem is well posed, if the solution:

1. exists

2. is unique

3. depends continuously on the data.

If a problem violates any of these conditions, then it is ill posed. It is condition 3 that causes the main problem with digital signals. The finite nature of the data means that there are many permissible solutions to the problem. As a consequence, we are faced with the problem of having to select one particular reconstruction. To overcome this inherent ambiguity, prior knowledge must be used to reduce the class of allowed solutions. For this reason, the use of prior information in the treatment of ill posed problems of this nature is essential.

In addition to prior information, the discrete nature of the data forces one to employ mathematical models for f. In principle, an unlimited number of different models that can be used which accounts for the wide variety and diversity of algorithms that have been designed to cope with problems of this kind. Since all such algorithms attempt to solve the same basic problem, attention should focus on designs which are simple to implement and compute, data adaptive and reliable in the presence of noise of a varying dynamic range.

Because sampled data are always insufficient to specify a unique, correct solution and because no algorithm is able to reconstruct equally well all characteristics of the object, it is essential that the user is able to play a role in the design of the algorithm that is employed and incorporate maximum knowledge of the expected features in the object. This allows optimum use to be made of the available data together with the user's experience, judgement and intuition. Hence, models for the object and conditions for the reconstruction should be utilized which are amenable to modification as knowledge about the object improves. This provides the opportunity for the user to participate in the design of an algorithm by choosing a condition for the reconstruction which is best suited to his or her particular application.

10.2 LINEAR LEAST SQUARES METHODS

Our problem is to solve for f given the data S_n in equation (10.1.2). Let us start by considering a linear polynomial model for $f(x)$ of the following form,

$$f(x) = \sum_n A_n \exp(ik_n x) \tag{10.2.1}$$

where

$$\sum_n \equiv \sum_{n=-N/2}^{N/2}$$

This model for f is just a Fourier series. Clearly, in order to compute f, the coefficients A_n (which are complex numbers) must be known. Hence, given the model above, our problem is reduced to finding a method of computing A_n. How this is done depends on the criterion for the reconstruction that is chosen. The choice depends on a number of factors, such as the nature of the data, the complexity of the resulting algorithm and its computational cost. To start with and as a useful introduction to the problem, we shall consider the least mean square approach. The application of this approach for spectral extrapolation is known as the Gerchberg-Papoulis method. In this case, A_n are chosen in such a way that the mean square error

$$e = \int_{-X}^{X} \mid s(x) - f(x) \mid^2 dx \tag{10.2.2}$$

is a minimum. Since $s = f + n$ this is equivalent to minimizing the noise in the signal. Substituting equation (10.2.1) into equation (10.2.2) and differentiating with respect to A_m we get (using the orthogonality principle)

$$\frac{\partial e}{\partial A_m} = -\int_{-X}^{X} \left(s - \sum_n A_n \exp(ik_n x) \right) \exp(-ik_m x) = 0$$

Using this result, by interchanging the order of integration and summation, we obtain the following equation

$$\int_{-X}^{X} s(x) \exp(-ik_m x) dx = \sum_n A_n \int_{-X}^{X} \exp[-i(k_m - k_n)x] dx \tag{10.2.3}$$

The left hand side of this equation is just the discrete Fourier data that is provided $S(k_n)$ and the integral on the right hand side of this equation gives a sinc function,

$$\int_{-X}^{X} \exp[-i(k_m - k_n)x] dx = 2X \operatorname{sinc}[(k_m - k_n)X]$$

By solving equation (10.2.3) for A_n, the object function $f(x)$ can be obtained from equation (10.2.1). This solution for the object function is a least squares approximation for $f(x)$. To compute A_n from $S(k_n)$, the value of X (the support of the object) needs to be known. We can therefore write $f(x)$ in the closed form,

$$f(x) = w(x) \sum_n A_n \exp(ik_n x) \qquad (10.2.4)$$

where we have introduced the weighting function

$$w(x) = \begin{cases} 1, & \mid x \mid \le X \\ 0, & \mid x \mid > X \end{cases}$$

This function is a simple form of prior information. In this case it is information about the finite extent of the object.

Incorporation of *a priori* **information**

The algebraic form of equation (10.2.4), suggests that the function $w(x)$ is used to incorporate more general prior knowledge about the object. We therefore consider the case where we are given the data $S(k_n)$ defined by equation (10.1.2) together with some form of prior knowledge on the structure of $f(x)$ that can be used to construct a suitable weighting function $w(x)$. This weighting function is then used to compute $f(x)$ as follows:

$$f(x) = w(x) \sum_n A_n \exp(ik_n x) \qquad (10.2.5)$$

Substituting equation (10.2.5) into equation (10.2.2), we find that the error is a minimum when

$$\int_{-X}^{X} s(x)w(x)\exp(-ik_m x)dx = \sum_n A_n \int_{-X}^{X} [w(x)]^2 \exp[-i(k_m - k_n)x]dx$$

Here, we run into a problem which is that for arbitrary functions w (which is what we must assume if different types of prior information are to be incorporated), the integral on the left hand side of the above equation is not the same as the data provided $S(k_n)$. In other words, the equation above cannot be solved from the available data: it is not 'data-consistent'. One way of overcoming this difficulty is to modify equation (10.2.2) and introduce the inverse weighted mean square error

$$e = \int\limits_{-X}^{X} \mid s(x) - f(x) \mid^2 \frac{1}{w(x)} dx \qquad (10.2.6)$$

This is a weighted Hilbert space, designed to provide data consistency. It is a minimum when

$$\int\limits_{-X}^{X} s(x) \exp(-ik_m x) dx = \sum_n A_n \int\limits_{-X}^{X} w(x) \exp[-i(k_m - k_n)x] dx$$

Here, the data on the left hand side of the above equation is equal to $S(k_n)$. We therefore have a data-consistent equation of the form

$$S(k_m) = \sum_n A_n W(k_m - k_n) \qquad (10.2.7)$$

where

$$W(k_m) = \int\limits_{-X}^{X} w(x) \exp(-ik_m x) dx, \quad \mid k_m \mid \le K$$

This method provides a solution which allows arbitrary weighting functions $w(x)$ containing additional prior information on the structure of f to be introduced. The method can be summarized as follows:

1. Given the data $S(k_n)$, construct a weighting function $w(x)$ that is obtained from prior knowledge on the structure of $f(x)$.

2. Compute $W(k_n)$ from $w(x)$.

3. Solve the equation

$$\sum_n A_n W(k_m - k_n) = S(k_m)$$

to obtain the coefficients A_n.

4. Compute the estimate $w(x) \sum_n A_n \exp(ik_n x)$

This algorithm is based on minimizing the inverse weighted mean square error function given by equation (10.2.6). Note, that the algebraic form of this error indicates that w should be greater than zero to avoid singularities occuring in $1/w$. Also note, that when

$$w(x) = 1, \quad \mid x \mid \le X$$

the former least squares estimate is obtained.

Practical considerations

In practice, the data $S(k_n)$ is obtained by taking the discrete Fourier transform (DFT) of some band limited signal $s_{BL}(x)$. The data $W(k_n)$ is obtained by computing the discrete Fourier transform of $w(x)$ and reducing the bandwidth of the spectrum so that it is the same as $S(k_n)$. We then solve equation (10.2.7) to obtain $A(k_n) \equiv A_n$. This equation is just a discrete convolution in Fourier space, i.e.

$$S(k_n) = A(k_n) \otimes W(k_n)$$

where $\otimes$ denotes the convolution sum. Hence, using the convolution theorem, we can write

$$s_{BL}(x) = a(x)w_{BL}(x)$$

where s_{BL} and w_{BL} are bandlimited estimates of $s(x)$ and $w(x)$ respectively given by

$$s_{BL}(x) = \sum_n S(k_n) \exp(ik_n x)$$

$$w_{BL}(x) = \sum_n W(k_n) \exp(ik_n x)$$

and

$$a(x) = \sum_n A(k_n) \exp(ik_n x)$$

From equation (10.2.5) we then have

$$f(x) = w(x) \sum_n A(k_n) \exp(ik_n x) = w(x)a(x)$$

Hence, the minimum mean square estimate of f can be written as

$$f(x) = \frac{w(x)}{w_{BL}(x)} s_{BL}(x)$$

From this equation, it is easy to compute f given s_{BL} and w. All that is required is a DFT to obtain w_{BL} from w. Furthermore, because the orthogonality principle can be applied to two-dimensional problems, the equations listed above may be used to extrapolate the spectrum of a two-dimensional bandlimited signal. A flow diagram of the basic steps that are involved in this process is given in figure 10.1.

The mean square approximation is a linear algebraic method. We shall now examin some nonlinear techniques which are known collectively as Bayes estimates. These include the maximum likelihood and maximum *a posteriori* estimates which have already been discussed in Chapter 9 where Bayesian estimation was used to design deconvolution algorithms. Unlike the minimum mean square method, Bayes estimation allows and indeed depends on prior information about the statistical behaviour of the object function f and the noise n.

10.3 BAYESIAN AND MAXIMUM ENTROPY ESTIMATION

Maximum Likelihood (ML) estimate

To obtain the MAP estimate, the pdf for f must be known *a priori*. Because the ML estimate ignores this information, it is in general, easier to compute. For this reason, the ML estimate shall be considered first. We shall use the same model for the object function as before, i.e.,

$$f(x) = w(x) \sum_n A_n \exp(ik_n x) \qquad (10.3.1)$$

The ML estimate is then obtained by finding the coefficients A_n which satisfy the condition

$$\frac{\partial}{\partial A_m} \ln P(\mathbf{s} \mid \mathbf{f}) = 0$$

Gaussian statistics

The probability of measuring s given f is determined by the noise since

$$n(x) = s(x) - f(x)$$

297

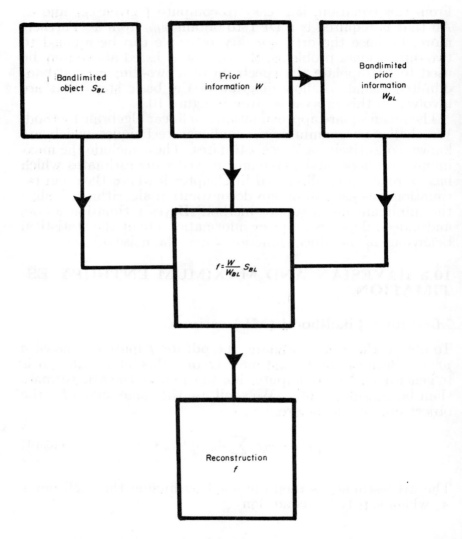

Figure 10.1 Flow diagram of the basic steps involved in the least squares method of spectral extrapolation using prior information

If the noise is zero-mean Gaussian with standard deviation σ_n^2, then,

$$P(\mathbf{s} \mid \mathbf{f}) = \frac{1}{\sqrt{2\pi\sigma_n^2}} \exp\left(-\frac{1}{2\sigma_n^2} \int_{-X}^{X} |s(x) - f(x)|^2 \, dx\right) \qquad (10.3.2)$$

Substituting equation (10.3.1) into equation (10.3.2), the ML estimate is given by solving the equation

$$\frac{\partial}{\partial A_m} \ln P(\mathbf{s} \mid \mathbf{f}) = -\frac{1}{2\sigma_n^2} \frac{\partial}{\partial A_m} \int_{-X}^{X} |s(x) - w(x) \sum_n A_n \exp(ik_n x)|^2 \, dx = 0$$

for A_n. Differentiating, we get

$$\int_{-X}^{X} s(x)w(x) \exp(-ik_m x) dx = \sum_n A_n \int_{-X}^{X} [w(x)]^2 \exp[-i(k_m - k_n)x] dx$$

Here, we run into exactly the same type of problem as that encountered in section 10.2: the equation above is not data-consistent. As in section 10.2, this problem can be overcome by designing a suitable Hilbert space. By introducing an inverse weighted pdf of the form

$$P(\mathbf{f} \mid \mathbf{s}) = \frac{1}{\sqrt{2\pi\sigma_n^2}} \exp\left(-\frac{1}{2\sigma_n^2} \int_{-X}^{X} |s(x) - f(x)|^2 \frac{1}{w(x)} dx\right)$$

and repeating the calculation above we obtain the data-consistent result

$$S(k_m) = \sum_n A_n W(k_m - k_n)$$

Using the convolution theorem, we have

$$s_{BL}(x) = a(x)w_{BL}(x)$$

and hence, from equation (10.3.1), the ML estimate is

$$f_{ML}(x) = \frac{w(x)}{w_{BL}(x)} s_{BL}(x)$$

Note, that this result is identical to the least mean square approximation.

Rayleigh statistics

A very common and generally accurate model for the random amplitude fluctuations a of a signal is the Rayleigh distribution

$$P(a) = \frac{1}{\sigma_a^2} a \exp\left(-\frac{a^2}{2\sigma_a^2}\right) ; a \geq 0$$

It is an accurate representation of the statistical fluctuations of the amplitude modulations of many radar, sonar, ultrasonic and seismic signals for example. If the signal s is taken to represent amplitude modulations then the functions f and n are necessarily real and non-negative. Hence, in this case we can utilize an inverse weighted pdf of the form,

$$P(\mathbf{s} \mid \mathbf{f}) = \frac{1}{\sigma_n^2} \int\limits_{-X}^{X} [s(x) - f(x)]dx \exp\left(-\frac{1}{2\sigma_n^2} \int\limits_{-X}^{X} [s(x) - f(x)]^2 \frac{1}{w(x)} dx\right)$$

The ML estimate is then given by finding the coefficients A_n which satisfy the equation

$$\frac{\partial}{\partial A_m} \ln P(\mathbf{s} \mid \mathbf{f}) = -\frac{W(k_m)}{N(0)} + \frac{1}{\sigma_n^2}\left(S(k_m) - \sum_n A_n W(k_m - k_n)\right) = 0$$

where $N(0)$ is the DC level of the noise, i.e.

$$N(0) = \int\limits_{-X}^{X} [s(x) - f(x)]dx = \int\limits_{-X}^{X} n(x)dx$$

From this equation we get (using the convolution theorem)

$$-\frac{\sigma_n^2}{N(0)} w_{BL}(x) + s_{BL}(x) = a(x)w_{BL}(x)$$

and hence, the ML estimate for a Rayleigh distribution becomes

$$f_{ML}(x) = w(x)\left(\frac{s_{BL}}{w_{BL}} - \frac{\sigma_n^2}{N(0)}\right)$$

Observe, that when $\sigma_n = 0$, the ML estimate for Rayleigh statistics reduces to the ML estimate for Gaussian statistics.

Maximum *a posteriori* (MAP) estimate

The MAP estimate is obtained by finding the coefficients A_m which satisfies the equation

$$\frac{\partial}{\partial A_m} \ln P(\mathbf{s} \mid \mathbf{f}) + \frac{\partial}{\partial A_m} \ln P(\mathbf{f}) = 0 \qquad (10.3.3)$$

where

$$f(x) = w(x) \sum_n A_n \exp(ik_n x) \qquad (10.3.5)$$

Gaussian statistics

Consider the case where

$$P(\mathbf{s} \mid \mathbf{f}) = \frac{1}{\sqrt{2\pi\sigma_n^2}} \exp\left(-\frac{1}{2\sigma_n^2} \int\limits_{-X}^{X} |\, s(x) - f(x)\,|^2 \frac{1}{w(x)} dx\right)$$

and

$$P(\mathbf{f}) = \frac{1}{\sqrt{2\pi\sigma_f^2}} \exp\left(-\frac{1}{2\sigma_f^2} \int\limits_{-X}^{X} |\, f(x) - \bar{f}(x)\,|^2 \frac{1}{w(x)} dx\right)$$

where $\bar{f}$ is the average value of f at a point x. Substituting these expressions for the pdfs into equation (10.3.3) we have

$$-\frac{1}{2\sigma_n^2} \frac{\partial}{\partial A_m} \int\limits_{-X}^{X} |\, s(x) - w(x) \sum_n A_n \exp(ik_n x)\,|^2 \frac{1}{w(x)} dx$$

$$-\frac{1}{2\sigma_f^2} \frac{\partial}{\partial A_m} \int\limits_{-X}^{X} |\, w(x) \sum_n A_n \exp(ik_n) - \bar{f}(x)\,|^2 \frac{1}{w(x)} dx = 0$$

Differentiating, we get

$$\frac{1}{\sigma_n^2} \int\limits_{-X}^{X} [s(x) - w(x) \sum_n A_n \exp(ik_n x)] \exp(-ik_m x) dx$$

Quantitative coherent imaging

$$-\frac{1}{\sigma_f^2} \int\limits_{-X}^{X} [w(x) \sum_n A_n \exp(ik_n x) - \bar{f}(x)] \exp(-ik_m x) dx = 0$$

or

$$\frac{1}{\sigma_n^2} S(k_m) - \frac{1}{\sigma_n^2} \sum_n A_n W(k_m - k_n) - \frac{1}{\sigma_f^2} \sum_n A_n W(k_m - k_n) + \frac{1}{\sigma_f^2} \bar{F}(k_m) = 0$$

where

$$\bar{F}(k_m) = \int\limits_{-X}^{X} \bar{f}(x) \exp(-ik_m x) dx$$

Using the convolution theorem, we then obtain

$$\left(\frac{1}{\sigma_n^2} + \frac{1}{\sigma_f^2}\right) a(x) w_{BL}(x) = \frac{1}{\sigma_n^2} s_{BL}(x) + \frac{1}{\sigma_f^2} \bar{f}(x)$$

Rearranging, from equation (10.3.5), the MAP estimate for Gaussian statistics is given by

$$f_{MAP}(x) = \frac{1}{1+\Gamma^2} \frac{w(x)}{w_{BL}(x)} \left(\bar{f}(x) + \Gamma^2 s_{BL}(x)\right)$$

where Γ is the signal to noise ratio

$$\Gamma = \frac{\sigma_f}{\sigma_n}$$

Rayleigh statistics

For Rayleigh statistics, we choose pdf's of the form (s and f taken to be real and positive)

$$P(\mathbf{s} \mid \mathbf{f}) = \frac{1}{\sigma_n^2} \int\limits_{-X}^{X} [s(x) - f(x)] dx \exp\left(-\frac{1}{2\sigma_n^2} \int\limits_{-X}^{X} [s(x) - f(x)]^2 \frac{1}{w(x)} dx\right)$$

and

$$P(\mathbf{f}) = \frac{1}{\sigma_f^2} \int\limits_{-X}^{X} f(x) dx \exp\left(-\frac{1}{2\sigma_f^2} \int\limits_{-X}^{X} [f(x)]^2 \frac{1}{w(x)} dx\right)$$

In this case

$$\frac{\partial}{\partial A_m} \ln P(\mathbf{f}) = \frac{W(k_m)}{F(0)} - \frac{1}{\sigma_f^2} \sum_n A_n W(k_m - k_n)$$

where $F(0)$ is the DC level of $F(k_m)$,

$$F(0) = \int_{-X}^{X} f(x)dx$$

and

$$\frac{\partial}{\partial A_m} \ln P(\mathbf{s} \mid \mathbf{f}) = -\frac{W(k_m)}{N(0)} + \frac{1}{\sigma_n^2} \left(S(k_m) - \sum_n A_n W(k_m - k_n) \right)$$

where $N(0)$ is the DC level of $N(k_m)$,

$$N(0) = \int_{-X}^{X} n(x)dx$$

It is then easy to show, that the MAP estimate for Rayleigh statistics is given by

$$f_{MAP}(x) = \frac{1}{1 + \Gamma^2} \frac{w(x)}{w_{BL}(x)} \left[\Gamma^2 s_{BL}(x) + \sigma_f^2 w_{BL}(x) \left(\frac{1}{F(0)} - \frac{1}{N(0)} \right) \right]$$

Maximum entropy estimation

Maximum entropy estimation is usually based on modelling the object itself as a pdf using Maxwell-Boltzmann statistics. A reconstruction is found for f such that

$$E = \int_{-X}^{X} f(x) \ln f(x)dx$$

is a maximum. If we use a model for f of the form

$$f(x) = w(x) \sum_n A_n \exp(ik_n x)$$

then the problem is reduced to finding the coefficients A_n which maximizes E. This requires that f is both real and non-negative. Another way in which the object can be reconstructed is by choosing the coefficients A_n is such a way that the entropy of the amplitude spectrum $| A_n |$ is a maximum. The entropy of this spectrum is given by

$$E = \sum_n | A_n | \ln | A_n |$$

Because $s = f + n$, we can write

$$\lambda \left[\int_{-X}^{X} | s(x) - f(x) |^2 \frac{1}{w(x)} dx - \int_{-X}^{X} | n(x) |^2 \frac{1}{w(x)} dx \right] = 0$$

where λ is the Lagrange multiplier. Thus, we may write the entropy of $| A_n |$ as

$$E = \sum_n | A_n | \ln | A_n | + \lambda \left[\int_{-X}^{X} | s(x) - f(x) |^2 \frac{1}{w(x)} dx \right.$$

$$\left. - \int_{-X}^{X} | n(x) |^2 \frac{1}{w(x)} dx \right] \qquad (10.3.6)$$

This entropy is a function of the coefficients A_m that we want to compute and is therefore a maximum when

$$\frac{\partial E}{\partial A_m} = 0$$

Substituting our model for $f(x)$ into equation (10.3.6) and differentiating with respect to A_m, we get

$$(1 + \ln | A_m |) \frac{A_m}{2 | A_m |}$$

$$- \lambda \left(\int_{-X}^{X} [s(x) - w(x) \sum_n A_n \exp(ik_n x)] \exp(-ik_m x) dx \right) = 0$$

Noting that A_m can be written as

$$A_m =| A_m | \exp(i\phi_m)$$

where $| A_m |$ and ϕ_m are the amplitude and phase spectra of A_m respectively, we have

$$(1 + \ln | A_m |) \exp(i\phi_m) = \lambda \left(S(k_m) - \sum_n A_n W(k_m - k_n) \right)$$

or

$$| A_m |= \exp \left[-1 + \lambda \exp(-i\phi_m) \left(S(k_m) - \sum_n A_n W(k_m - k_n) \right) \right]$$

This equation is transcendental in A_m and as such requires that A_m is evaluated iteratively, i.e.

$$| A_m^{k+1} |= \exp \left[-1 + \lambda \exp(-i\phi_m^k) \left(S(k_m) - \sum_n A_n^k W(k_m - k_n) \right) \right]$$

where

$$\phi_m^k = \text{Im}[\ln A_m^k]$$

A useful approximation to this maximum extropy estimate can be obtained by linearizing the above equation. This is obtained by expanding the exponential function and retaining the linear terms giving

$$| A_m |\simeq \lambda \exp(-i\phi_m) \left(S(k_m) - \sum_n A_n W(k_m - k_n) \right)$$

or

$$\frac{A_m}{\lambda} \simeq S(k_m) - \sum_n A_n W(k_m - k_n)$$

From the last equation, it follows that (taking the inverse Fourier transform and using the convolution theorem)

$$a(x) \simeq \frac{s_{BL}(x)}{w_{BL}(x) + 1/\lambda}$$

Table 10.1 Estimates used to extrapolate the spectrum of a bandlimited signal with additive noise. (The symbols are defined below)

Name of estimate f	Formula	Conditions
Least mean square	$f = \dfrac{w}{w_{BL}} s_{BL}$	Minimum noise
Maximum likelihood	$f = \dfrac{w}{w_{BL}} s_{BL}$	Gaussian statistics
	$f = w\left(\dfrac{s_{BL}}{w_{BL}} - \dfrac{2\sigma_n^2}{N(0)}\right)$	Rayleigh statistics
		s_{BL} real and > 0
Maximum *a posteriori*	$f = \dfrac{1}{1+\Gamma^2}\dfrac{w}{w_{BL}}(\bar{f}+\Gamma^2 s_{BL})$	Gaussian statistics for n
		Gaussian statistics for f
	$f = \dfrac{1}{1+\Gamma^2}\dfrac{w}{w_{BL}}\Bigg[\Gamma^2 s_{BL}$	Rayleigh statistics for n
	$\qquad + \sigma_f^2 w_{BL}\left(\dfrac{1}{F(0)} - \dfrac{1}{N(0)}\right)\Bigg]$	Rayleigh statistics for f
		s_{BL} real and > 0
Maximum entropy	$f \simeq \dfrac{w s_{BL}}{w_{BL} + 1/\lambda}$	Linear approximation

f estimate
s_{BL} Bandlimited signal
w Prior information (w is real and > 0)
w_{BL} Bandlimited prior information
$\bar{f}$ Average value of f
σ_f Standard deviation of the signal f
σ_n Standard deviation of the noise n
Γ Signal to noise ratio $= \sigma_f/\sigma_n$
λ Lagrange multiplier

and hence

$$f(x) = \frac{w(x)s_{BL}(x)}{w_{BL}(x) + 1/\lambda}$$

Discussion

Table 10.1 lists the different estimates discussed in this chapter. Observe that the algebraic form of these estimates is very similar. As the standard deviation of the noise tends to zero, they reduce to the same basic result, i.e.

$$f(x) = \frac{w(x)}{w_{BL}(x)} s_{BL}(x)$$

As always with ill posed problems of this kind, a condition for the reconstruction is chosen which is both physically reasonable and yields a manageable set of equations that can be solved at a reasonable computational cost. Since there is no unique solution to a problem of this type, the decision about which estimate to use must be guided by the user. For this reason, simplicity and data adaptability are essential if the final algorithm is going to be of any practical use. In this chapter we have presented estimates which are based on a variety of different conditions. In each case, the estimate is data adaptive and easy to implement. All that is required to compute these estimates is a discrete Fourier transform to generate w_{BL} from w. In practice, this can be achieved using a Fast Fourier transform algorithm such as the one provided in section 2.11.

Some numerical examples

At this stage, the opportunity is taken to provide some examples which serve to demonstrate the performance of the basic reconstruction formula

$$\text{Reconstruction} = \text{Bandlimited data}$$
$$\times \frac{\text{prior information}}{\text{Bandlimited Prior Information}}$$

Figure 10.2 is a demostration of the reconstruction formula given above when the bandlimited data is real and nonnegative. In this example, an object has been chosen which consists of 64 × 64 pixels and is composed of a boundary in the form of a thin annular layer enclosing a region of uniform density and three discs. The bandwidth of this object has been reduced to just 4 pixels using a square lowpass filter giving the data shown. Prior information is chosen which includes the support of the original object but does not reflect its internal structure (i.e. the three discs). Application of the formula above provides the reconstruction shown.

In this example, it is assumed that the user has access to a limited but accurate form of information about the structure of

307

Object

Data

Prior information

Reconstruction

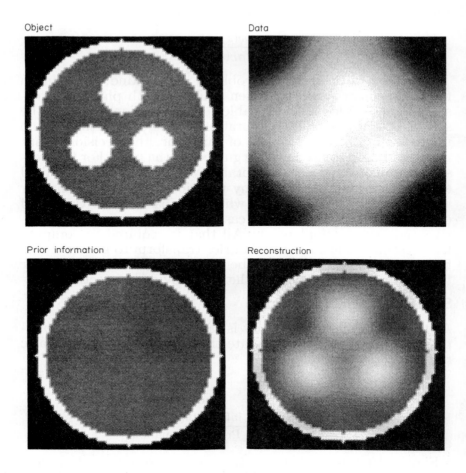

Figure 10.2 Reconstruction of a test object from bandlimited data using prior information. The level of noise in this example is zero (i.e. the standard deviation of the noise σ_n is zero). Hence, from Table 10.1, this reconstruction is a minimum mean square, a maximum likelihood and a maximum *a posteriori* estimate. It is also a linear approximation to the maximum entropy estimate for $\lambda \gg 1$

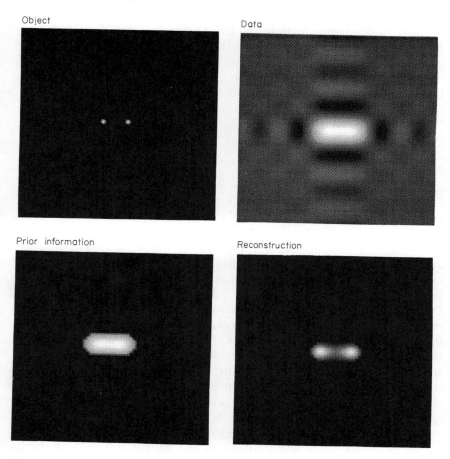

Figure 10.3 Reconstruction of two points from bandlimited data. In this example, the prior information on the support of the object (i.e. the approximate location of the two points in the image scene) has been obtained by thresholding the bandlimited data

the object. In many application this is a reasonable assumption particularly in cases when the object can, to a limited extent, be inspected visually. In other cases, no detailed prior information may be available. In such cases, prior information on the support of the object must be estimated for the data alone. One simple way of doing this is to threshold the data, i.e. apply the following process:

if $v_{in}(i,j)$ >threshold

then

$v_{out}(i,j) = v_{in}(i,j)$

else

$v_{out}(i,j) = 0.$

endif

An example of this is given in figure 10.3. Here, an object consisting of two points has been severely bandlimited by applying a square lowpass filter. In this case, the data is real but of alternating polarity. Thresholding this data provides an estimate of the support of the object (i.e. prior information on the location of the two points in the image scene) which is then used to obtain the reconstruction shown using the formula above. Exactly the same technique has been used to obtain the reconstruction given in figure 10.4, which is an example of a synthetic aperture radar or SAR image. The object at the centre of the picture is a ship. The data for this image were obtained using the Seasat satellite. The SAR image given in figure 10.4 is a display of the amplitude modulations after the bandwidth of the complex data (i.e. the real signals plus their Hilbert transforms) has been reduced to remove some of the high frequencies which give rise to an effect called 'speckle'. In this example, the speckle has been caused primarily by scattering from the sea surface. By thresholding the amplitude modulations, prior information about the location of the object in the image scene is obtained together with some additional structural information. Application of the formula above provides the reconstruction shown.

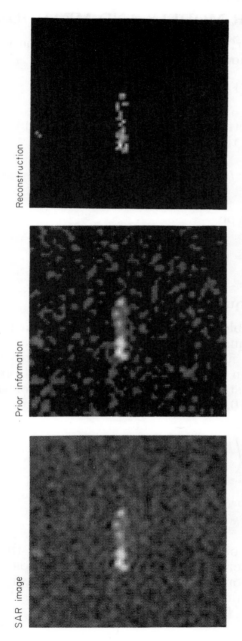

SAR image

Prior information

Reconstruction

Figure 10.4 Super resolution of a SAR image. The complex data have been low pass filtered to remove the speckle. The SAR image is a display of the amplitude modulations in these data. The blurred object at the centre of this image is a ship. By thresholding this image, an estimate of the support of this object is acquired. This prior information on the location of the object in the image scene is then used to extrapolate the spectrum of the bandlimited (complex) data

10.4 NONLINEAR MODELS AND METHODS

So far in this chapter, we have only made use of the weighted linear polynolmial model

$$f(x) = w(x) \sum_n A_n \exp(ik_n x)$$

Another class of spectral estimator can be acquired by utilizing nonlinear models on the inverse type

$$f(x) = \frac{w(x)}{\sum_n A_n \exp(ik_n x)} \tag{10.4.1}$$

or the exponential type

$$f(x) = w(x) \exp\left(\sum_n A_n \exp(ik_n x)\right) \tag{10.4.2}$$

The least mean squares method

By designing a suitable least squares error, nonlinear models of the type given by equations (10.4.1) and (10.4.2) can be used. As in sections 10.2 and 10.3, the basic trick is to design a Hilbert space (i.e. an expression for the error function) which yields a data- consistent equation. For a model of the type given by equation (10.4.1), we use the following error function

$$e = \int_{-X}^{X} | \frac{1}{s(x)} - \frac{1}{f(x)} |^2 w^2(x)s(x)dx$$

$$= \int_{-X}^{X} | \frac{w(x)}{s(x)} - \sum_n A_n \exp(ik_n x) |^2 s(x)dx$$

The algebraic form of this error function requires that s and f are greater than zero so that singularities are avoided in $1/s$ and $1/f$. Using the orthogonality principle, the error function defined above is a minimum when

$$\frac{\partial e}{\partial A_m} = \int_{-X}^{X} \left(\frac{w(x)}{s(x)} - \sum_n A_n \exp(ik_n x)\right) \exp(-ik_m x)s(x)dx = 0$$

or

$$A_n \otimes S_n = W_n$$

In image space, the last equation is

$$a(x)s_{BL}(x) = w_{BL}(x)$$

and hence, from equation (10.4.1), we get

$$f(x) = \frac{w(x)}{a(x)} = w(x)\frac{s_{BL}(x)}{w_{BL}(x)}$$

This result is identical to the minimum mean square method used in conjuction with the linear polynomial model discussed in section 10.2.

For a model of the exponential type given by equation (10.4.2), we introduce an error function of the form

$$e = \int_{-X}^{X} | \frac{s(x)}{w(x)} - \ln\left(\frac{f(x)}{w(x)}\right) |^2 w(x)dx$$

$$= \int_{-X}^{X} | \frac{s(x)}{w(x)} - \sum_n A_n \exp(ik_n x) |^2 w(x)dx$$

where $w > 0$ and s and f are non-negative functions. Using the orthogonality principle, this error is a minimum when

$$S_n - A_n \otimes W_n = 0$$

or in image space, when

$$a(x)w_{BL}(x) = s_{BL}(x)$$

Form equation (10.4.2), we then get

$$f(x) = w(x)\exp\left(\frac{s_{BL}(x)}{w_{BL}(x)}\right)$$

SUMMARY OF IMPORTANT RESULTS

Basic problem (super resolution of bandlimited signals)

Given the band limited signal

$$s_{BL}(x) = \text{sinc}(\alpha x) \otimes f(x) + n(x)$$

where n is noise, find a solution for the object function f.

Basic solution

$$f(x) = \frac{w(x)}{w_{BL}(x)} s_{BL}(x)$$

w - prior information on the functional behaviour of f.

w_{BL} - bandlimited prior information.

FURTHER READING

Papoulis A, *Signal Analysis*, McGraw-Hill, 1977. Bandlimited functions are discussed in chapter 7. Spectral extrapolation using the Gerchberg- Papoulis algorithm is also discussed in chpater 7.

Byrne C L, Fitzgerald R M, Fiddy M A, Hall T J and Darling A M, *Image Restoration and Resolution Enhancement*, Journal of the Optical Society of America, 1983, Volume 73, Number 11, Pages 1481-1487. This paper uses both linear and nonlinear weighted polynomial models to extrapolate the spectra of bandlimited data.

Cheng L M, Ho A S and Burge R E, *Use of a Priori Knowledge in Image Reconstruction*, Journal of the optical Society of America, 1984, Volume 1, Number 4, Pages 386-391. This paper uses the ideas presented in the paper above together with the product theorem to establish a simple algebraic reconstruction formula of the type presented in this chapter (i.e. $f = w s_{BL}/w_{BL}$).

314

11 Image enhancement

The goal of image enhancement is literally to make the image look better. For this reason, image enhancement is a rather subjective matter because what 'looks better' depends on the type of details and contrasts in the image that the user is hoping to to acquire. In turn, these properties depend on the physical characteristics of the image, the prior knowledge that the user may have on certain features in the image, coupled with the user's experience, intuition and judgement. Hence, not surprisingly, there have evolved a wide variety of techniques for enhancing images which are based as much on the quality of the results that are achieved as on the criterion for enhancement. In this chapter, some of the more commonly used methods are discussed.

11.1 SIMPLE TRANSFORMS

Simple transformations can be used to enhance details in an image which occur in dark or light regions of the image. They are trivial to compute and in some cases have a physical significance.

Logarithmic transform

The logarithmic transform is of the general form

$$v_{out}(i, j) = \ln v_{in}(i, j)$$

where v is the value of a pixel at a location (i, j). The portion of the logarithmic curve over which this transform is required can be adjusted by introducing a scaling parameter α and employing the transform

$$v_{out}(i, j) = \frac{1}{\alpha} \ln[1 + (e^{\alpha} - 1)v_{in}(i, j)]$$

The addition of 1 is included to prevent problems occuring if $v_{in} = 0$. The effect of this transform is to increase the dynamic range of dark regions in an image and decrease the dynamic range of light regions.

The logarithmic transform is a relatively simple method of adjusting the visual quality of an image in favour of those features which have low grey level values. In some cases, using a logarithmic transform of this kind to enhance an image can be justified physically. For example, with X-ray images, the value of a pixel at (i, j) is given by the intensity of the X-rays I as they emerge from an object of varying thickness and density. The distribution in intensity is given by

$$I(i, j) = I_0 \exp[-f(i, j)]$$

where I_0 is the intensity of the X-ray source and f is a function of the X-ray attenuating properties of the material which in turn depend on the thickness and density of the material. If we apply the logarithmic transform to an X-ray image of this kind, we get

$$\ln I_{out}(i, j) = \ln I_0 - f(i, j)$$

In this case, the logarithmic transform provides an image which is a linear mapping of the X-ray attenuating properties of the material described by f. This technique is often employed in X-ray radiography.

Exponential transform

The exponential transform is the inverse of the logarithmic transform and has an inverse effect on the image, i.e. it enhances detail in the light regions of the image while decreasing the dynamic range of grey levels in dark regions of the image. The basic transform is

$$v_{\text{out}}(i, j) = \exp[v_{\text{in}}(i, j)]$$

Bases other that the exponential can also be used for this purpose by employing the transform

$$v_{\text{out}}(i, j) = \frac{1}{\alpha}[(1 + \alpha)^{v_{\text{in}}(i,j)} - 1]$$

where α is a variable scaling parameter defined by the user.

11.2 HISTOGRAM EQUALIZATION

Another way of enhancing an image is to apply a transform which modifies the histogram of the image in a predetermined and desired fashion. A histogram is just a plot of the number of times a particular grey level occurs against the grey level. This provides a global description of the appearance of the image in terms of the characteristic probability distribution function of grey levels. The profile or 'shape' of the histogram describes the density of grey levels in the image. If the histogram peaks at a low grey level, then the image is relatively dark, and if the histogram has a concentration of pixels with a high grey level, then the image is relatively light.

Histogram equalization attempts to generate an image whose histogram is uniform (i.e. an image where each grey level occurs an equal number of times: hence the term 'equalization'). The effect is to increase the dynamic range of grey levels. This has a considerable influence on the visual appearance of the image, enhancing the detail of many features in both the dark and light regions of the image.

In mathematical terms, we can formulate the problem in the following way: Let v represent the value of a pixel which is confined to the range

$$0 \leq v \leq 1$$

where 0 represents black and 1 represents white. The pixels are quantized into L grey levels so that their range of values is now

$$0 \leq v_k \leq L, \quad k = 0, 1, 2, ..., L$$

where $v_0 = 0, v_1 = 1, v_2 = 2$ and so on. The probability of a grey level occurring with value v_k is given by

$$P(v_k) = \frac{n_k}{N}$$

where n_k is the number of times a pixel occurs with value v_k in the image and N is the total number of pixels. The histogram is a plot of $P(v_k)$ against v_k. To equalize the histogram we require a transform $\hat{T}$ which produces a range of values

$$v_k^{\text{out}} = \hat{T}[v_k^{\text{in}}]$$

such that

$$P(v_k^{\text{out}}) = 1$$

In these terms, it is clear that the basic problem is to find $\hat{T}$. This is done by using an equation which is a consequence of probability theory. The equation is

$$C(v_k^{\text{out}}) = C(v_k^{\text{in}}) \tag{11.2.1}$$

where $C(v_k^{\text{out}})$ and $C(v_k^{\text{in}})$ are known as the cumulative histograms given by

$$C(v_k^{\text{out}}) = \sum_{i=0}^{k} P(v_i^{\text{out}})$$

and

$$C(v_k^{\text{in}}) = \sum_{i=0}^{k} P(v_i^{\text{in}})$$

respectively. The transform is then obtained by noting that if

$$P(v_i^{\text{out}}) = 1 \forall i$$

then

$$C(v_k^{\text{out}}) = \sum_{i=0}^{k} P(v_i^{\text{out}}) = v_k^{\text{out}}$$

From equation (11.2.1), we then have,

$$v_k^{\text{out}} = C(v_k^{\text{in}})$$

which can computed directly from the original image. Thus, to enhance an image by histogram equalization we carry out the following procedure:

1. Normalize the image so that the largest pixel value is 1.

2. Quantize the pixels into L levels (defined by the user).

3. Compute the histogram of the image $P(v_k^{\text{in}})$.

4. Compute the cumulative histogram of the image $C(v_k^{\text{in}}) = \sum_{i=0}^{k} P(v_i^{\text{in}})$.

5. Normalize this cumulative histogram and then quantize it into the same number of levels L.

6. Assign the value of $C(v_k^{\text{in}})$ to all the pixels with an original grey level of v_k^{in}.

A FORTRAN program to perform these operations is given below. On input X is the original image and on output X is the histogram equalized image. The size of the image is N×N (maximum value being set at 64×64) and L is the number of grey levels into which the image is quantized (specified by the user).

```
      SUBROUTINE HE(X,N,L)
C
C FUNCTION: THIS SUBROUTINE ENHANCES AN IMAGE
C           BY EQUALIZING ITS HISTOGRAM.
C
      DIMENSION X(64,64),V(65),P(65),C(65)
      REAL MAX
C
C X IS THE INPUT/OUPUT IMAGE AND N x N IS THE
C NUMBER OF PIXELS.
C L IS THE NUMBER OF GREY LEVELS.
C V IS THE NUMBER OF PIXELS WITH GREY LEVEL K.
C P IS THE PROBABILITY OF A PIXEL
C HAVING GREY LEVEL K.
```

```
C C IS THE CUMULATIVE PROBABILITY OF A PIXEL
C HAVING GREY LEVEL K.
C
C FIND THE MAXIMUM GREY LEVEL IN THE IMAGE.
C
      MAX=0.
      DO J=1,N
      DO I=1,N
      IF(X(I,J).GT.MAX)MAX=X(I,J)
      ENDDO
      ENDDO
C
C NORMALIZE THE IMAGE BY DIVIDING THROUGH BY MAX
C AND THEN QUANTIZE INTO L SEPARATE (INTEGER)
C VALUES BY APPLYING THE ANINT FUNCTION WHICH
C PROVIDES THE NEAREST WHOLE NUMBER.
C
      DO J=1,N
      DO I=1,N
      X(I,J)=X(I,J)/MAX !NORMALIZATION
      X(I,J)=ANINT(X(I,J)*FLOAT(L)) !QUANTIZATION
      ENDDO
      ENDDO
C
C INITIALIZE V (SET ALL VALUES OF V TO ZERO).
C
      DO K=1,L+1
      V(K)=0.
      ENDDO
C
C FIND THE NUMBER OF GREY LEVELS WITH VALUE
C K (BETWEEN 0 AND L).
C
      DO K=1,L+1
      DO J=1,N
      DO I=1,N
      IF(X(I,J).EQ.FLOAT(K-1))V(K)=V(K)+1.
      ENDDO
      ENDDO
      ENDDO
C
C COMPUTE THE PROBABILITY DISTRIBUTION
```

```
C FUNCTION OF GREY LEVELS.
C
      DO K=1,L+1
      P(K)=V(K)/(N*N)
      ENDDO
C
C COMPUTE THE CUMULATIVE PROBABILITY
C DISTRIBUTION FUNCTION.
C
      C(1)=P(1)
      DO K=2,L+1
      C(K)=C(K-1)+P(K)
      ENDDO
C
C FIND THE MAXIMUM VALUE OF C AND THEN
C NORMALIZE AND QUANTIZE.
C
      MAX=0.
      DO K=1,L+1
      IF(C(K).GT.MAX)MAX=C(K)
      ENDDO
      DO K=1,L+1
      C(K)=C(K)/MAX
      C(K)=ANINT(C(K)*FLOAT(L))
      ENDDO
C
C  ASSIGN THE VALUE OF C(K) TO ALL
C  PIXELS WITH ORIGINAL VALUE K.
C
      DO K=1,L+1
      DO J=1,N
      DO I=1,N
      IF(X(I,J).EQ.FLOAT(K-1))XX(I,J)=C(K)
      ENDDO
      ENDDO
      ENDDO
C
C FINALLY, WRITE OUTPUT (HISTOGRAM EQUALIZED IMAGE).
C
      DO J=1,N
      DO I=1,N
      X(I,J)=XX(I,J)
```

Histogram of grey levels

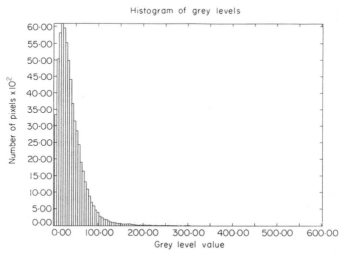

Fig. 11.1 (a)

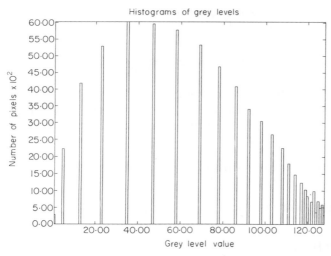

Fig. 11.1 (b)

```
      ENDDO
      ENDDO
C

      RETURN
      END
```

An example of histogram equalization (using the above subroutine) is given in figure 11.1. This figure shows two synthetic aperture radar images of junction 15 on the UK M1 motorway (see figure 7.1) before (a) and after (b) histogram equalization together with their associated histograms. The image in figure 11.1(a) is composed of a narrow Rayleigh-type distribution of grey levels which is characteristic of SAR images in general. Figure 11.1(b) illustrates how the equalization process spreads the distribution of grey levels in the image.

11.3 HOMOMORPHIC FILTERING

Homomorphic filtering is based on using the properties of the logarithm to transform a multiplicative processes into an additive process.

Physical model

This method of filtering assumes an illumination-reflection model for the image of the form

$$f(x, y) = i(x, y)r(x, y)$$

where r is the reflection component, i is the illumination and f is the intensity distribution. In general, this model has two important features which homomorphic filtering relies upon. They are:

1. The illumination component is composed of low spatial frequencies.

2. The reflection component is composed of high spatial frequencies.

Basic method

The objective of homomorphic filtering is to separate the reflection component from the illumination component. This is

324

done by computing the logarithm of f, i.e.

$$\ln f(x,y) = \ln i(x,y) + \ln r(x,y)$$

The illumination and reflection components then become additive where:

1. $\ln i$ is composed of low spatial frequencies.

2. $\ln r$ is composed of high spatial frequencies.

Because of 1 and 2 above, by applying a suitable (user defined and controlled) high pass filter (HPF) to reduce the contribution of $\ln i$ to $\ln f$, $\ln r$ can be extracted, i.e.

$$\ln r(x,y) \simeq \text{HPF}[\ln f(x,y)]$$

Performing an exponentiation to convert the process back into an intensity distribution then provides the reflection component

$$r(x,y) \simeq \exp\Big(\text{HPF}[\ln f(x,y)]\Big)$$

This method of image enhancement is known as homomorphic filtering. It requires specification of the HPF. A variety of filters can be used for this purpose.

The ideal high pass filter

The ideal high pass filter is given by

$$H(k_x, k_y) = \begin{cases} 0, & \sqrt{k_x^2 + k_y^2} \leq K \\ \\ 1, & \sqrt{k_x^2 + k_y^2} > K \end{cases}$$

where K is the cut-off distance measured from the origin (the point in Fourier space where $k_x = k_y = 0$). This filter attenuates completely (i.e. sets to zero) all those spatial frequencies that are less than or equal to the cut-off frequency and passes without modification all those spatial frequencies that are greater than the cut-off frequency.

The Butterworth high pass filter

The Butterworth high pass filter (BHPF) is an approximation to the ideal filter. It is a continuous and circularly symmetric filter given by

$$B(k_x, k_y) = \frac{1}{1 + \left(\frac{K}{\sqrt{k_x^2 + k_y^2}}\right)^{2n}}$$

The parameter n is a user-defined positive integer called the order of the filter. As the value of n increases, the BHPF approaches the ideal filter. Image enhancement by homomorphic filtering is usually carried out using the BHPF. In practice, a 2D FFT is used to carry out the filtering operation and the user may repeat this enhancing process for different values of K and n.

The following program is designed to enhance an image using the homomorphic filtering technique discussed above. On input X is the image of size N×N where N is less than or equal to 64 and an integer power of 2. Larger images may of course be used by declaring arrays which are larger than 64×64 but again, the size of the arrays must be an integer power of 2 so that FFT2D can be used.

```
      SUBROUTINE HMF(X,N,CUT,ORD)
C
C FUNCTION: THIS SUBROUTINE ENHANCES AN IMAGE
C           BY HOMOMORPHIC FILTERING USING A
C           BUTTERWORTH HIGHPASS FILTER.
C
      DIMENSION X(64,64),XR(64,64),XI(64,64)
      DIMENSION FXR(64,64),FXI(64,64),B(64,64)
      INTEGER CUT,ORD
C
C X - IMAGE.
C ORD - ORDER OF BHPF.
C CUT - CUT-OFF FREQUENCY OF BHPF SPECIFIED
C IN TERMS OF THE NUMBER OF PIXELS FROM
C THE CENTRE OF THE SPECTRUM.
C
C FIRST, TAKE THE LOGARITHM OF THE IMAGE X.
C 1 IS ADDED TO THE IMAGE AT THIS STAGE TO
```

326

```
C ELIMINATE ANY ZEROS THAT MAY BE PRESENT.
C
      DO J=1,N
      DO I=1,N
      XR(I,J)=LOG(1.+X(I,J))  !  REAL PART
      XI(I,J)=0.  !IMAGINARY PART SET TO ZERO.
      ENDDO
      ENDDO
C
C TAKE THE FOURIER TRANSFORM OF XR.
C
      CALL FFT2D(XR,XI,N,-1)
C
C COMPUTE BHPF.
C
      NH=N/2+1
      DO J=1,N
      DO I=1,N
      A=(FLOAT(I-NH)**2.+FLOAT(J-NH)**2.)**0.5
      IF(A.EQ.0.)THEN
      B(I,J)=0.
      ELSE
      B(I,J)=1./(1.+(CUT/A)**(2.*ORD))
      ENDIF
      ENDDO
      ENDDO
C
C PERFORM THE FILTERING OPERATION.
C
      DO J=1,N
      DO I=1,N
      FXR(I,J)=XR(I,J)*B(I,J)
      FXI(I,J)=XI(I,J)*B(I,J)
      ENDDO
      ENDDO
C
C TRANSFORM BACK INTO IMAGE SPACE BY
C INVERSE FOURIER TRANSFORMING.
C
      CALL FFT2D(FXR,FXI,N,1)
C
C EXPONENTIATE THE BHPF IMAGE AND
```

```
C WRITE THE RESULT TO OUTPUT.
C
      DO J=1,N
      DO I=1,N
      X(I,J)=EXP(FXR(I,J))
      ENDDO
      ENDDO
C
      RETURN
      END
```

11.4 HIGH EMPHASIS FILTERING

High emphasis filtering is based on computing the Laplacian of a blurred image and then subtracting the result from the image. This process povides a reconstruction which is particularly good at restoring the edges of the blurred image. This is important because the human visual system operates in a way that appears to make use of the outlines or edges of a feature for the purposes of recognition and the perception of distance and orientation.

The high emphasis filtered image (which shall be denoted by g) is related to the blurred image f by the formula

$$g(x, y) = f(x, y) - \nabla^2 f(x, y)$$

The effect of the Laplacian is to amplify the high spatial frequencies in the image while leaving the low spatial frequencies relatively unchanged. This is easy to see from the relationship

$$\nabla^2 f(x, y) \Longleftrightarrow (k_x^2 + k_y^2) F(k_x, k_y)$$

By subtracting $\nabla^2 f$ from f, the low frequencies are virtually cancelled out while the high frequencies remain relatively unchanged.

Physical model

High emphasis filtering is based on a physical model for the image which assumes that the blurring has occurred via a process of diffusion. This process is described by the following partial differential equation (the diffusion equation)

$$\frac{\partial}{\partial t} f(x, y, t) = K \nabla^2 f(x, y, t)$$

where $K > 0$ is a constant which determines the rate of diffusion and

$$f(x, y, t) = g(x, y, t), \quad t = 0$$

At any time $t > 0$, it is assumed that a diffusion process is responsible for blurring the image g. As time increases, this image becomes progressively blurred. The problem is to find g from f at some time $t > 0$. High emphasis filtering is based on a solution to this problem that uses an approximation to the Taylor series expansion for f.

Suppose that we record the diffusion blurred image f at a time $t = T$. The Taylor series for f at $t = 0$ may then be written as

$$f(x, y, 0) = f(x, y, T) - T \left[\frac{\partial}{\partial t} f(x, y, t) \right]_{t=T} + \frac{T^2}{2!} \left[\frac{\partial^2}{\partial t^2} f(x, y, t) \right]_{t=T} + \ldots$$

We then approximate this function be neglecting all terms after the second term. Using the diffusion equation, we obtain

$$f(x, y, 0) \simeq f(x, y, T) - T \left[\frac{\partial}{\partial t} f(x, y, t) \right]_{t=T}$$

$$= f(x, y, T) - TK\nabla^2 f(x, y, T)$$

Now, since

$$f(x, y, 0) = g(x, y, 0)$$

we have

$$g(x, y, 0) = f(x, y, T) - TK\nabla^2 f(x, y, T)$$

The equation for high emphasis filtering given earlier applies to the case when $TK = 1$ but the value of TK can be changed if the user requires some control over the process. Introducing the scaling factor α we can use the equation

$$g(x, y) = f(x, y) - \alpha \nabla^2 f(x, y), \quad t = T \qquad (11.4.1)$$

The effect of increasing the value of α is to amplify the high frequency content of f. By lowering the value of α the influence of the high frequencies in f on g is decreased.

Computation

Image enhancement by high emphasis filtering is usually achieved by computing the digital Laplacian. This is given by

$$\nabla^2 f(i,j) = f(i+1,j) + f(i-1,j) + f(i,j+1) + f(i,j-1) - 4f(i,j)$$

From this result, we have

$$g(i,j) = f(i,j) - \nabla^2 f(i,j)$$

$$= 5f(i,j) - f(i+1,j) - f(i-1,j) - f(i,j+1) - f(i,j-1)$$

This operation is easy to compute using a digital computer. However, the values of the pixels at the edges of the image must be specified. The value of these pixels can be set to the value of their nearest neighbour, i.e.

$$g(i,1) = g(i,2)$$

$$g(i,N) = g(i,N-1)$$

and

$$g(1,j) = g(2,j)$$

$$g(N,j) = g(N-1,j)$$

High emphasis filtering using the FFT

The digital Laplacian is a shift invariant linear operation. Applying this operation to a digital image $f(i,j)$ is the same as convolving the image with the two-dimensional array

$$\begin{array}{ccc} & 1 & \\ 1 & -4 & 1 \\ & 1 & \end{array}$$

where all other points in the array are zero (N.B. -4 is taken to occur at the centre of the array). Hence, computing $g(i,j)$ is the same as convolving $f(i,j)$ with the array

$$\begin{array}{ccc} & -1 & \\ -1 & 5 & -1 \\ & -1 & \end{array}$$

These arrays are called masks and we can write

$$g(i,j) = \text{mask}(i,j) \,\otimes\otimes\, f(i,j)$$

where

$$\text{mask}(i,j) = \begin{matrix} & -1 & \\ -1 & 5 & -1 \\ & -1 & \end{matrix}$$

If the scaling parameter α is included, then the mask above becomes

$$\text{mask}(i,j) = \begin{matrix} & -\alpha & \\ -\alpha & 4+\alpha & -\alpha \\ & -\alpha & \end{matrix}$$

The convolution of an image with the mask can be carried out using an FFT. A subroutine to compute the high emphasis filter using this method is given below. In this case, the user must specify the value of the scaling parameter ALPHA.

```
      SUBROUTINE HEF(X,N,ALPHA)
C
C FUNCTION:  THIS SUBROUTINE USES A FFT TO ENHANCE
C            AN IMAGE USING THE HIGH EMPHASIS FILTER.
C
      DIMENSION X(64,64),XR(64,64),XI(64,64)
      DIMENSION G(64,64),GR(64,64),GI(64,64)
      REAL MASK(64,64),MASKR(64,64),MASKI(64,64)
C
C X - INPUT/OUTPUT IMAGE, SIZE N x N.
C ALPHA - SCALING PARAMETER.
C
C COMPUTE THE APPROPRIATE MASK.
C
      DO J=1,N
      DO I=1,N
      MASK(I,J)=0.
      ENDDO
      ENDDO
      NN=N/2
      MASK(NN,NN)=4.+ALPHA
      MASK(NN-1,NN)=-ALPHA
      MASK(NN+1,NN)=-ALPHA
      MASK(NN,NN-1)=-ALPHA
```

331

```
      MASK(NN,NN+1)=-ALPHA
C
C TAKE THE FOURIER TRANSFORM OF MASK AND X.
C
      DO J=1,N
      DO I=1,N
      XR(I,J)=X(I,J)
      XI(I,J)=0.
      MASKR(I,J)=MASK(I,J)
      MASKI(I,J)=0.
      ENDDO
      ENDDO
      CALL FFT2D(XR,XI,N,-1)
      CALL FFT2D(MASKR,MASKI,N,-1)
C
C MULTIPLY COMPLEX SPECTRA TOGETHER.
C
      DO J=1,N
      DO I=1,N
      GR(I,J)=XR(I,J)*MASKR(I,J)-XI(I,J)*MASKI(I,J)
      GI(I,J)=XR(I,J)*MASKI(I,J)+XI(,J)*MASKR(I,J)
      ENDDO
      ENDDO
C
C TAKE THE INVERSE FOURIER TRANSFORM.
C
      CALL FFT2D(GR,GI,N,1)
C
C WRITE OUTPUT.
C
      DO J=1,N
      DO I=1,N
      X(I,J)=GR(I,J)
      ENDDO
      ENDDO
C
      RETURN
      END
```

Exact solution

If we record an image at a time $t = T$ then by Taylor expanding f at $t = 0$ we can write

$$g(x, y, 0) = f(x, y, T) + \sum_{n=1}^{\infty} \frac{(-1)^n}{n!} T^n \left[\frac{\partial^n}{\partial t^n} f(x, y, t) \right]_{t=T}$$

The high emphasis filter is derived by neglecting terms in the series above for $n > 1$ giving an approximate solution for the deblurred image g. If we include all the terms in this series, then an exact solution for g can be obtained. This can be done by noting that (from the diffusion equation)

$$\frac{\partial^2 f}{\partial t^2} = K \nabla^2 \frac{\partial f}{\partial t} = K^2 \nabla^4 f$$

$$\frac{\partial^3 f}{\partial t^3} = K \nabla^2 \frac{\partial^2 f}{\partial t^2} = K^3 \nabla^6 f$$

and so on. In general we can write

$$\left[\frac{\partial^n}{\partial t^n} f(x, y, t) \right]_{t=T} = K^n \nabla^{2n} f(x, y, T)$$

Substituting this result into the series for g given above, we get

$$g(x, y) = f(x, y) + \sum_{n=1}^{\infty} \frac{(-1)^n}{n!} (TK)^n \nabla^{2n} f(x, y), \qquad t = T$$

11.5 AM, FM AND PHASE IMAGING

AM imaging

AM imaging is based on observing a grey scale or colour coded display of the amplitude modulations (AM) in a stack of signals.

If s is the analytic signal given by

$$s = f + iq \qquad (11.5.1)$$

where s, f and q are all function of time t and

$$q = \frac{1}{\pi t} \otimes f$$

then, the amplitude modulations A in the signal are given by

$$A = \mid s \mid = \sqrt{f^2 + q^2}$$

This parameter is easy to compute and is used to display data (processed or otherwise) in many coherent imaging systems. Another way of constructing a coherent image is by computing the instantaneous phase of the data. This leads to the concept of phase imaging.

Phase imaging

The analytic signal can be written in the form

$$s = A \exp(i\theta) \tag{11.5.2}$$

where θ is the instantaneous phase. This parameter measures the phase of a signal at a given point in time and phase imaging is based on observing the behaviour of this parameter as a function of time in a stack of signals. An important property of the instantaneous phase is its derivative with respect to time. This measures the instantaneous frequency of the signal (i.e. variations in the rate of change of phase as a function of time). By taking the natural logarithm of equation (11.5.2), we get

$$\ln s = \ln A + i\theta$$

Thus, we can write

$$\theta = \text{Im}[\ln s]$$

If we now take the derivative of the last equation, we obtain

$$\frac{d\theta}{dt} = \text{Im}\left[\frac{d\ln s}{dt}\right] = \text{Im}\left[\frac{1}{s}\frac{ds}{dt}\right]$$

Substituting equation (11.5.1) into the above equation, we can then write

$$\psi = \frac{d\theta}{dt} = \frac{1}{A^2}\left(f\frac{dq}{dt} - q\frac{df}{dt}\right) \tag{11.5.3}$$

From this result, the instantaneous phase can be obtained by integration, i.e.

$$\theta = \theta_0 + \int^t \psi(t')dt'$$

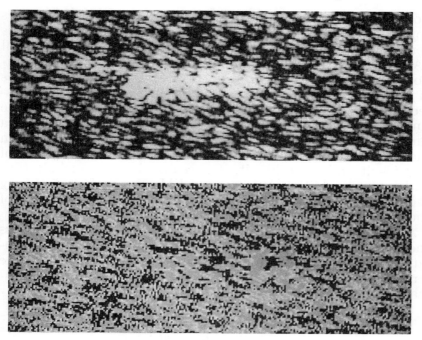

Figure 11.2 AM (*upper*) and FM (*lower*) images of a ship obtained with a 24 cm wavelength synthetic aperture radar

where

$$\theta_0 = \theta(t = 0)$$

This phase function is known as the unwrapped phase.

FM imaging

Another interesting parameter associated with the analytic signal is the frequency modulation (FM) given by $|\dot{\psi}|$. By constructing a grey level display of this parameter, a FM image is obtained.

In practice, the nonlinear dependence of ψ on A in equation (11.5.3) means that $\dot{\psi}$ is very sensitive to relatively small scale variation in A. Hence, a straight forward display of the frequency modulations tends to 'highlight' those positions in time where A is small. The problem with this is that it produces an image that is entirely contrary to conventional AM imaging.

Consequently, in comparison with an AM image, FM images appear to bear little relation to the object structure. This is demonstrated in figure 11.2. In this example, a conventional SAR image of a ship (i.e. a display of the amplitude modulations) is compared with a display of the frequency modulations in the same data. The ship has a relatively large radar cross-section and in the AM image, is easy to distinguish from the surrounding clutter which is caused by scattering from the sea surface. However, in the FM image, it is not possible to discern the areas of high and low radar cross-section. On the basis of this result and those like it, it is reasonable to conclude that without any additional processing FM images do not convey useful information on the structure of a scatterer in terms of the visual display of the data on the scattered field.

A variety of different techniques can be used to pre-process the data in a form suitable to display the frequency modulations. One of the simplest methods involves smoothing the amplitude modulations and then computing the modified instantaneous frequency

$$\psi_s = \frac{1}{A_s^2} \left(f \frac{dq}{dt} - q \frac{df}{dt} \right)$$

where A_s is the smoothed amplitude envelope obtained by applying a suitable low pass filter. The effect of doing this is to reduce the high frequency content of A and hence lower the dynamic range of $1/A^2$. In this case, the smoothed FM image is given by $|\psi_s|$ and the smoothed phase image is obtained by integrating ψ_s.

Real zero conversion

Another way of overcoming the problem asociated with FM and phase imaging is to real zero convert the signals.

If we write a real valued signal as a polynomial of the form

$$f(z) = a_0 + a_1 z + a_2 z^2 + \ldots + a_N z^N$$

then it is clear that we can associate N roots with this signal by solving the equation $f(z) = 0$ where z is a complex variable. If the roots of this equation are $z_1, z_2, \ldots, z_N$, then it can be written in the factored form

$$a_N (z - z_1)(z - z_2) \ldots (z - z_N) = 0$$

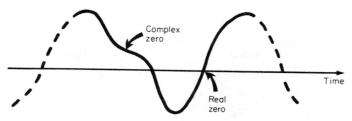

Figure 11.3 Features in a real valued signal that correspond to its real and complex zeros

In general, these roots can have both real or complex values and in signal analysis are referred to as the real and complex zeros of the signal respectively. In addition to Fourier analysis, a digital signal can be analysed by studying the location and distribution of its zeros. This is known as complex zero analysis. The real zeros of a signal are just the positions in time where it changes polarity and therefore passes through zero (i.e. they are the points in time where the amplitude of the signal vanishes). The complex zeros of a signal correspond to those more subtle attributes where the amplitude is modulated but the polarity of the signal remains the same. This is illustrated in figure 11.3. Complex zero signals are among the most common types of signals to be found especially in coherent imaging. A signal of this type can be uniquely determined from its zeros.

In terms of a descriptive framework, frequency modulations access the information encoded primarily in the real zeros of a signal. It is therefore appropriate to modify the information contained in the original signal in such a way that it is completely encoded in the real zeros as shown in figure 11.3. Signals of this form are known as real zero signals, and methods of analysing and processing them can be developed which are based entirely on the zero-crossings of the signal. The conversion of a complex zero signal to a real zero signal is known as real zero conversion or RZC. Compared to the complex zeros, the real roots of a digital signal are relatively straightforward to obtain. One simply has to evaluate the points in time where the amplitude of the signal changes sign.

There are two ways by which a signal can be real zero con-

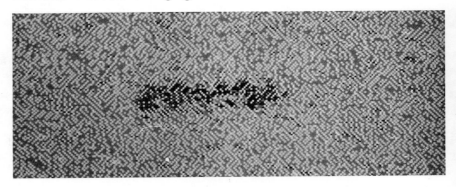

Figure 11.4 Real zero converted FM image using the same SAR data whose AM image is given in Figure 11.2

verted. One way is to successively differentiate the signal. The problem with this method is that in practice it is not very successful because multiple differentiation requires extremely sharp filters to control out-of-band noise. Also, multiple differentiation is not strictly invertable because of the loss of addition constants. The second and more practical method (if only because of its sheer simplicity) of generating a RZC signal is to add a sine wave $a\sin(\omega_0 t)$ of known frequency (ω_0) and amplitude a equal to or greater than the highest frequency and amplitude present in the data respectively. Given a real signal f whose spectrum is $F(\omega), |\omega| \leq \Omega$, the corresponding RZC signal is given by

$$f_{RZC} = f + a\sin(\omega_0 t), \quad a \geq |f|_{max}, \quad \omega_0 \geq \Omega$$

This method of real zero conversion is very easy to perform in analogue or digital form. A RZC signal which is produced in this way amounts to a sine wave with 'jitter' in the position of its real zeros. The jitter is determined by both the amplitude and frequency modulations in the original signal. The information on the original signal is completely encoded in the displacement of the zeros from the regular sine wave locations. We can therefore consider a RZC signal as a sine wave (whose amplitude and frequency modulations are constant in time), perturbed by a signal whose amplitude and frequency modulations vary in time. The result is to produce a signal with

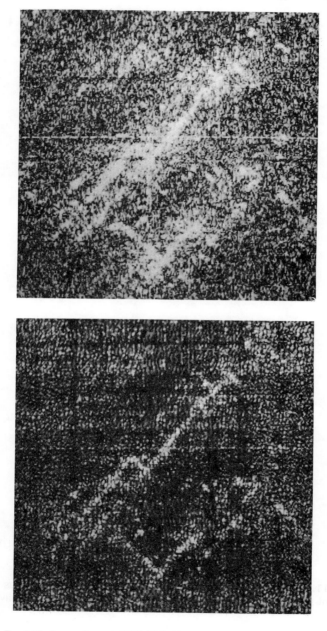

Figure 11.5 AM (*upper*) and RZC FM (*lower*) images of a building imaged with an airborne SAR system

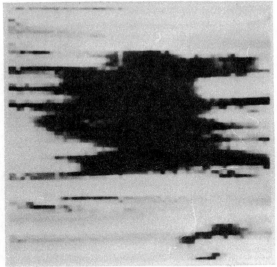

Figure 11.6 Ultrasonic AM (*upper*) and RZC FM (*lower*) images of a tissue equivalent phantom (similar in acoustical properties to the human liver)

fluctuations in the amplitude envelope A about a, fluctuations in ψ about ω_0, and changes in the phase which perturb an otherwise linear phase function $\omega_0 t$. By adjusting the magnitude of a to an appropriate value, information encoded in the frequency modulations and phase of the original signal can be assessed in terms of how they perturb the regular sine wave.

By real zero converting each signal in a stack of signals and computing the frequency modulations, the 'RZC FM' image can be obtained. Figure 11.4 is a RZC FM image obtained from the data whose AM image is given in figure 11.2. Compared to the FM image in figure 11.2, the area of high radar cross-section (i.e. the ship) is now easy to distinguish. This is essentially just another way of displaying the data. However, it offers a degree of freedom which can result in an improved visualization of the scatterer. A further example of this, using some airborne SAR data, is given in figure 11.5. This shows the AM and RZC FM images of a small building with a relatively large radar cross-section due to its partial construction form sheet metal panels. Figure 11.6 shows the AM and RZC FM images for a sample of ultrasonic data obtained in a pulse-echo experiment on a tissue-equivalent phantom (similar in acoustical properties to human liver) using a 3.5 MHz centre frequency transducer. In this case, the ultrasonic signals were only partially real zero converted by lowering the magnitude of the added sine wave so that it did not lie above the original signal envelope for its entire duration. The boundary delineation between the low and high scatter regions exhibited in figure 11.6 demonstrates that, in comparison with the AM image, an improved visualization of the known object structure can be obtained by displaying the RZC FM image. Finally, figure 11.7 shows a CDP stack of seismic signals and the corresponding instantaneous frequency after real zero conversion. In seismology, a display of the instantaneous frequency has an application in direct detection techniques because it is often observed that a shift towards lower frequencies occurs immediately below hydrocarbon-bearing structures.

SUMMARY OF IMPORTANT RESULTS

Histogram equalization

The basic process is

$$v_k^{out} = \sum_{i=0}^{k} P(v_k^{in})$$

where v is the value of a pixel located at $[i,j]$ and P is the probability of a grey level occurring with value v_k.

Homomorphic filtering

The basic problem is: Given

$$f(x,y) = i(x,y)r(x,y)$$

where f is the data, i is the illumination component and r is the reflection component, recover r. The solution to this problem is as follows:

1. Apply the homomorphic process

$$\ln f = \ln i + \ln r$$

2. Apply a highpass filter to recover $\ln r$

$$\ln r \simeq \text{HPF}[\ln f(x)]$$

3. Apply exponentiation to recover r

$$r = \exp(\ln r) \simeq \exp[\text{HPF}(\ln f)]$$

High emphasis filter

Assumes that the blur in an image is due to a process of diffusion rather than convolution. The restored image g is given by

$$g(x,y) = f(x,y) - \nabla^2 f(x,y)$$

where f is the blurred image.

342

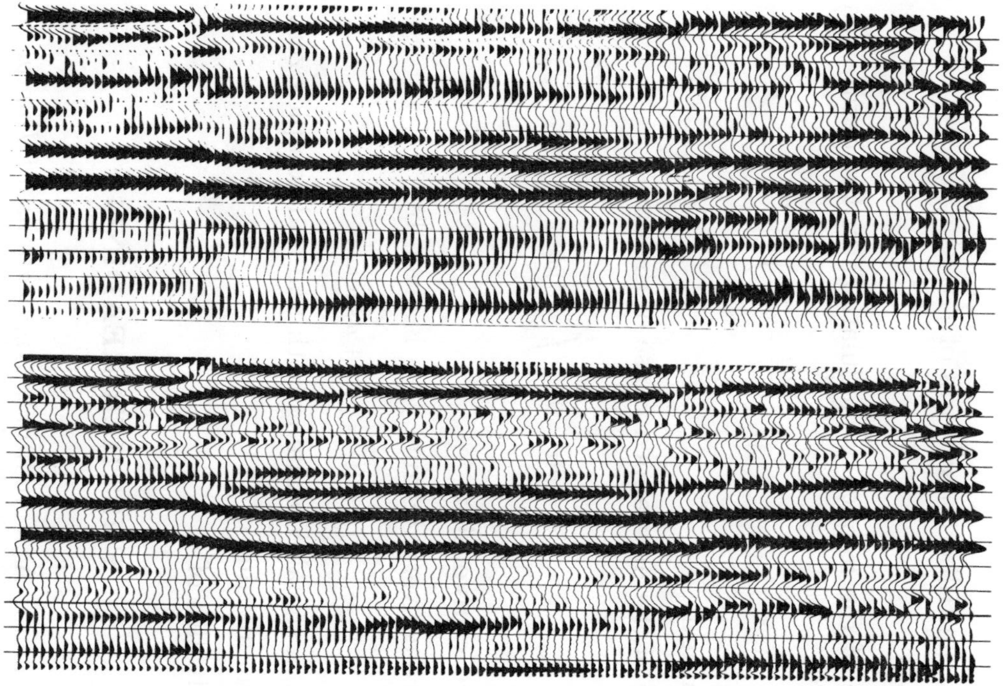

Figure 11.7 Conventional seismic image (CDP stack; *upper*) and RZC instantaneous frequency (*lower*)

AM image

An image of the amplitude modulations in the data. If f is the real valued signal, then the amplitude modulations are given by

$$A = \sqrt{f^2 + q^2}$$

where q is the Hilbert transform of f.

FM image

An image of the frequency modulations in the data given by $|\psi|$, where

$$\psi = \frac{1}{A^2} \left(f \frac{dq}{dt} - q \frac{df}{dt} \right)$$

Phase image

An image of the unwrapped phase of the data,

$$\theta = \theta(t = 0) + \int^{t} \psi(t') dt'$$

Real zero conversion

A real zero converted signal f_{RZC} is given by

$$f_{RZC}(t) = f(t) + a \sin(\omega_0 t)$$

where f is a signal containing both real and complex zeros,

$a \geq$ maximum value of $|f|$

$\omega_0 \geq$ bandwidth of f.

FURTHER READING

1. Oppenheim A V (editor), *Applications of Digital Signal Processing*, Prentice-Hall, Signal Processing Series, 1978. Image enhancement is discussed in chapter 4 which includes other methods of digital processing. This book is collection of papers on various applications and includes detailed discussions on the processing of radar, sonar and seismic signals.

2.   Rosenfeld A and Kak A C, *Digital Picture Processing*, Computer Science and Applied Mathematics, Academic Press, 1980. Image enhancement is discussed in chapter 11.

3. Seggie D A, Doherty C M and Leeman S, *Pulse-Echo Imaging Via Zero Manipulation*, Journal of the Acoustical Society of America, 1987, Volume 81, Number 5, Pages 1465-1470. This is one of the first papers to introduce the idea of real zero conversion for FM imaging using ultrasound.

4. Blackledge J M, Burge R E and Barrett N R, *Phase Imaging by Real Zero Conversion and its Application to Synthetic Aperture Radar*, Journal of Physics D: Applied Physics, Volume 20, Number 11, Pages 1438-1444. This paper applies the method presented in the paper above by Seggie et al. to Synthetic Aperture Radar Imaging.

12 Noise reduction

Noise refers to a variety of unwanted disturbances due to measuring and recording errors of all types and interference from external sources. All signals and images have some degree of noise present in them. The amplitude of the noise may vary considerably. Also, depending on the type of experiment that is conducted, noise may be confined to a range of frequencies or exist over the entire spectrum. In the latter case, the noise is referred to as white noise in analogy with white light which is composed of a range of different frequencies (in the visible part of the electromagnetic spectrum). Noise which is confined to a band of frequencies is sometimes referred to as coloured noise. The contamination of signals and images by noise has important consequences for all types of processing.

The aim of a noise reduction algorithm is primarily to enhance the visual quality of an image by eliminating features which are random and uncorrelated. In practice, noise tends to corrupt the high frequency content of most data where the energy of the data spectrum is usually low. Thus, one way of reducing noise is by attenuating the high frequency components of the data over a range of frequencies which can be selected and adjusted by the user to provide optimum results. This can be achieved by applying a low pass filter.

12.1 THE LOW PASS FILTER

As the name suggests, the low pass filter passes the low frequencies of the data spectrum and attenuates the high frequencies.

The ideal low pass filter

The ideal low pass filter is given by

$$
H(k_x, k_y) = \begin{cases} 1, & \sqrt{k_x^2 + k_y^2} \leq K \\ \\ 0, & \sqrt{k_x^2 + k_y^2} > K \end{cases}
$$

where K is the cut-off frequency. This type of filter attenuates completely all the spatial frequencies above the cut-off frequency and retains without modification all those frequencies less than or equal to the cut-off frequency.

The Butterworth low pass filter

The discontinuous nature of the ideal low pass filter causes ringing to occur in the filtered output. This phenomenon is known as the Gibbs effect and can be reduced by employing low pass filters which are continuous funtions. A well known and widely used filter of this type is the Butterworth low pass filter (BLPF) which is given by

$$
B(k_x, k_y) = \frac{1}{1 + \left(\frac{\sqrt{k_x^2 + k_y^2}}{K} \right)^{2n}}
$$

In this expression, n is referred to as the order of the filter. This parameter is a positive integer and determines the rate at which the filter approaches zero. An example of a program which employs the BLPF to reduce high frequency noise is given below.

```
        SUBROUTINE BLPF(X,N,CUT,ORD)
C
C FUNCTION:  THIS PROGRAM USES THE BUTTERWORTH LOW
C            PASS FILTER TO REDUCE HIGH FREQUENCY
```

347

```
C             NOISE IN AN IMAGE.
C
      DIMENSION X(64,64),XR(64,64),XI(64,64)
      DIMENSION YR(64,64),YI(64,64),B(64,64)
      INTEGER CUT,ORD
C
C X - INPUT/OUTPUT IMAGE OF SIZE N x N.
C CUT - CUT-OFF FREQUENCY IN PIXELS.
C ORD - ORDER OF FILTER.
C
C COMPUTE THE BLPF AND THE REAL AND IMAGINARY ARRAYS
C THAT WILL BE USED LATER IN FFT2D.
C
      NH=N/2+1
      DO J=1,N
      DO I=1,N
      A=(FLOAT(I-NH)**2.+FLOAT(J-NH)**2.)**.5
      B(I,J)=1./(1.+(A/CUT)**(2.*ORD))
      XR(I,J)=X(I,J)
      XI(I,J)=0.
      ENDDO
      ENDDO
C
C TAKE THE FOURIER TRANSFORM OF THE IMAGE.
C
      CALL FFT2D(XR,XI,N,-1)
C
C MULTIPLY THE COMPLEX SPECTRUM OF THE
C IMAGE WITH THE BLPF (ARRAY B).
C
      DO J=1,N
      DO I=1,N
      YR(I,J)=XR(I,J)*B(I,J)
      YI(I,J)=XI(I,J)*B(I,J)
      ENDDO
      ENDDO
C
C TAKE THE INVERSE FOURIER TRANSFORM
C AND WRITE THE OUTPUT.
C
      CALL FFT2D(YR,YI,N,1)
C
```

```
      DO J=1,N
      DO I=1,N
      X(I,J)=YR(I,J)
      ENDDO
      ENDDO
C

      RETURN
      END
```

12.2 THE NEIGHBOURHOOD AVERAGING FILTER

The neighbourhood averaging filter is a spatial domain technique. A window is chosen which encloses a predetermined neighbourhood of pixels. The average value of the pixels enclosed by this window is then computed and assigned to the pixel at the centre of the neighbourhood. By moving the window and repeating this process, a neighbourhood averaged image is obtained. The size of the neighbourhood is defined by the user. Although different-shaped windows can be employed, a square window is easier to use in practice. The size of the neighbourhoods is typically 3×3, 7×7, 9×9 etc. The effect of computing the average of a neighbourhood of pixels is to eliminate any sudden jumps in the grey level which could be caused by some noise process. This is demonstrated in the following example: Suppose we have the 3×3 neighbourhood

$$
\begin{array}{ccc}
2 & 2 & 3 \\
3 & 30 & 2 \\
1 & 3 & 2
\end{array}
$$

Compared to the numbers 1,2 and 3, the number 30 is relatively large and can be taken to be a digital representation of a noise spike. The average value of this group of numbers is 5.3. By assigning this value to the central pixel we obtain the neighbourhood

$$
\begin{array}{ccc}
2 & 2 & 3 \\
3 & 5.3 & 2 \\
1 & 3 & 2
\end{array}
$$

The value of the central pixel is now compatible with its neighbours. Hence, the noise spike is removed. In mathematical terms, we can express the neighbourhood averaging process as

$$g(i,j) = \frac{1}{M} \sum_{(n,m) \in S} f(n,m) \qquad (12.2.1)$$

where S is the window enclosing $n \times m$ neighbours whose centre is located at (i,j) and M is the total number of pixels (enclosed by S). A computer program for performing this process using a 5×5 window is given below.

```
        SUBROUTINE NAF(X,N)
C
C FUNCTION:  THIS SUBROUTINE REDUCES THE NOISE IN AN IMAGE
C            USING THE  NEIGHBOURHOOD AVERAGING PROCESS
C            WITH A 5 x 5 WINDOW.
C
        DIMENSION X(64,64),Y(68,68),Z(68,68)
        DIMENSION A(5,5),B(25),C(25)
C
C X - INPUT/OUTPUT OF SIZE N x N.
C
C FIRST, FRAME THE IMAGE X WITH AN ARRAY OF ZEROS
C 2 PIXELS WIDE.  THE FRAMED IMAGE IS STORED
C IN THE N+2 x N+2 ARRAY Y.
C
        M=N+4
        DO J=1,M
        DO I=1,M
        Y(I,J)=0.    !INITIALIZE.
        Z(I,J)=0.
        ENDDO
        ENDDO
        DO J=1,N
        DO I=1,N
        Y(I+2,J+2)=X(I,J)
        ENDDO
        ENDDO
C
C
C START PROCESS.
C
        DO J=3,M-2
```

```
      DO I=3,M-2
C
C FIND THE 5 x 5 NEIGHBOURHOOD OF PIXELS AT CENTRE (I,J)
C AND STORE THE RESULT IN ARRAY A.
C
      DO K=1,5
      DO KK=1,5
      A(KK,K)=Y(I-3+KK,J-3+K)
      ENDDO
      ENDDO
C
C CONVERT ARRAY A INTO ROW VECTOR B
C FOR LATER USE.
C
      KKK=1
      DO K=1,5
      DO KK=1,5
      B(KKK)=A(KK,K)
      KKK=KKK+1
      ENDDO
      ENDDO
C
C COMPUTE THE AVERAGE VALUE OF B.
C
      DO K=1,25
      C(K)=0.  !INTIALIZE.
      ENDDO
      C(1)=B(1) !INITIAL VALUE.
      DO K=2,25
      C(K)=C(K-1)+B(K) !SUM OF B.
      ENDDO
      AV=C(25)/25 !AVERAGE.
C
C STORE THE AVERAGE VALUE OF THE NEIGHBOURHOOD IN Z(I,J).
C
      Z(I,J)=AV
C
C REPEAT THE PROCESS, I.E., MOVE ON TO NEXT CENTRE (I,J).
C
      ENDDO
      ENDDO
C
```

```
C EXTRACT THE NEIGHBOURHOOD AVERAGED IMAGE X FROM Z(I,J).
C
      DO J=1,N
      DO I=1,N
      X(I,J)=Z(I+2,J+2)
      ENDDO
      ENDDO
C

      RETURN
      END
```

As explained in program above, the problem of computing the neighbourhood average of the pixels at the extreme edge of the image is overcome by adding a frame of zeros. For a 5×5 mask the frame must be 2 pixels wide. The original image is then extracted after completing the neighbourhood averaging process.

Deblurring

The main problem with neighbourhood averaging is that it tends to blur the image. It therefore has a similar effect to the low pass filter in that high frequency noise is reduced at the expense of image sharpness. One way of reducing this effect is by using a thresholding process to leave unchanged those regions of an image with large variations in the grey level. This can be done by employing the following process:

if $| f(i,j) - g(i,j) | <$ threshold

$h(i,j) = g(i,j)$

else

$h(i,j) = f(i,j)$

endif

where $g(i,j)$ is given by equation (12.2.1) and $h(i,j)$ is the output. If $| f - g |$ is greater or equal to the threshold, then the image remains unchanged. Regions of the image where $| f - g |$ is large correspond to places where there is an abrupt change in the value of the grey level. For this reason, application of the thresholding process given above helps to reduce high frequency noise while preserving the original sharpness of the image and therefore important features such as its edges.

12.3 THE MEDIAN FILTER

The aim of all noise-reducing processes is to suppress noise without blurring or degrading the original image. With low pass filters, achieving optimum results often requires a considerable amount of trial and error. In the case of neighbourhood averaging, the application of a threshold can go some way to preserving image sharpness. However, once again, choosing the right threshold involves the user having to test a range of different values. This is both time consuming and can be computationally expensive. These problems can be overcome to a limited extent be employing another filter known as the median filter. The basic idea is the same as the neighbourhood averaging filter except that instead of computing the average of the neighbourhood we compute the median of the neighbourhood.

The median

The median m of a set of numbers is such that half of the numbers in the set are less than m and half are greater than m. Thus, suppose we have a set of five numbers say

$$(1, 2, 3, 4, 5)$$

then the median of these numbers is 3. Similarly, the median of the numbers

$$(7, 19, 20, 30, 31, 49, 69, 72, 81)$$

is 31 because it is the fifth largest value of the set (there are four numbers less than 31 and four numbers greater than 31).

Basic method

As with neighbourhood averaging, the size of the neighbourhood is defined by the user - typically 3×3, 7×7, 9×9 etc. In a 3×3 neighbourhood, the median is the 5th largest value. In a 5×5 neighbourhood, the median is the 13th largest value and so on. In practice, the median of a neighbourhood of pixels can be found by reordering them as a sequence of increasing numbers. For example, suppose we have the following 3×3 neighbourhood of pixels

$$
\begin{array}{ccc}
2 & 6 & 3 \\
14 & 81 & 12 \\
13 & 4 & 1
\end{array}
$$

First, we convert this 3×3 matrix into the row vector

$$(2, 6, 3, 14, 81, 12, 13, 4, 1)$$

Then, we reorder these numbers as a sequence of increasing values

$$(1, 2, 3, 4, 6, 12, 13, 14, 81)$$

The median of this sequence is then the fifth largest value which is 6. This example is a good illustration of why median filtering reduces noise. In comparison with the other numbers in the neighbourhood above, 81 is relatively large and can be taken to represent a noise spike. The median filter replaces this value with the median of the neighbourhood, i.e., 81 is replaced by 6 and the neighbourhood becomes

$$
\begin{array}{ccc}
2 & 6 & 3 \\
14 & 6 & 12 \\
13 & 4 & 1
\end{array}
$$

If some of the numbers in the set are the same, then the equal values are grouped together. For example, suppose we have the set

$$(5, 6, 20, 10, 11, 10, 12, 13, 10)$$

where the number 10 occurs three times. Reordering these numbers in ascending values, the three 10s are grouped together thus:

$$(5, 6, 10, 10, 10, 11, 12, 13, 20)$$

The median of this set is still the fifth largest value which in this example is 10.

The examples given above demonstrate that the principal function of a median filter is to force pixels with very distinct values to be more like their neighbours. The program given below uses a 5×5 window to median filter a N×N image (the maximum value of N being set at 64). The problem of computing the median of those pixels at the extreme edge of the image is dealt with in exactly the same way as in the neighbourhood averaging filter program given earlier.

```
      SUBROUTINE MF(X,N)
C
C FUNCTION: THIS PROGRAM REDUCES THE NOISE IN AN IMAGE
C           USING A MEDIAN FILTER WITH A 5 x 5 WINDOW.
C
      DIMENSION X(64,64),Y(68,68),Z(68,68)
      DIMENSION A(5,5),B(25),C(25)
      REAL MAX
C
C X - INPUT/OUTPUT, SIZE N x N.
C
C FRAME THE IMAGE WITH AN ARRAY
C OF ZEROS 2 PIXELS WIDE.
C
      M=N+4
      DO J=1,M
      DO I=1,M
      Y(I,J)=0.   !INITIALIZE
      Z(I,J)=0.
      ENDDO
      ENDDO
      DO J=1,N
      DO I=1,N
      Y(I+2,J+2)=X(I,J)
      ENDDO
      ENDDO
C
C START PROCESS.
C
      DO J=3,M-2
      DO I=3,M-2
C
C FIND THE 5 x 5 NEIGHBOURHOOD OF PIXELS AT
C CENTRE (I,J) AND STORE THE RESULT IN A.
C
      DO K=1,5
      DO KK=1,5
      A(KK,K)=Y(I-3+KK,J-3+K)
      ENDDO
```

```
      ENDDO
C
C CONVERT A(K,KK) INTO ROW VECTOR B(KKK).
C
      KKK=1
      DO K=1,5
      DO KK=1,5
      B(KKK)=A(KK,K)
      KKK=KKK+1
      ENDDO
      ENDDO
C
C REORDER B(K) INTO A SEQUENCE OF NUMBERS OF
C INCREASING VALUE BY EMPLOYING THE FOLLOWING
C PROCESS (KNOWN AS A BUBBLE SORT):
C
C 1.    FIND THE LARGEST VALUE OF B(K).
C 2.    ASSIGN THIS VALUE TO C(25).
C 3.    SET THIS VALUE OF B(K) TO ZERO.
C 4.    FIND THE SECOND LARGEST VALUE OF B(K).
C 5.    ALLOCATE THIS VALUE TO C(24).
C 6.    SET THIS VALUE OF B(K) TO ZERO.
C 7.    REPEAT PROCESS FOR ALL VALUES OF B(K).
C
      DO K=1,25
      MAX=0.
      DO KK=1,25
      IF(B(KK).GT.MAX)MAX=B(KK)
      ENDDO
      DO KK=1,25
      IF(B(KK).EQ.MAX)THEN
      C(26-K)=MAX
      B(KK)=0.
      ENDIF
      ENDDO
      ENDDO
C
C STORE MEDIAN OF THE NEIGHBOURHOOD IN Z(I,J).
C
      Z(I,J)=C(13)
C
C MOVE ONTO THE NEXT CENTRE (I,J) AND
```

```
C REPEAT THE PROCESS.
C
      ENDDO
      ENDDO
C
C EXTRACT THE MEDIAN FILTERED IMAGE X (THE OUTPUT)
C FROM Z(I,J).
C
      DO J=1,N
      DO I=1,N
      X(I,J)=Z(I+2,J+2)
      ENDDO
      ENDDO
C
      RETURN
      END
```

SUMMARY OF IMPORTANT RESULTS

Butterworth low pass filter

$$B(k_x, k_y) = \frac{1}{1 + \left(\frac{\sqrt{k_x^2 + k_y^2}}{K} \right)^{2n}}$$

where K is the cut-off frequency and n is the order of the filter (a user-defined positive integer).

Neighbourhood averaging filter

$$g(i,j) = \frac{1}{M} \sum_{(n,m) \in S} f(n,m)$$

where S is the window containing $n \times m$ pixels whose centre is located at $[i,j]$ and M is the total number of pixels in the image.

Median filter

The median m of a set of numbers is such that half the numbers are less than m and half the numbers are greater than

m. The median filter operates in the same way as the neighbourhood averaging filter except that instead of computing the average of the neighbourhood, it computes the median of the neighbourhood.

FURTHER READING

1. Gonzalez R C and Wintz P, *Digital Image Processing*, Addison-Wesley, 1987. Noise reduction by low pass filtering, neighbourhood averaging and median filtering are discussed in chapter 4.

2. Huang T S (editor), *Two-Dimensional Digital Signal Processing*, Topics in Applied Physics, Volume 43, Springer-Verlag, 1981. Part 2 of this series discusses the statistical and deterministic properties of the median filter.

INDEX

Index

Index